The Energy
Disruption Triangle

The Energy Disruption Triangle

Three Sectors That Will Change How We Generate, Use, and Store Energy

David C. Fessler

WILEY

Published by John Wiley & Sons, Inc., Hoboken, New Jersey.
Published simultaneously in Canada.

For general information on our other products and services or for technical support,
please contact our Customer Care Department within the United States at
(800) 762-2974, outside the United States at (317) 572-3993, or fax (317) 572-4002.

Wiley publishes in a variety of print and electronic formats and by print-on-demand.
Some material included with standard print versions of this book may not be included
in e-books or in print-on-demand. If this book refers to media such as a CD or DVD
that is not included in the version you purchased, you may download this material
at http://booksupport.wiley.com. For more information about Wiley products, visit
www.wiley.com.

Library of Congress Cataloging-in-Publication Data

Names: Fessler, Dave, 1953- author.
Title: The energy disruption triangle : three sectors that will change how we generate,
  use, and store energy / Dave Fessler.
Description: Hoboken, New Jersey : John Wiley & Sons, Inc., [2019] | Includes index. |
  Identifiers: LCCN 2018045785 (print) | LCCN 2018047877 (ebook) | ISBN
  9781119347132 (ePub) | ISBN 9781119347125 (ePDF) | ISBN 9781119347118
  (hardcover)
Subjects: LCSH: Energy industries. | Energy consumption. | Energy development.
Classification: LCC HD9502.A2 (ebook) | LCC HD9502.A2 F47 2019 (print) |
  DDC 333.79—dc23
LC record available at https://lccn.loc.gov/2018045785

Cover Design: Wiley
Cover Image: © mikalajn/Shutterstock, © mr. teerapon tiuekhom/Shutterstock,
© Diyana Dimitrova/Shutterstock

Printed in the United States of America.
V10007113_122218

To my dear wife, Anne, and my devoted sons, Jared and Noah.
With you at my side, anything is possible.

If you do not change direction, you may end up where you are heading.

—Lao Tzu

Contents

Foreword

It has often and rightly been said that you never fully appreciate something until it's gone. This is particularly true of energy.

We take it for granted when we flick the light switch that we'll get illumination. Or that the car will start when we turn the key. Or that the room will get cooler when we hit the air conditioner.

It's only when those things don't happen that we're reminded just how dependent we are on safe, reliable energy. And if we fail to appreciate energy in our day-to-day lives, we don't adequately recognize how different life was in the past without it.

Imagine, for example, that the Roman statesman Cicero – from 18 centuries earlier – magically decided to visit Thomas Jefferson at Monticello.

How would that happen?

He would start by sending Jefferson a letter informing him of his intended visit. (And given the quality of the transatlantic postal service 200 years ago, he might easily arrive before his letter.)

He would then take a horse to a Mediterranean port. He would sail on a wind-driven wooden boat to the United States. He would arrive in Charlottesville on horseback. And he would find Jefferson in a mountaintop home heated by fire and reading at night by candlelight.

In other words, almost two millennia would have passed and yet an aristocrat like Jefferson lived just like the citizens of ancient Rome.

This underscores just how mistaken it is to assume that human history has been one long upward-sloping arc of progress. It hasn't. Our lives only began to really improve with the advent of science – and the successful harnessing of energy.

Energy powered the Industrial Revolution. And that has been an unalloyed good for humanity. It made it possible to feed billions, double life spans, slash extreme poverty, and replace human sweat and misery with machinery.

As societies got richer, life was no longer a struggle for subsistence. People no longer spent their days trying to meet basic needs. Indeed, energy has played an incalculable role in making us richer, safer, healthier, and freer than our ancestors.

The folks who work in the resource sector – and the investors who finance them – make our affluent lives possible. And the high returns they deliver is a good reason energy stocks deserve a place in your portfolio.

Yes, there is a downside to our prodigious energy use. Fossil fuels create waste. They damage the environment. Carbon emissions get trapped in the atmosphere.

Yet some people don't see the big picture. And I mean really don't get it.

Author Bill McKibben writes, "We need to view the fossil-fuel industry in a new light. It has become a rogue industry, reckless like no other force on Earth. It is Public Enemy Number One to the survival of our planetary civilization."[1]

James Hansen, a prominent climate scientist, says oil company CEOs should be "tried for high crimes against humanity and nature."[2]

And in a *New York Times* review of Naomi Klein's book *This Changes Everything: Capitalism vs. the Climate*, Rob Nixon openly laments that we are unable to bankrupt the major oil companies.[3]

This is not environmentalism. It is mindless anti-corporatism.

How will you drive or fly, heat and cool your home, or operate your smart phone and computer without fossil fuels?

I'm not insensitive to environmentalists' concerns. Climate change is real and human carbon emissions play a major role. Yet the voices of some prominent environmentalists aren't just shrill. They're counterproductive.

They don't understand that scientific innovation and capitalism will ultimately help solve our climate problems, not self-righteous finger wagging.

My long-time friend and colleague Dave Fessler knows the history of energy and how it created modern prosperity.

Raw materials and fossil fuels drive economic development and increase our standard of living. What resource companies unlock from the earth are inside the buildings you live and work in, the planes you fly in, the cars you drive, the bridges you cross, and the computers and smartphones that keep you connected.

Construction, communications, transportation, recreation, retailing, finance and healthcare – among many other industries – all rely on what natural resource companies supply, chiefly energy. Approximately 87 percent of our energy needs are met by fossil fuels.

And while the volume of fossil-fuel consumption keeps increasing (atleast for now), it has an encouraging environmental trend: The increase is slowing, and we're emitting less carbon dioxide per unit of energy produced.

The biggest contributor to this decarbonization is the switch from high-carbon coal to lower-carbon gas in electricity generation. New technologies – particularly hydraulic fracturing and horizontal drilling – have made formerly inaccessible formations economically viable. They have also made the United States the world's leading energy producer, topping Saudi Arabia in oil and Russia in gas. Though many people don't realize it, this environmentally friendly trend in energy is not something new.

When coal replaced wood, it reversed the deforestation of Europe and North America. Oil extraction halted the slaughter of the world's whales and seals for their blubber. That's why Greenpeace should display a picture of John D. Rockefeller on the walls of every office.

Fertilizer manufactured with gas halved the amount of land needed to produce a given amount of crops, thus feeding the world's burgeoning population while increasing the amount of land available for wildlife.

As economic historian Deirdre McCloskey points out,[4] there has been a roughly 9,000 percent increase in the value of goods and services available to the average American since 1800, virtually all of them made of, made with, or powered by fossil fuels.

You'd think people everywhere would celebrate this fact. Yet... lend an ear to Professor Roy Scranton of Notre Dame.

In a recent column in the *New York Times*, he said, "the only truly moral response to global climate change is suicide. There is simply no other more effective way to shrink your carbon footprint. Once you're dead, you won't use any more electricity, you won't eat any more meat, you won't burn any more gasoline, and you certainly won't have any more children. If you really want to save the planet, you should die."[5]

I'm guessing that Dr. Scranton is not a big hit at children's parties.

Yet he's hardly alone. He is simply a part of what is commonly known as the Romantic Green Movement. These are cult-like members of an apocalyptic movement that shows a shocking indifference to starvation, indulges in ghoulish fantasies about a depopulated planet, and makes Nazi-like comparisons of human beings to vermin and pathogens.

They aren't just anti-progress. They are anti-human – and stupendously ill informed.

The data clearly shows that as countries get richer – they would call it more "consumerist" or "materialistic" – they also get cleaner.

The most polluted nations in the world are the poor ones, not the rich ones. It's only when people live comfortable lives that they start to care more deeply about the quality of their environment. And while it's true that richer countries are bigger carbon emitters, they are also the ones most focused on doing something about it.

Abundant, affordable, and reliable energy is vital to human flourishing. Yet I regularly hear folks claim that the earth is running out of oil and gas and that our fossil-fueled civilization is "unsustainable."

If we were truly running out of oil and gas, you might reasonably wonder why both are far cheaper today than they were a few years ago. These folks seem unaware that technological innovations like horizontal drilling and hydraulic fracturing have greatly increased the available supply.

Despite the growing global economy, a major factor is reducing the price and total demand for energy. It's called dematerialization.

Technological progress allows us to do more with less.

For example, mobile phones don't require thousands of miles of telephone poles and wires. The digital revolution replaced shelves full of books with a single tablet and crates of records and CDs with an MP3 player. Many people now prefer to read magazines and newspapers online. And a terabyte of storage makes a 10-ream box of paper obsolete.

And consider all the material devices that have been replaced by your smartphone: a telephone, answering machine, phone book, Rolodex, camera, camcorder, radio, alarm clock, calculator, dictionary, street maps, compass, flashlight, fax machine, and thermometer, to name just a few.

Thanks to gains in efficiency and emission control, Western countries have learned how to get the most energy with the least emission of greenhouse gases.

As we climbed the energy ladder from wood to coal to oil to gas, the ratio of carbon to hydrogen in our energy sources fell steadily.

As a result, fewer cities are now shrouded in a smoggy haze. Urban waterways that had been left for dead – Puget Sound, Chesapeake Bay, Boston Harbor, Lake Erie, and many others – have been recolonized by birds, fish, marine mammals, and intrepid swimmers.

For decades, ecologists have told us that environmental protection will require smaller populations and slower economic growth.

Turns out that just the opposite is true. The wealthiest countries have the cleanest environments. And as the poor ones get wealthier, they get cleaner too. Environmental problems, like other problems, are solvable.

One of the greatest challenges facing humanity, however, is that we dump 38 billion tons of carbon dioxide into the atmosphere each year. Fossil fuels provide 86 percent of the world's energy, powering our cars, trucks, planes, ships, tractors, furnaces, and factories, in addition to most of our electricity plants.

There are many ways that human ingenuity and free markets will solve our most pressing energy needs. Dave Fessler is familiar with most of them – if not all.

He knows that new technologies are inherently disruptive and transformative, that US energy production has never been stronger, that solar and wind installations are on the rise, and the smart grid is getting smarter.

In the pages ahead, he explains the how and why of all of this. He also points to the very best ways to take advantage of it.

Dave is one of the savviest and most knowledgeable energy and infrastructure analysts I know. His insights are always worth hearing.

And his investment recommendations? I've followed them for over a decade now. They work.

It requires energy to produce and maintain human prosperity. Dave Fessler's specialty is taking this basic truth and turning it into unusually large profits.

In short, you are in very good hands here. Enjoy . . .

Alexander Green

NOTES

1. https://www.rollingstone.com/politics/politics-news/global-warmings-terrifying-new-math-188550/
2. https://www.nytimes.com/2014/11/09/books/review/naomi-klein-this-changes-everything-review.html
3. https://www.nytimes.com/2014/11/09/books/review/naomi-klein-this-changes-everything-review.html
4. https://www.wsj.com/articles/fossil-fuels-will-save-the-world-really-1426282420
5. https://www.nytimes.com/2018/07/16/opinion/climate-change-parenting.html

Introduction

There's a big disruption coming to the world of energy. Actually, it's a combination of three separate, yet connected developments, which are each disruptions in their own right. I call it the Energy Disruption Triangle. It's going to completely change the way we generate, use, and store energy. It's a "black swan" event that few people see coming.

The disruption coming to energy is going to affect nearly all of humanity. So, this book is for everyone. Reading this book will give you an excellent understanding of just how life changing this disruption will be. If you drive a car, within 20 years, you'll probably be driving an electric one. Two or three decades from now, most of the electricity you use won't come from **fossil fuel** or **nuclear power** plants. The ability to economically store electricity and use it when we want to is something we've never been able to do since the dawn of the electric age.

I decided to write this book now primarily because no one has written about this before. There have been bits and pieces, but no one has pulled all three sides of the Energy Disruption Triangle together . . . until now. I think it's important for everyone to understand the magnitude of the disruption and the positive changes that come along for the ride. Global warming will become a thing of the past. That's right, **greenhouse gas** emissions will start dropping rapidly, as the use of fossil fuels declines. The air in our cities will clear up. The morning "**smog** report" in Los Angeles will continually improve, even more than it has already. The world needs to fully understand that one of the largest disruptions in history is upon us. This disruption is full of positive benefits and no negative ones.

This isn't the first disruption associated with electricity. There have been several big disruptions that preceded the ones I'm writing about in this book.

Electricity has been around since the dawn of time. However, it's only been in the past 250 years or so that people have been able to harness and use its power. In June 1752, Benjamin Franklin's famous kite experiment was one of the first attempts to show that we might eventually harness and use electricity. Unbeknownst to Franklin, several French electricians verified the same theory.

But it was nearly 80 years later, in 1831, when Michael Faraday, a British scientist, discovered how to *generate* electricity. Faraday, starting with Franklin's experiments and those of other scientists, eventually made a key discovery. He found that he could create or "induce" an electrical current by moving a magnet inside a coiled copper wire. The discovery of **electromagnetic** induction is widely credited to Faraday.

It was a disruptive event, in that it allowed electrical production anytime. That same process is still in use today, although it is very different from Faraday's small handheld device. Massive generators powered by a water or steam **turbine** produce huge amounts of electricity that flow onto the world's **power grids**. Faraday's discovery started the world of electricity.

The first application of electricity came only six years after Faraday's discovery. In 1837, Samuel Morse developed and patented the electrical telegraph. Alfred Vail, working with Morse, developed the Morse code, a system of "dots and dashes" that represented the alphabet. Now anyone could "talk" to anyone else with a telegraph machine. In a few decades after its invention, the telegraph network became global. Suddenly, people and businesses around the world could communicate at the speed of light . . . in the 1800s! The telegraph was another early disruptor in the world of electricity.

In parallel with the invention and deployment of the telegraph, was harnessing electrical power to produce light. In 1803, British scientist Humphry Davy demonstrated the first arc lamp to the Royal Institute in Great Britain. The lighting system consisted of a bank of batteries powering an arc, or spark, of light that continuously flowed between two charcoal rods. These arc lamps were popular as the first street lamps to brighten city streets at night. But arc lamps were expensive and required constant replacement of the charcoal or carbon rods.

Fast-forward to 1835, when the first constant light was developed. But it was Thomas Alva Edison, an American working in his shop in West Orange, New Jersey, who really revolutionized electrical power.

In 1879, Edison developed the first practical, long-lasting light bulb. He also demonstrated the first system of electrical generation and distribution with his Pearl Street Station in Lower Manhattan, which started operation in September 1882.[1]

Initially, J. P. Morgan and a few other customers of means in New York City hired Edison to provide lighting for their homes. While Edison's generating stations were rudimentary compared to today's behemoths that can produce hundreds of megawatts (MW), they were state-of-the-art at the time. All of a sudden, Edison was introducing Americans to an entirely new form of energy: electricity.

Electricity caused a huge disruption and became an outright threat to the booming gas lighting companies that were widespread in New York City at the time. Electrical lighting soon became all the rage. By the 1900s, there were more than 30 competing companies generating and distributing electricity in New York City.

While one of Edison's projects was the continual improvement in generating and distributing electricity, he was busy with other related projects, too. Edison and others in the same business of distributing electricity had to find a way to see how much each customer was using. So Edison got to work again. He developed and patented an electric meter. But it was difficult to read, as it involved the weighing of a copper strip at the end of each billing period.

The latter half of the nineteenth century saw many discoveries in the area of electromagnetism turned into practical applications. Motors, transformers, meters, lamps, and generators (called dynamos) all appeared one after the other. The time was ripe, not just here in the United States but in Europe as well, and electricians and scientists developed many of the above items nearly simultaneously in both places.

A great example of a European invention was the replacement of **carbon filaments** in **incandescent** bulbs with filaments made from tungsten. These lamps were much brighter than lamps with carbon filaments and lasted far longer. Lamp manufacturers would go on to produce the tungsten filament lamp for more than a century.

The next big disruption in the world of electricity has been more of a series of slow improvements, but it is becoming clear that the demand for electricity is booming. By 2050, economists expect the world's population to reach nine billion. In order to meet mid-twenty-first-century world energy demands, supply has to grow by 80 percent. That means that in a mere 33 years, our energy supplies will have to nearly double. Most experts agree that simply isn't possible.

A 2012 Royal Dutch Shell plc study assumed advances in technology, competition, and geology will boost energy supplies by 50 percent and demand would decrease by 20 percent. Higher prices and smarter urban development will contribute to this. The Shell study showed that a "Zone of Uncertainty" between energy supply and demand would still exist. That uncertainty could equal the entire worldwide energy output in 2000. Shell concluded that even if a brand new energy technology landed in our laps today, it wouldn't make much of a difference. According to the Shell researchers, "[it would] require thirty years of sustained double-digit growth to build industrial capacity and grow sufficiently to feature at even 1–2% of the energy system."[2]

It was clear that efforts to improve energy efficiency needed to start right away. Over the past decade, energy efficiency efforts have really started to gain traction. The US federal government has issued a series of energy efficiency mandates. Improving energy efficiency of lights, motors, and other electrical equipment is an easy way to reduce the carbon footprint on a per-person basis.

The Department of Energy (DOE) decided to go after the low-hanging fruit first. It set its sights on the lowly 100-watt incandescent bulb. It was a mandate that was part of the Energy Independence and Security Act quietly passed by Congress in December 2007. It banned the production and sale of 100-watt incandescent bulbs after December 31, 2011. Two years later, the law banished the 60-watt and 40-watt bulbs.

The first answer to Congress's incandescent ban was the compact **fluorescent** lamp, or CFL for short. CFLs – or swirl bulbs – emit the same amount of light as incandescents, but they use 75 to 80 percent less energy. Manufacturers quoted lifetimes of 10,000 hours. CFLs seemed like a great idea at the time, but their lifetime was to be short-lived.

It turns out CFLs contained mercury, which the bulb requires to produce light. But mercury is a heavy metal, and as such, presented a disposal problem. Even though bulb packages advised consumers to properly dispose of used bulbs, most just threw them in the trash when they failed. And premature failure, especially of cheaply made Chinese-imported CFL bulbs, was a big problem.

Thomas Edison once said, "There's a better way to do it. Find it." So engineers at Cree, Inc. set out to do just that. They took high-intensity light-emitting diodes (LEDs) and migrated them from flashlights to light bulbs.

When manufacturers first introduced LED bulbs in about 2010, a 60-watt-equivalent bulb cost $40. With the introduction of high-volume manufacturing, 60-watt-equivalent LED bulbs now cost less than $2.50 each. Instead of drawing 60 watts of power, an LED version draws 9 watts, or about 15 percent of an incandescent version. Cree's bulbs come with a 10-year warranty, are dimmable, and have an estimated 25,000-hour lifetime.

Depending on how many hours a day it's on, an LED bulb can pay for itself in as little as a few months. Over the past several years, LED replacement bulbs are available in just about every shape and size. There are even LED replacement tubes for 4- and 8-foot fluorescent lights. Now, when you go into a big-box store, CFL bulbs are harder to find. Instead, store shelves are flooded with LED bulbs.

How disruptive are LED light bulbs? If every US household replaced one 60-watt incandescent bulb with an LED-equivalent version, we could turn off one average-sized **power plant**.

Since the beginning of the age of electricity more than a century ago, its generation, distribution, and use have changed little. Customers use electricity as soon as utilities generate it. That's because we haven't had a cost-effective means of *storing* electricity.

But that's rapidly changing. Utilities, industrial users, commercial users, and homeowners are able to cheaply store electricity and use it at the time of their choosing. While that may not sound like a big change, it has huge ramifications for the entire energy sector, including oil and natural gas, utilities, and their customers.

In this book, I'm going to delve into the Energy Disruption Triangle in detail. I'm going to show you its effects, both positive and negative, for all the players involved. When all the dust settles, our ability to store energy and use it when we need it is going to have profound and positive effects on our way of life that most people can't possibly imagine today.

Others, like Elon Musk for instance, already get it. When reporters have asked Musk about Tesla, he usually says something like: "I'm not building an electric car company. I'm building a sustainable energy company." Sustainable energy. Up until recently, it wasn't something most people thought about twice. The Energy Disruption Triangle is the intersection of three elements: solar energy, electric vehicles (EVs), and battery storage. Together, these three elements are disrupting the way we generate, use, and, now, store electricity.

No discussion of technology would be complete without the views of entrepreneur, inventor, and visionary Ray Kurzweil. The *Wall Street Journal* described him as "the restless genius," and *Forbes* dubbed him "the ultimate thinking machine." *Inc.* magazine called him "the rightful heir to Thomas Edison," ranking him #8 among US entrepreneurs. Among other things, Kurzweil invented omni-font optical character recognition, the CCD flatbed scanner, the first music synthesizer, the first print-to-speech reader for blind people, and the first commercially available speech recognition software.

In a TED Talk recorded in February 2005[3] titled "The Accelerating Power of Technology," Kurzweil shared some of his views on technology. "Technology grows in an exponential manner. It's not linear. And our intuition is linear. It's hardwired in our brains." That's why we humans tend to vastly underestimate the pace of technology.

Technology fascinates me. I spent much of my adult career as an electrical engineer working in the **semiconductor** industry. In college, I was the first engineering student to have a scientific calculator. Until that point, we were all using slide rules. Ask a current engineering student what a slide rule is and you'll likely get a blank, quizzical look.

Initially, my teachers didn't permit me to use my new calculator on tests, as it gave me an unfair advantage over the rest of my classmates, who still used slide rules. However, by the end of the semester every student had one. Just think about the difference in the speed of computing power between a slide rule and even the slowest handheld scientific calculators. It was hundreds of orders of magnitude. It was another huge disruption, driven by technology.

This illustrates what I call **Fessler's First Law of Technology:** "Technology marches on." While politicians and the media may think it stops periodically, engineers and scientists know it never does. Advances in technology are recession-proof. The Great Depression didn't slow the advancement of the exponential progression of technology one bit. During that time, we had the invention of traffic signals, frozen food, insulin, Band-Aids, aerosol cans, electric shavers, Scotch tape, car radios, penicillin, and jet engines.

When I was in college, no one had a personal computer. They didn't exist. In fact, the only computer in the school of engineering was housed in one lab. It was an old Hewlett-Packard, and it had a grand total of 16,384 bytes of memory. Compare that to today's smartphones, some of which come equipped with one terabyte of memory. That's 61 million times more memory than our "massive" computer in the lab.

By today's standards, that old HP really couldn't do much of anything, except talk to an ITT Teletype terminal. But as fledgling engineering students, its power fascinated us. To program it, we used IBM punch cards or rolls of punched paper tape. Fast-forward to 2016. We now carry more computing power around in our pocket than the astronauts had who first landed on the moon. Technology marches on.

The way we communicate is another great example of technological advances. When I was growing up, my parents' first telephone line was a "party" line. We shared it with two other families. It made for some interesting conversations. Especially if you really needed to make a phone call, and the other party didn't want to give up the line.

In July 2015, the Centers for Disease Control published a study on telephones. It found that 41 percent of Americans have just a cellphone, 48 percent have both a cellphone and a landline, 9 percent have just a landline, and 2 percent have no phone at all.

A decade from now, I'm sure more people will just have cellphones. People are shunning landlines for one reason: freedom. With a cellphone, you are reachable just about anywhere. With a handheld satellite phone, you can be reached anywhere in the world. Technology marches on.

These are just a few examples of technology in action. Now I'm going to introduce **Fessler's Second Law of Technology:** "When it comes to technology, changes happen much faster than anyone expects they will."

This one is obvious when you look at any 10-year forecast involving something to do with technology. Wait two or three years, and then go back and look at that forecast again. More than likely, it will be wrong. There's a good chance that regardless of what the forecast was measuring, it turned out to be conservative.

Technological advances happen fast. I witnessed it firsthand in the world of semiconductors. In 1965, the cofounder of Intel, Gordon

Moore, made an observation and a prediction. He observed that the quantity of transistors on one square inch of integrated circuits had doubled every 24 months since the invention of the integrated circuit. He predicted that this doubling effect would continue every 24 months for the foreseeable future (see Figure I.1).

Here we are in 2017, and some analysts wonder if Moore's law is about to run out of steam. Intel's original **microprocessor**, the 4004, had 2,300 **transistors** on it. The chip was just 12 square millimeters in size. The gap between transistors was "just" 10,000 nanometers (billionths of a meter).

Intel's Skylake processors are 10 times as big as the old 4004. While the number of transistors on a Skylake chip is proprietary, they are only 14 nanometers apart. The transistors aren't viewable by the human eye, even with the most powerful optical microscope. That's because the size of the transistors are much smaller than the wavelengths of light humans and microscopes can detect.

FIGURE I.1 **MICROPROCESSOR TRANSISTOR COUNTS 1971–2017 AND MOORE'S LAW**

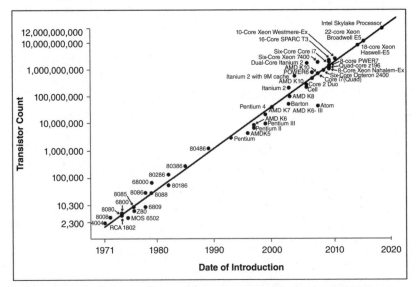

Data source: en.wikipedia.org/wiki/Transistor_count (accessed September 9, 2016) and personal estimate for the Intel Skylake processor, based on 14-nanometer transistor line width.

We could guess how many chips a Skylake processor has based on Intel's last generation chip, the 18-core Xeon Haswell E-5. It had 5.56 billion transistors, spaced just 22 nanometers apart. It's a safe bet that the Skylake probably has over 12 billion transistors.

How much longer will Moore's law hold up? No one knows, but one thing is certain: No one would have ever guessed back in 1971 that it would hold up for the next 44 years.

Is there a Moore's law for solar? Not specifically. If there were, it would be about solar energy's drop in price. Electricity production from solar is the first "side" of the energy disruption triangle. Residential solar energy systems have now reached the affordability range for most American homeowners. Americans are installing solar energy systems like never before. The sector is growing 50 percent annually, due almost entirely to high-volume manufacturing of **solar cells** and panels.

Figure I.2 is logarithmic. Every point translates into a doubling of the amount of energy we're producing from solar. That doubling was happening every two years through 2013. As of 2013, worldwide solar installations totaled about 150 gigawatts (GW). From there, all we need

FIGURE I.2   WORLD CUMULATIVE PHOTOVOLTAIC PRODUCTION (1975–2020E)

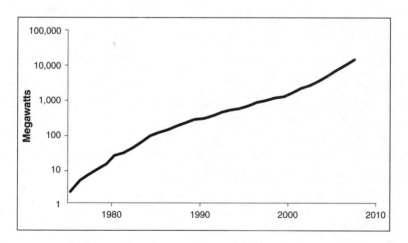

Data sources: www.kurzweilai.net/photovoltaic-production (accessed September 9, 2016), www.greentechmedia.com/articles/read/gtm-research-global-solar-pv-installations-grew-34-in-2015 (accessed September 9, 2016).

is five more doublings and solar will provide 100 percent of the world's energy needs. Unfortunately, the solar doubling every two years stopped at the end of 2013. Many countries reduced or eliminated government incentives in 2014, resulting in less growth than 2013. By the end of 2015, total global installed solar **photovoltaic (PV)** was 256 GW.[4]

A November 2015 IHS estimate[5] predicts the global installed base of solar PV will increase by an additional 272.4 GW. It expects 65 GW, 65.5 GW, 68.4 GW, and 73.5 GW to be added in 2016, 2017, 2018, and 2019, respectively. That's more than double from the end of 2015. A 2015 study by GlobalData predicts that by 2025, total global installed solar PV will hit 652 GW.[6] A January 2016 study by GTM Research was even more optimistic. It estimates we'll hit 750 GW by 2020, roughly five of the eight doublings needed. At current installation rates, installed solar capacity should hit eight doublings (6,400 GW) sometime before 2040. The sun's energy is there, waiting for us to capture and use it. And there's plenty of it: Every day, the sun's energy hitting earth is 10,000 times more than we use annually.[7]

The next few years are going to be banner years for solar here in the United States. In late 2015, Congress gave solar a boost by extending the 30 percent solar investment tax credit (ITC) through the end of 2019. In 2020, the credit drops to 20 percent and then to 10 percent in 2021 and thereafter. In June 2018, the Department of the Treasury issued IRS Notice 2018-59. It clarifies eligibility for the ITC as any project that begins construction before the end of 2019.[8] By then, mass adoption of solar on mid-to-high-level homes will be the norm, not the exception.

The same thing is happening with EVs (electric vehicles), the second side of the energy disruption triangle. They are still in an "exception" phase because they are still a year or two away from becoming cost-effective and probably a decade away from becoming a mainstream purchase for the car-buying public.

That hasn't stopped nearly every carmaker from investing billions to make them. Ten years ago, Tesla was the only company with a roadmap to a cost-effective EV. Now, nearly every carmaker is producing EVs, or has plans to do so. There's no question that Tesla has a big head start, and has set the quality, features, and options quite high for the competition. Even the process of buying a Tesla without a dealer could eventually make new car dealers obsolete.

This brings me to **Fessler's Third Law of Technology:** "New technology is almost always disruptive and transformative." A perfect example is today's smartphone. Where would you be without yours? Most of what users do with them now doesn't involve talking to someone. We now use them to pay for items in the store, check-in at the airport, reserve a table at a restaurant, and order a car to take us somewhere. Talk about disruptive.

While both solar and EVs are on their way to disruptive status, it's the third side of the energy disruption triangle that will be the biggest disruptor of all three. I'm talking about cheap battery storage. In 2016, the energy storage market shifted to a commercially viable market. And now, prices are just dropping like a stone. Elon Musk and Tesla are building a gigafactory in Nevada that will be one of the largest factories on the planet. And all it will be doing is making batteries for EVs and energy storage systems.

For the last decade or so, engineers have been hard at work improving storage batteries. This is especially true for lithium-ion batteries, which are in cellphones, laptops, and EVs—and in all of them, have become the batteries of choice—for good reason. Lithium-ion battery chemistry works over a wide temperature range. This is important for EVs, residential and commercial solar/storage, and utility-scale storage systems.

Think about it. An EV in Alaska is going to perform differently than an EV in Florida. The batteries need to work well in both environments. The same is true for a residential home storage system. If installed as part of a solar-plus-storage system, the battery unit will likely be outside or in an unheated garage. Utility-scale storage systems are all outdoor units.

Another advantage of lithium-ion batteries is their ability to be recharged thousands of times. They don't suffer from the "memory effect" that plagues other rechargeable battery technologies like nickel-cadmium or nickel-metal-hydride.

Lastly, battery engineers have been hard at work increasing the energy *density* of lithium-ion cells. Energy density is the amount of energy available from a given size battery. Increasing the energy density ultimately boosts the amount of energy each cell can store.

That's especially important for EVs. The higher the energy density of an EV battery pack, the further it can go on a single charge. It's also important for battery storage units designed to work with residential or utility-scale solar power systems.

One of the biggest challenges battery engineers face is reducing cost. The easiest way to reduce cost is to scale manufacturing to very high levels. An automated, high-speed manufacturing plant can produce billions of batteries. That's exactly what Tesla, Inc. is doing. Its "Gigafactory 1" is open for production but still under construction near Las Vegas; its Gigafactory 2 now operates in Buffalo, New York.

Every Tesla EV has groups of cells packaged together to form battery modules. Groups of modules connect to electric motors that run the car. Tesla is also using lithium-ion batteries produced at its Gigafactory in its home energy storage system, Powerwall. The company sold out of its original Powerwall system through mid-2016. It received more than 38,000 reservations, totaling $800 million. Tesla also manufactures storage systems for utility-scale customers. Since 2015, Tesla has installed over one gigawatt of energy storage.[9]

It's clear from the numbers that 2015 was the year energy storage began a rapid ramp upward. The residential and utility energy storage markets are just starting what will likely be a decades-long period of incredible growth. The fourth quarter of 2015 saw 112 megawatts (MW) of storage deployed. That was more than all of the battery storage installed in 2013 and 2014 combined. The total installed for all of 2015 was 221 MW. That was a record 243 percent growth rate over the previous year. But energy storage is still in the starting gate.

Research firm IHS Inc. said that in the fourth quarter of 2015, utility-scale energy storage projects increased 400 MW over the previous quarter. That's a quarter-over-quarter increase of 45 percent. The firm expected utility-scale energy storage projects to add another 900 MW to the grid in 2016. That's double the total energy storage capacity of the previous year.

According to GTM Research studies conducted in 2015, utility-scale – also referred to as front-of-meter storage – accounted for 85 percent of all storage installed that year. The rest of the storage market consisted of residential and nonresidential that combined are the behind-the-meter market.

While it is far smaller than the front-of-meter market, the behind-the-meter segment grew a whopping 405 percent in 2015. At current growth rates, GTM research projects the annual storage market in the United States to hit 1 GW by 2019. By 2020, GTM says, it will nearly double to 1.7 GW, with an annual valuation of $2.5 billion.

For at least the next decade, energy storage, both behind-the-meter and front-of-meter, will see exponential growth. Lithium-ion battery prices have dropped from $490/kilowatt-hour (kWh) in 2014 to $225/kWh in 2018. Further drops are predicted with further increases in supply. However, as of this writing, supply constraints at Tesla and other manufacturers are keeping prices at current levels.[10] It's what utilities have been waiting for. Peaks and dips in demand will slowly disappear with the strategic deployment of utility-scale storage. Energy storage promises to augment and financially justify the connection of both wind and solar generation to the distribution side of the grid.

In the chapters that follow, we'll examine the rise of solar, electric vehicles, and energy storage. As you'll see, the combination of all three will truly be a disruptive event that will bring positive and lasting changes to our energy supply and how we use it.

NOTES

1. instituteforenergyresearch.org/history-electricity/
2. www.shell.com/media/news-and-media-releases/2011/scenarios-signals-signposts/_jcr_content/par/textimage.stream/1441290243973/c391c923bdbf7a73e3e00313ecf588ac627d5f039704c1fbe3a4b6a1e35a9ae9/signals-signposts.pdf
3. www.ted.com/talks/ray_kurzweil_on_how_technology_will_transform_us?language=en
4. www.greentechmedia.com/articles/read/gtm-research-global-solar-pv-installations-grew-34-in-2015
5. www.pv-magazine.com/news/details/beitrag/ihs-272-gw-of-solar-installs-from-2016-2019_100021902/#axzz4FdKIyUb9
6. cleantechnica.com/2015/09/01/global-solar-pv-installed-capacity-expected-reach-652-gw-2025-globaldata/
7. www.ted.com/talks/ray_kurzweil_announces_singularity_university/transcript?language=en
8. https://www.jdsupra.com/legalnews/irs-notice-2018-59-clarifies-rules-on-37668/
9. https://www.fastcompany.com/40580693/exclusive-tesla-has-installed-a-truly-huge-amount-of-energy-storage
10. https://www.pv-magazine.com/2018/09/06/us-triples-energy-storage-installations/

Acknowledgments

There are many people who have helped and influenced me during my life, and during the process of writing this book.

To Julia Guth, who took a chance on a guy with no writing experience and gave me an inspiring and fulfilling encore career. You'll never know how much your support has meant to me.

To Alexander Green, investment guru, wonderful friend, extraordinary writer, and mentor to me over the past decade. Your continued encouragement has guided my success as a writer.

To Bob Williams, friend and motivator. Your faith in my abilities kept me on the right track.

To Louis Basenese and Carl Delfeld, thank you for pulling me out of the ocean and saving my life.

To Alison Kleeman. Thank you for your skill, attentive work, and rapid turnaround on the graphics for this book. You make it look so easy.

To Steven King, thanks for all you do, and your extraordinary attention to detail.

To Jan Carver, thanks for your support and interest in sustainability.

To all my friends and colleagues at the Oxford Club. Thanks to all of you for your unwavering support. The enthusiasm and drive you have as a group is unparalleled. Keep striving to raise the bar.

To Jeff Acopian, a devoted, lifelong friend who believes in sustainability. Thanks for taking us for a ride in your Tesla. You're a great salesman and early adopter.

To Steven Lee, provider of the best customer service and technical support on the planet. Thanks for helping to advance the sustainability movement. I love your little "black box."

To Elon Musk, a true visionary and the world's ambassador for sustainable living. I love my Tesla.

To Jenny Barnett Hauber, an angel of mercy who continues to help me navigate my road to recovery.

To Rick Schall. You are an amazing man, and so inspirational to so many. I think about you every day.

To all my friends at the Easton Anglers' Association. Thanks for your camaraderie and for allowing me to share in the stewardship of such a special place.

To everyone at the Good Shepherd Rehabilitation Hospital. You are a special, caring family of remarkable people. I wouldn't be where I am if it weren't for your undying support. You've shown me that anything is possible.

To Jessie Miller, Melissa Ward, Kelly Ward, and Rose Tavianini. Thanks for all your help with my research and typing. Your laughter and enthusiasm have made my work a real pleasure.

To Debbie Gryta. Where would I be without your care, attentiveness, and company? Your presence and gentle prodding make all the difference.

To my mother and father, who encouraged me to think that anything is possible.

To my brother Steve, I couldn't ask for a more devoted brother. You help me more than you'll ever know.

To my sons, Jared and Noah. I couldn't be more proud of the men you've become.

To my wife, Anne. You are my rock.

About the Author

 David C. Fessler is the editor of "Fessler's Flash Profits," a premium research service published by the Oxford Club.

The Oxford Club is one of the world's most exclusive and prestigious networks of private investors. He's their energy, infrastructure, and technology expert.

A prolific writer, David is also co-editor of the free e-letter, "Energy & Resource Digest," a focused overview of the energy and infrastructure markets appearing three times per week.

He's the co-editor of the "Strategic Trends Investor," a paid newsletter that delivers unique investment opportunities from a diverse range of industries and sectors.

His articles are syndicated widely. Seeking Alpha has listed Dave in the group of the top 100 fastest growing authors, and one of its Top Ten Commodities authors by readership.

David has appeared on the Fox News Channel, where he was one of the first journalists to break the story on the 2008 commercial real estate crash. David has also appeared on Moneyshow.com and The Real Estate Guys radio network.

Before retiring at the age of 47, David served as Vice President for Strategic Business at LTX Corporation. He was also Vice President of Operations, Sales & Marketing for Quality Telecommunications, Inc.

His success as an investor spans 45 years in the technology and energy sectors. He has owned and operated two successful businesses.

He's a degreed Electrical Engineer, and is a renowned specialist in the semiconductor, telecommunications, energy, and infrastructure sectors.

David, his wife Anne, and their sons, Jared and Noah, live on a 68-acre farm in northeast Pennsylvania. He generates most of his electricity via a ground-mounted solar array. He and his wife drive a Tesla Model X EV.

The US Solar Build Out: Disrupting Energy Supplies

CHAPTER ONE

The History of Solar Energy

About 4.5 billion years ago, Earth's Sun was born. It sits at the center of our solar system, 93 million miles away from Earth. It's also about 30,000 light years away from the center of the Milky Way galaxy. Our solar system is located in one of the Milky Way's spiral arms. Just as all of our planets rotate around the Sun, our solar system rotates around the center of the galaxy. It takes a mere 250 million years to do so.

Unlike the earth, the sun is entirely gaseous. It's approximately 74 percent hydrogen, 25 percent helium, and 1 percent other. A constant nuclear chain reaction produces the light and heat given off by the sun's layers. The sun's luminosity, or brightness, is the same as that produced by four trillion-trillion (4,000,000,000,000,000,000,000,000,000) 100-watt lightbulbs. The sun will continue to get brighter and larger for another five billion years.

In the meantime, humanity benefits from the solar energy that reaches the earth. We receive just one-billionth of the total energy generated by the sun. About 174,000 terawatts (TW) of radiation hits the earth's upper atmosphere. It reflects roughly 30 percent back into space. Oceans, landmasses, and clouds absorb the rest. The wavelengths of the solar radiation we receive are in the visible, ultraviolet, and near infrared spectrums. To put the amount of solar energy the earth gets into perspective, we receive more energy from the sun in one hour than the world uses in an entire year. It's roughly two times as much as all the energy that we will ever get from all of the oil, coal, natural gas, and uranium combined.[1]

However, the amount of energy actually available to generate electricity is less than what reaches the earth's surface. This is due to limiting factors such as cloud cover and geography. Landmasses closer to the equator receive far more solar radiation (called insolation) than lands closer to the polar regions.

THE MAGIC OF THE PHOTOVOLTAIC EFFECT

The French physicist A. E. Becquerel observed the photovoltaic effect for the first time in 1839. A voltage or electric current is created when various materials are exposed to light. It is both a chemical and physical phenomenon. When the light is absorbed, it causes the excitation of an electron to a state of higher energy. A voltage or electric potential is created by the separation of charges. The light hitting the material has to contain enough energy to surpass the potential excitation barrier. In the case of the sun, this isn't a problem.

Back in 1839, Becquerel's first experiment used an electrochemical cell to create the photovoltaic effect. But today we can observe the photovoltaic effect in solid-state semiconductor devices. These are either **photodiodes** or devices commonly called solar cells. When sunlight strikes the surface of a photodiode, electrons on the surface of the material absorb **photons** from the sunlight. The excited electrons jump to the conduction band and become free. They then diffuse into the material. Some will reach what is known as a rectifying junction (commonly called a **p-n junction**). The Galvani potential accelerates these into a different material. This process generates an electromotive force, thereby converting some of the original sunlight into electricity.

Now that we've established the vast potential of the sun's radiation, let's delve into man's quest to harness that radiation to produce useful energy. It all started in a small town in France, more than 150 years ago. Augustin Mouchot, a nineteenth-century French schoolteacher and inventor, was concerned about his country's increasingly dependent use of coal. He astutely believed that this natural resource would eventually run out, bringing the world's booming Industrial Revolution to a grinding halt. So, he began to investigate alternative energy

FIGURE 1.1 AUGUSTIN MOUCHOT AND ABEL PIFRE'S PARABOLIC
SOLAR-POWERED STEAM GENERATOR

Source: https://commons.wikimedia.org/wiki/File:Mouchot1878x.jpg.

sources that could replace the dirty fossil fuel. This ultimately led him to conduct experiments in solar energy.

His first experiments involved cooking with solar energy. He then demonstrated the ability to produce steam from a water-filled glass cauldron. He used this to power a small steam engine. Mouchot postured that if he could concentrate solar energy, he could produce even more steam. In 1866, he successfully designed the first parabolic solar collector (Figure 1.1). In 1869, he published his book *Solar Heat and Its Industrial Applications*.[2] That same year, Mouchot displayed the largest solar-powered steam engine he had ever built.

Mouchot's solar "motor" was a big hit. He worked for six years to improve his invention. He added a solar tracking mechanism that enabled the mirror to continually adjust to the sun's azimuth and altitude. This provided him with virtually uninterrupted and maximum reception of the sun's radiation. In 1872, he displayed his newly updated machine at his home in Tours. At this point, his solar motor was capable of producing one-half horsepower.

Mouchot tabulated his findings and results and reported them to the French Academy of Science. The French government was excited about Mouchot's invention. They decided that the best place to make the best use of it would be in the extremely hot and tropical climate of Algeria, which was a French protectorate at the time. Their reasoning was simple. Algeria had nearly constant sunshine, the perfect location for Mouchot's solar-powered steam motor. Before Mouchot's invention, steam engines in Algeria were entirely dependent on imported coal, a commodity that was prohibitively expensive in North Africa.

In 1878, Mouchot had yet again redesigned his solar steam motor. He attached this version to a refrigeration device. To an amazed audience, Mouchot demonstrated that it was possible to make ice using solar power. The French government awarded Mouchot a medal for his efforts. In 1881, it dispatched two commissioners from the French Ministry of Public Works to assess the cost efficiency of Mouchot's machine. They reported it was a technical success, but a failure in practice.

Unfortunately, for Mouchot, something else happened that was the deathblow for his invention. The French and English governments had vastly improved their working relationship. That meant that English coal, upon which the French were entirely dependent, became more readily and cheaply available. Mouchot, convinced this was a fool's errand, expressed his opinion in 1880 after one of his demonstrations of solar thermal energy: "Eventually industry will no longer find in Europe the resources to satisfy its prodigious expansion ... Coal will undoubtedly be used up. What will industry do then?"[3] The French government decided energy alternatives were no longer required and dropped Mouchot's research funding. Unable to find anyone else to fund his research and development, a frustrated Mouchot returned to teaching.

Mouchot had a young partner by the name of Abel Pifre. Upon returning to teaching, Mouchot sold Pifre his patents. Pifre perfected Mouchot's original designs and increased their performance. In 1882, Pifre tested one of his improved generators at the Tuileries Gardens in Paris. It generated enough steam to power a Marinoni printing press that printed 500 newspapers per hour.

At this point, Pifre's solar-powered steam motor caught the attention of an Englishman by the name of William Grylls Adams, a professor of natural philosophy at King's College in London. Adams was convinced he could make improvements to Pifre's design that would greatly increase its power. He changed out Pifre's original parabolic dish-shaped reflector for 72 individual 10-inch by 17-inch flat mirrors. He aimed each one individually toward the central boiler. Adams' design produced enough steam to run a 2.5 horsepower steam engine, five times as big as Pifre's design.

Shortly thereafter, Adams's experimentation ended. Historians believe Adams lacked the enthusiasm to pursue further commercialization of his machine. But his design is the same basic concept used in today's **concentrated solar power** tower systems. The only difference is that the steam produced from today's systems powers a turbine shaft that connects to an electrical generator.

However, Adams had another experiment unrelated to his experiments on improving Pifre's solar steam-powered motor. In 1876, Adams, teamed with one of his students, Richard Evans Day, discovered that when light struck one of two metal plates immersed in a dilute acid, it produced a weak electrical signal. The two plates were selenium and platinum, and illuminating their junction produced a photovoltaic effect, a chemical and physical phenomenon.

Werner von Siemens, one of the nineteenth century's greatest experts in the field of electricity, said Adams and Day's discovery was "scientifically of the most far-reaching importance." The selenium/platinum "solar cell" was far from efficient. Nevertheless, this was the very first demonstration that a junction of two metals, exposed to light, could directly produce electricity.

Albert Einstein was the first to explain the **photoelectric** effect in 1905. Einstein postulated that a new quantum theory of light explained the effect. He wrote an extensive paper on the subject and received the 1921 Nobel Prize in Physics for his efforts. In 1913, William Coblentz, a research scientist at the National Bureau of Standards, received the very first US patent (no. 1077219) for a "solar cell."

It would be almost 70 years after Adams's and Day's early experiments with selenium and platinum cells before scientists would discover the modern silicon solar cell, also known as the silicon photovoltaic (PV) cell. In 1954, three Bell Laboratory scientists, D. M. Chapin, C. S. Fuller, and G. L. Pearson, demonstrated the first silicon-based solar cell. Their paper, "A New Silicon p-n Junction Photocell for Converting Solar Radiation into Electrical Power," appeared in the May 1954 issue of the *Journal of Applied Physics*.

The initial silicon solar cells produced by the trio were only 6 percent efficient. After their unveiling to the public, the *New York Times* proclaimed the discovery was "the beginning of a new era, leading eventually to the realization of harnessing the almost limitless energy of the sun for the uses of civilization."[4] A year later, AT&T's manufacturing arm, the Western Electric Company, licensed the technology. In 1956, the first commercial solar cells became available. At $300 for a 1-watt cell, the cost was prohibitively expensive for most applications. Another company, Hoffman Electronics, created a commercial silicon-based PV cell with an efficiency of 2 percent. Each cell cost $25, and 71 of them were required to produce 1 watt of power.[5]

At this point, the only customers for those expensive solar cells were companies building satellites for communications and military purposes. In 1958, the US Signal Corps Laboratory developed a silicon solar cell design that was highly resistant to radiation damage in space. Later that same year, the United States launched the Vanguard I, the very first solar-powered satellite. Its solar panel was just 100 square centimeters, or about 2.5 inches on a side. It produced just 0.1 watts of power.[6]

The 1960s and 1970s saw continued improvements in solar cell efficiency and use. By 1960, Hoffman Electronics created a silicon solar cell with 14 percent efficiency. In 1962, the United States launched the Telstar communications satellite, powered by solar. In 1967, the Soviet Union launched Soyuz 1, the first solar-powered, manned spacecraft. A year later saw the introduction of a solar wristwatch and in 1973, the United States launched Skylab, the first US-manned orbiting spacelab powered by solar cells.[7] Finally, in the late 1970s, in addition to solar-powered calculators, solar got a big boost in public interest as a result of the "energy crisis." The Iran-Iraq war triggered it, and it led to a significant drop in Iran's oil output.

The 1980s and 1990s saw even more interest and improvements in solar technology. In 1982, Kyocera Corporation was the first company to mass-produce silicon solar cells. It used the casting method, a manufacturing technique that is still today's industry standard. By 1983, the worldwide cumulative PV production had reached 21.3 megawatts and sales hit $250 million.[8]

In 1984, the very first rooftop PV installation sat on the roof of the Intercultural Center at Georgetown University. The rooftop array totaled 30,000 square feet and to this day produces an average of 1 megawatt-hour of electricity daily. By 1985, solar was under development around the world. At the University of New South Wales School for Photovoltaic Engineering, researchers created the first solar cells to reach 20 percent efficiency.[9]

In 1991, solar energy in the United States got a big boost. President George H. W. Bush announced the creation of the National Renewable Energy Laboratory (NREL) under the US Department of Energy. In 1993, the NREL established the Solar Energy Research Facility. By the end of the decade, worldwide PV installations reached a cumulative 1 gigawatt (1,000 megawatts). Solar was well on the way to becoming more than just a science experiment.

THE NEW MILLENNIUM USHERS IN RENEWABLE ENERGY

Since 2000, the continued development of solar cell efficiency and automated, high-speed manufacturing technology has enabled solar energy to flourish. It is now a mainstream energy source in the United States, and globally as well. In 2003, President George W. Bush had a 9-kW PV solar energy system and a thermal solar hot water system installed on the grounds-keeping building on the White House grounds.

However, what really got solar off the ground in the United States has been a continuing series of state mandates for renewable energy. These consist of an individual state requiring its electric utilities to have a given percentage of its generated power come from renewables by a certain date.

California has clearly led the US charge toward renewable energy. It started in 2004 with Governor Arnold Schwarzenegger. Through his Solar Roofs Initiative, he proposed that California have one million solar roofs by 2017. Through June 30, 2018, according to the Solar Energy Industries Association, the state led the nation with 863,266 solar projects installed. That equates to 22.77 GW of PV solar power.[10]

California recently approved a law that requires most new homes built in the state starting in 2020 have solar rooftop panels installed.[11]

Also in 2004, Governor Kathleen Sebelius issued a state mandate for 1 GW of renewable power in Kansas by 2015. Next came the Renewable Energy Standards Act, HB 2369, passed by the Kansas legislature in 2009, which created the state's first renewable portfolio standard (RPS). It required the state's investor-owned utilities to buy or generate at least 20 percent of its peak electrical demand from renewable sources starting in 2020.[12]

Then, in May 2015, the Kansas state legislature approved SB 91, which made the 2009 goal voluntary. This was somewhat ironic, because by 2014, wind power generation alone already accounted for 21.7 percent of the state's electricity mix. Regardless, SB 91 is viewed as a backward step for renewable energy in Kansas.

Polysilicon was primarily used in the fabrication of integrated circuits and other semiconductors until 2006, when the use of polysilicon for solar exceeded all other uses for the first time ever. That same year, the California Public Utilities Commission approved a program to keep polysilicon use for solar on the rise. The California Solar Initiative was a $2.8 billion, comprehensive program providing incentives for solar project development over the next 11 years.[13]

In 2007, the Vatican and Google both announced they would install solar energy systems to reduce their dependence on fossil fuel–generated electricity. That same year, the University of Delaware claimed it set a new world record in solar cell efficiency at 42.8 percent, although another laboratory has never independently confirmed this. In 2008, the NREL set a confirmed world record of 40.8 percent in solar cell efficiency, but it used a light concentrator to focus the equivalent energy of 326 suns on the solar cell.[14]

Even though some of the new techniques for improving efficiency were not cost-effective, it was clear that solar energy was on the rise. In 2010, President Barack Obama added additional solar panels and thermal solar water heating on the White House.

By 2011, a number of rapidly growing factories in China pushed PV solar panel manufacturing costs down to $1.25 per watt. By the end of the year, utilities and homeowners had installed roughly 70 GW of solar generating capacity worldwide. That was a 204 percent jump in just two years.[15]

By 2016, researchers at the University of New South Wales set a new world record for solar cell efficiency at 34.5 percent. Their cell was a single solar cell using unfocused sunlight embedded in a prism. That extracted the maximum energy from the sunlight by splitting it into four separate bands. Engineers used a four-junction receiver to capture and produce electricity from each band.[16]

In parallel to the development of silicon PV cells, **thin-film solar cells** were also under development. To make thin-film PV cells, engineers deposit one or more thin-film layers on a substrate of glass, metal, or plastic. There are three thin-film technologies. They are amorphous thin-film silicon (a-Si, TF-Si), cadmium telluride (CdTe), and copper indium gallium diselenide (CIGS). These technologies and their future applications are discussed in more detail in Chapter 5.

Cells made using thin-film technology are far thinner than cells made using crystalline silicon (c-Si). The advantage of thin-film, especially when using plastic substrates, is that the cells and panels can be flexible, semitransparent, and much lower in weight. Building integrated PV (BIPV) systems, where roof shingles and building siding can act as solar gathering devices, use thin-film technology. Given their transparent nature, thin-film solar can be laminated onto window glass.

But the thin-film technologies are mainly attractive because they are far less costly than conventional c-Si cells and modules. Today, some of the largest commercial, utility-scale power plants use thin-film solar panels. While cell efficiencies of thin-film have lagged those of c-Si, recent lab cell efficiencies for CdTe and CIGS are beyond 21 percent. Under accelerated life testing conditions, however, thin-film modules and panels seem to degrade faster than c-Si panels. Typically, c-Si panels come with a 25-year warranty, whereas thin-film panels have an expected lifetime of 20 years.[17]

During their heyday, thin-film solar panels commanded as much as 20 percent of the solar panel market but have now receded to about 9 percent of the overall solar panel market. The story of the rise and fall of thin-film solar technology is an interesting one. No history of solar energy would be complete without it.

It all started in 2007. The increasing demand for solar panels was straining the ability of crystalline silicon wafer manufacturers to keep up. While manufacturers of crystalline silicon ingots were building additional capacity, it was clear that it was lagging the exploding

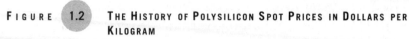

FIGURE 1.2   THE HISTORY OF POLYSILICON SPOT PRICES IN DOLLARS PER
              KILOGRAM

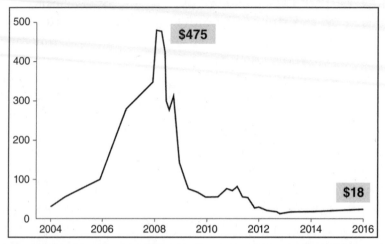

Source: commons.wikimedia.org/wiki/File:Polysilicon_prices_history_since_2004.svg and: pv.energytrend.com/pricequotes.html.

demand for solar panels. As you can see from Figure 1.2, the cost for raw polysilicon hit $475 per kilogram ($1,045 per pound) back in early 2008.

Clearly, something had to be done. Enter a company called Solyndra. It offered what was then a novel, CIGS, thin-film solar panel. But Solyndra wasn't the only company betting on thin-film technology. In a presentation I gave in 2009, I said there were no less than 143 companies making or planning to make thin-film solar panels. Most are out of business today. What happened?

As you can see from Figure 1.2, the unthinkable, but in hindsight very predictable, thing happened. Manufacturing capacity for polysilicon crystal mushroomed. When that happened, prices for raw polysilicon fell dramatically. And that killed the economic models of nearly every would-be thin-film solar panel manufacturer. Their long-term viability was completely dependent on the price of raw polysilicon remaining high. Nonetheless, an increase in demand for any commodity is eventually met with an increase in supply. That's what happened a decade ago and it spelled the end for most thin-film manufacturers.

The case of Solyndra was notable for several reasons. Solyndra was founded in Fremont, California, in 2005. It designed, manufactured, and sold CIGS-based thin-film solar panels. But its panels were unique in the industry. Each 1 × 2 meter panel contained a rack of 40 cylindrical tubes. Each tube was actually a CIGS thin-film solar module containing up to 200 CIGS cells.[18] Solyndra believed its revolutionary cylindrical design could produce significantly more electricity than conventional panels. That's because Solyndra claimed its panels always had some of its face directly perpendicular to the sun's rays.

In September 2009, Solyndra received a $535 million loan guarantee from the US Department of Energy to build and equip a 450-MW thin-film panel-manufacturing factory. Known as Fab 2, this facility's total cost was $733 million. The remainder of its financing was put up by private investors. The plant was the size of five football fields, with a total of 300,000 square feet under roof. It was going to be highly automated with robotic assembly of individual panel assemblies. When completed in 2013, its projected annual production was 610 megawatts worth of panels.

After its peak in early 2008, however, the price of polysilicon, the raw material for Solyndra's competition, began dropping. By November 3, 2010, the writing was on the wall. Solyndra announced a layoff of 40 employees and the cancellation of contracts for 150 temporary workers. By mid-2011, the price of polysilicon had fallen 89 percent from its mid-2008 high. On August 31, 2011, Solyndra formally filed for Chapter 11 bankruptcy protection. It completely shut down all manufacturing and operations and laid off its remaining 1,100 employees.[19]

Given the amount of federal loan money involved, the US Treasury Department launched an investigation in September 2011. The FBI raided the company and the homes of Solyndra's CEO Brian Harrison, and its founder Chris Gronet. There was an immediate sense of company overspending.

An article originally published by *Bloomberg* reported that the Taj Mahal–like plant had robots whistling Disney tunes. The employee showers had "spa-like liquid crystal displays of the water temperature," and "glass-walled conference rooms."[20] It became obvious to investigators that Solyndra had designed and built a plant capable of building far more solar panels than it had orders for. Initially, it looked as though the Obama administration, and ultimately the US taxpayers, were going to be stuck with the defaulted loan. But by 2014, the US Department of Energy renewables loan program had recouped its losses, including Solyndra's $528 million blunder, and was profitable.

In 2018, demand for thin-film solar panels is a fraction of what it was during 2008, when polysilicon was in short supply. Currently, there is an oversupply of polysilicon for solar and semiconductor use, despite very strong demand in both semiconductor and solar markets. In January 2016, polysilicon prices hit near-record lows. Because of increased capacity built by existing manufacturers and Chinese capacity growth, the oversupply that was 7 percent in 2016 grew to 15 percent in 2018.[21] Based on the extension of the US renewables Investment Tax Credit, the Paris United Nations Conference on Climate Change (COP21) CO_2 limits, and higher solar growth in emerging markets, solar demand is outpacing even recent forecasts. You can clearly see this in Figure 1.3.

However, the ongoing trade war between China and the United States has affected the polysilicon market. Unfortunately, the United States has lost all access to Chinese polysilicon wafers. These are a key ingredient in the manufacture of solar cells, modules, and panels. In February 2016, polysilicon was selling for just $12 per kilogram,

FIGURE 1.3   PV DEMAND BY REGION

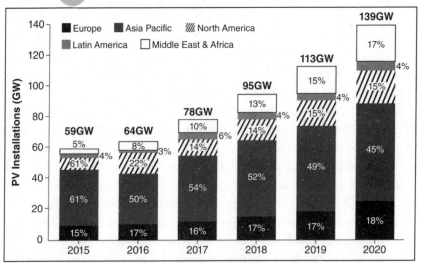

Data source: www.seia.org/research-resources/solar-market-insight-report-2015-q2.

FIGURE  1.4   POLYSILICON SUPPLY/DEMAND

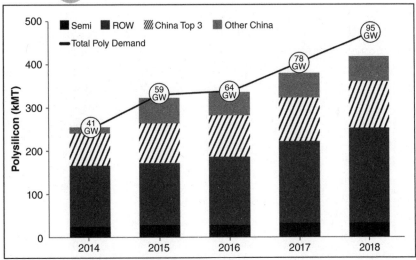

Data source: www.seia.org/research-resources/solar-market-insight-report-2015-q2.

near historic lows. But by April 2016, prices had risen to $19 per kilogram, a 58 percent increase in just three months. It turns out, according to IHS Markit, that some, if not all, of the price increase is due to demand in China.

The Chinese imposed a June 30, 2016, deadline, after which it cut solar feed-in tariff levels to large-scale wind and solar developers in China. The intent was to focus future installations on commercial and industrial sites, on the distributed side of the network. That created a rush to install new systems before the deadline. That also created a big spike in the demand for polysilicon.

Figure 1.4 shows polysilicon supply/demand and Figure 1.5 shows the market balance for polysilicon through 2018. This is predicated on a global PV demand forecast hitting 95 GW for 2018.[22]

Resolving the trade dispute with China makes sense for both countries. China will have better access to the US panel market. This is even more desirable since the investment tax credit extension (see the Introduction). It will eliminate US duty hikes on Chinese panels. Finally, it will eliminate the blooming polysilicon shortage in China.

For the United States, the reopening of the China market will help alleviate any shortage of polysilicon in China. Since most of the new

F I G U R E   1.5   POLYSILICON MARKET BALANCE

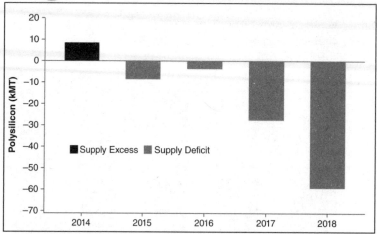

Data source: www.seia.org/research-resources/solar-market-insight-report-2015-q2.

polysilicon manufacturing capacity is being added outside of China, shortages for the rest of the world, including the United States are less likely to materialize.

The bottom line is solar energy is here to stay. While it took over 100 years to get to where we are today, it's clear that solar energy isn't just a science project anymore. Prices are competitive with conventional generation, and are already responsible for retiring fossil fuel-fired generating plants. Based on the above forecast from IHS, solar is set to pop 117 percent between now and 2020. Frankly, I believe that number could turn out to be conservative. We could see global demand come close to doubling by 2022.

NOTES

1. gcep.stanford.edu/research/exergycharts.html
2. books.google.com/books?id=IU5DAAAAIAAJ&source=gbs_navlinks_s
3. themindunleashed.org/2015/12/heres-how-long-weve-had-solar-power-technology-yet-have-chosen-to-use-coal-instead.html
4. www.experience.com/alumnus/article?channel_id=energy_utilities&source_page=additional_articles&article_id=article_1130427780670
5. en.wikipedia.org/wiki/Timeline_of_solar_cells
6. Ibid.

7. Ibid.
8. Ibid.
9. Ibid.
10. https://www.seia.org/states-map
11. www.californiasolarstatistics.ca.gov/
12. www.forbes.com/sites/williampentland/2015/05/29/kansas-makes-renewable-energy-standard-voluntary/—2514a52667a2
13. en.wikipedia.org/wiki/Timeline_of_solar_cells
14. Ibid.
15. Ibid.
16. Ibid.
17. en.wikipedia.org/wiki/Thin-film_solar_cell
18. www.greentechmedia.com/articles/read/solyndra-rolls-out-tube-shaped-thin-film-1542
19. en.wikipedia.org/wiki/Solyndra
20. www.bloomberg.com/news/articles/2011-09-28/solyndra-s-733-million-plant-had-whistling-robots-spa-showers
21. electroiq.com/2017/10/strong-solar-and-semiconductor-demand-but-still-a-sizeable-oversupply-of-polysilicon/
22. www.pv-tech.org/editors-blog/is-polysilicon-heading-for-shortage

CHAPTER TWO

The Workings of a Modern Solar Energy System

I n order to understand how a solar energy system works, I need to show you how a typical solar cell turns the sun's rays into an electrical current. The radiation emanating from the sun consists of photons. They travel to the earth at the speed of light. When photons hit a solar cell that's part of a solar panel, the silicon in the cell absorbs them. This causes electrons that were happily spinning around on their atomic orbit to get excited. Once a photon strike excites an electron, one of two things happens: The electron can dissipate the energy caused by the strike in the form of heat and return to its orbit, or the electron can move through the cell until it strikes an electrode. That strike generates an electric current. This current flows through the cell layers.

The vital part of the process is the chemical bonds of the various layers. There are usually two layers of silicon, one bonded with phosphorus and the other with boron. The two layers have different electrical charges, one positive and one negative. This difference allows electricity to flow between them as photons strike the surface of the cell. Solar cells create **direct current** (**DC**) electricity. Later in this chapter I'll discuss how DC electricity is converted to the **alternating current** (**AC**) electricity that we use at home and at work.

HOW POLYCRYSTALLINE SILICON SOLAR CELLS WORK

Scientists used silicon wafers to make the first generation of solar cells. Silicon is a very attractive raw material for solar cells. It has the ability to keep its semiconductor properties at high temperatures. In addition, silicon is abundant; however, purity levels required for both semiconductors and solar cells are very high. Roughly 90 percent of all solar panel applications use **polycrystalline silicon** solar cells. That's due to the high efficiencies you can achieve with polycrystalline silicon cells, compared to other solar cell technologies.

Figure 2.1 shows the composition of a typical p-n junction, polycrystalline silicon solar cell. The cell consists of four layers. The top layer (represented by the bars) is an antireflective coating. That's needed to keep photons from the sun's rays from reflecting before they can energize electrons. Below that are n-type and p-type silicon. The thin, gray layer conducts electrons. The thin line between the p-type semiconductor and the n-type semiconductor is the p-n junction.

When an n-type semiconductor layer is hit by light in the form of photons, each photon will free exactly one electron. This will leave a

FIGURE 2.1 COMPOSITION OF A TYPICAL p-n JUNCTION, POLYCRYSTALLINE SILICON SOLAR CELL

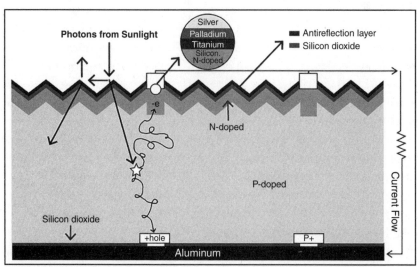

Data source: en.wikipedia.org/wiki/Solar_cell—/media/File:Silicon_Solar_cell_structure_and_mechanism.svg.

free hole. If this happens close by the electric field, it will drive the hole to the p side and the electron to the n side. If, as shown in Figure 2.1, there is an external electrical current path, electrons will flow through that path to the p side to fill holes that the electric field created there. This is a simple representation of the photoelectric effect, and the basic operation of a solar cell.

Individual solar cells are typically about four inches in diameter. A single cell produces 0.5 volts. The typical solar panel contains 96 solar cells connected in series. This produces a panel voltage of 48 volts DC. The panel's efficiency determines the power produced, and can range from 150 watts to 345 watts per panel.

SOLAR CELL MANUFACTURING PROCESS

In this section, I'll cover the manufacturing process and technology associated with polycrystalline silicon cell manufacturing. Later in this chapter, I'll touch on other cell technologies but won't get into other types of cell manufacturing. I believe polycrystalline silicon will remain the dominant cell technology as costs continue to decline.

As mentioned above, every polycrystalline silicon cell has as its base component a silicon wafer. A technician fills an electric carbon arc furnace with raw silicon, in the form of crushed quartz or quartzite gravel. The carbon releases the oxygen trapped in the quartz and the end products are molten silicon, a slag of impurities, and carbon dioxide.

Next, the machine lowers a half-inch diameter length of pure silicon (called the seed) into the molten silicon. It slowly rotates the seed and starts withdrawing a silicon ingot from the molten bath. The withdrawal rate determines the diameter of the resulting mono-crystal silicon ingot.

The silicon ingot is extremely pure. That's because the liquid bath tends to keep impurities in it. A diamond saw mills the ingot into a rectangular or hexagonal shape. This allows maximum space utilization when cells fit together on panels. A second diamond saw cuts the ingot into 0.5-millimeter-thick wafers. Special lapping machines polish the wafers to a mirror finish.

The next step in the cell manufacturing process is to "dope" the wafer. Doping intentionally adds impurities back into the silicon in order to change its electrical properties. Doped silicon is a much better conductor of electricity than pure silicon. Boron and phosphorous are typical dopants used on wafers destined to become solar cells.

From this point forward, the process is highly automated. Robots place wafers in a furnace. It heats them to 1,410°C (2,570°F), just below silicon's melting point. The furnace computer then introduces a small amount of phosphorous gas into the furnace chamber. The phosphorous atoms diffuse into the silicon as it is close to liquefying. The amount of phosphorous, temperature, and time are all carefully controlled. This creates a uniform diffusion depth. This process is very similar to doping processes used in the semiconductor industry.

The wafers then transfer to a screening machine. This machine screens thin lines of silver paste onto the wafers to create electrical connections on the front and back of the wafer. The final step is to heat the wafers in a furnace to temperatures ranging from 750–900°C (1,382–1,652°F). This firmly connects the silver to the front and back of the wafer. The lines have to be thin so as not to block sunlight to the cell surface.

The next step is to cover the cell surface with an antireflective coating. Pure silicon has a mirror-like finish and can reflect up to 35 percent of the incoming sunlight. This coating is typically silicon oxide or titanium dioxide. There are a number of different processes used to deposit this coating. The silicon wafers of the newest cells have a pyramid-shaped, grainy surface (Figure 2.2). These conduct as much as 70 percent of the available light. Scientists are using **nanotechnology** as a means to increase the surface area of a silicon wafer.

Finally, robots connect the finished cells to make a string of 36 or more. A tough glass top surface and a plastic back encapsulate the complete solar module. Glue attaches the module to an aluminum frame to allow mounting on rooftops or ground-mount assemblies.

SOLAR CELL AND MODULE EFFICIENCIES

The efficiency of a solar cell refers to the amount of sunlight the cell can convert into electricity. There are a number of factors that determine overall cell efficiency. **Reflectance efficiency** is a measure of the amount of light reflected back into the atmosphere from the cell surface.

FIGURE 2.2   SCANNING ELECTRON MICROSCOPE PHOTOGRAPH OF A TEXTURED SILICON SURFACE

Source: UNSW Photovoltaic and Renewable Energy Engineering. Reproduced with permission.

The thermodynamic efficiency is a measure of the amount of sunlight converted by the cell into electricity. The absolute maximum theoretically possible limit is 86 percent. However, in practice, limits for different technologies are far lower than that. For instance, a single junction silicon cell has a maximum thermodynamic efficiency limit of 31 percent.

Other factors affecting the overall efficiency of a solar cell are conduction efficiency and charge carrier separation efficiency. These parameters are difficult to measure, and their description is beyond the scope of this book.

The current world record for solar cell efficiency was set in December 2014. A multi-junction, light-concentrating solar cell achieved the remarkable efficiency of 46 percent. Scientists achieved this through the collaborative efforts of Fraunhofer ISE (Germany), CEA-Leti (France), and Soitec (France).

However, most solar cells used in today's photovoltaic systems have just one junction. This means they have a lower efficiency limit called the **ultimate efficiency**. Photons that are outside of the absorption range of the surface material cannot generate a flow of electrons that produces electricity. Instead, the light energy converts to heat. The ultimate efficiency for a single junction silicon photovoltaic cell is approximately 34 percent.

In February 2016, SunPower Corporation set a new record for solar module efficiency. In a National Renewable Energy Laboratory (NREL)–certified test, SunPower's latest module is 22.8 percent efficient. Then in June 2016, SunPower broke its own record introducing a module with an NREL-validated result of 24.1 percent. In March 2018, SunPower started selling its 22.8 percent efficient panels commercially.[1] There is absolutely no question in my mind that by the time you read this, this record will most certainly have been broken, either by SunPower or some other panel manufacturer. Technology marches on.

SOLAR PANEL MANUFACTURING

In order to make a solar panel, you must connect multiple solar cells together. The solar panel manufacturing process is highly automated. The modern solar-manufacturing plant employs robots, conveyors, and other automated machinery to lay out and construct each solar panel. To minimize contaminants, which could cause premature failure of the panel, the entire process happens in cleanroom conditions.

The first step in the process is to solder as many as 10 cells together into a string. This creates an electrical connection between the cells. Strings of cells are laid out in the form of a rectangular matrix containing 48, 60, or 72 cells. The next step is to connect the individual strings together via **soldering.**

The automated assembly line moves the cell matrix between two sheets of a special encapsulant. The assembly then moves to the next station, where one robot places a tough glass sheet over the top. A second robot places a highly durable backsheet made from a polymer-based material under the bottom encapsulant. The polymer backsheet has an access hole milled in it to allow the electrical conductors from the cell matrix to connect to a junction box. Heaters gently warm the entire assembly to activate both sheets of encapsulant. Slight pressure forces all layers together to create a complete encapsulation of the cell matrix. This protects them from harsh winter and summer weather.

Finally, a robot flips the assembly upside-down, and epoxies the junction box to the rear of the access hole and connects it electrically to the cell matrix. Robots then place a rigid aluminum frame around the entire assembly. They apply a waterproof glue to bond it to the glass surface. This provides structural rigidity to the panel, and facilitates mounting on a roof or ground-mounted racking system. The panel then proceeds to quality assurance testing and packaging for delivery.

THE PLUNGING COST OF SOLAR

One amazing graph tells the tale of solar and its future (see Figure 2.3). In 1975, solar energy production was primarily used by NASA to power satellites. Early solar cells were only about 4 percent efficient, and they were very expensive to make. At the time, no one seriously considered that polycrystalline silicon solar would ever develop into a serious mainstream energy source.

Engineers had to develop processes to purify silicon to a very high level. They then had to grow it into single crystal silicon ingots. Special saws cut each ingot into thin silicon wafers. Other machines polished them to a very smooth mirror-like finish. At the time, each cell produced just 0.5 watts of power. Connecting enough cells together and somehow creating solar panels at a reasonable price seemed impossible.

FIGURE 2.3 PRICE OF SOLAR PANELS IN WATTS AND TOTAL GLOBAL SOLAR INSTALLATION IN MEGAWATTS

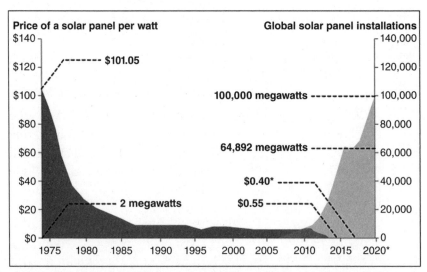

Source: www.treehugger.com/renewable-energy/striking-chart-showing-solar-power-will-take-over-world.html and new data from: www.greentechmedia.com/articles/read/gtm-research-global-solar-pv-installations-grew-34-in-2015 and cleantechnica.com/2015/01/29/solar-costs-will-fall-40-next-2-years-heres/.

As the cost of semiconductor wafers dropped over the next several decades, however, so did the cost of manufacturing solar cells. After all, a solar cell is just one giant semiconductor device. As prices dropped, cell efficiencies improved, too. Solar cells in production today have efficiencies as high as 24 percent. Back in 1975, solar panels cost $101.05 per watt of power produced. In October 2015, SolarCity announced a panel that produces power for $0.55 per watt.[2] But panels are going to get even cheaper. The International Renewable Energy Association predicts that prices will fall to $0.40 per watt by the end of 2017 or so.[3] Most large manufacturers are improving (reducing) cost per watt by 1–2 cents every quarter. It's certainly reasonable to think they'll reach $0.40 by the time this book is published.

A graph like the one shown in Figure 2.3 is quite familiar to any entrepreneur who's tried to launch a new product. The proof of concept phase is on the far left. The valley in between, often referred to in business as the "valley of death," can be longer and wider than a product developer's pockets. In the case of solar, it took three decades for the industry to really enter a viable commercial market.

The year 2000 was a notable one for the nascent solar industry. It had finally surpassed total panel production of 1 GW. That's the equivalent of a large, conventional coal or natural gas-fired power plant. By 2003, the solar industry was using more silicon wafer real estate than the semiconductor industry. Just four short years after it hit 1 GW of total panel production, the solar industry was producing 1-GW-worth of panels annually.

In just the past 10 years, solar installations have skyrocketed from about 5 GW of installed capacity worldwide to over 65 GW. Solar energy quickly became a mainstream option for utilities considering new capacity. A virtuous cycle of favorable government policies fueled increased installations. That drove manufacturers to invest in highly automated manufacturing lines, which drove costs down even more. That created even more demand and even lower prices, and so on.

It turns out there is a "Moore's law" for solar. It's **Swanson's law,** in honor of Richard Swanson. He is the founder of SunPower Corporation. Swanson's law states that every time there is a doubling of panel production and shipment, there is a 20 percent drop in panel costs. Swanson wrote a paper on this relationship back in 2006. Figure 2.4 is a chart depicting Swanson's law.

FIGURE **2.4** SWANSON'S LAW FOR PHOTOVOLTAICS

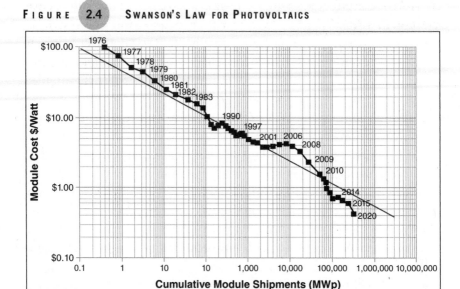

Source: en.wikipedia.org/wiki/Swanson%27s_law#/media/File:Swansons-law.png and updated with additional data provided by author.

As you can see from the figure, module costs have generally followed Swanson's law. In fact, by the end of 2015, panel costs had dropped to $0.55 per watt. By 2018, panel costs dropped to $0.37 per watt. By 2022, GTM Research projects that solar panel manufacturing costs will drop to $0.24 per watt. That's a drop of more than 100 percent in just seven years.[4] However, panel prices have fallen so far that they now represent less than half the total cost of a complete solar system at both the residential and utility scale. Most of the system now comprises **soft costs**. These are the inverters that change the direct current (DC) power into alternating current (AC) power that is grid-compatible. In addition to inverters, mounting hardware, grid connection fees and labor are also part of the soft costs.

From the present forward, it is now more appropriate to ask what is the cost reduction trend of solar-produced *electricity*. There will still be additional reductions in the cost of solar panels. But overall system costs, especially at the utility-scale level, will have the biggest impact on the cost of solar electricity.

For large utility-scale systems, having an executed **Power Purchase Agreement** (PPA) in place is almost a necessity before the system is constructed. A PPA is a long-term (usually 20 years) contract between the entity generating electricity (the seller) and a second party looking to purchase electricity (the buyer). The seller is generally the builder or developer of the utility-scale plant. The buyer is usually a utility; however, it may also be a building occupant, a government entity, a school, or a business.

Utility-scale solar installations are becoming increasingly popular. Due to the lack of a national energy plan, many states have passed renewable energy mandates. These require utilities to obtain a certain percentage of their power from renewable sources. The easiest way for utilities to comply is by executing PPAs with utility-scale solar plant developers. Banks or other entities providing financing for utility-scale projects almost always require that an executed PPA be in place before any money will be lent to build a project.

When it comes to PPAs, the seller typically seeks non-recourse project financing for the utility-scale project. This limits the seller's liability to the value of the project and the electricity produced. The PPA has clear definitions that define the expected power output of the solar project, and its associated revenue stream. In addition, the Federal Energy Regulatory Commission (FERC) regulates and reviews all PPAs in the United States.

Developers price PPAs in dollars per megawatt-hour (MWh) produced. As solar system prices have come down, so too have PPA prices, as seen in Figure 2.5.

Under the typical PPA, the seller is responsible for operation and maintenance of the utility-scale project. This typically includes regular inspections, any panel replacements if necessary, and cleaning of the panel surfaces. The seller is also required to install and maintain a metering device that measures the real-time and cumulative power output data. This is typically an automated system that the purchaser can access anytime.

The PPA also delineates the delivery point of the power (i.e. where the sale point is relative to the buyer and seller's location). With solar PPAs, the typical delivery is a **busbar** sale or delivery. That means the

FIGURE **2.5**   LEVELIZED US UTILITY-SCALE PPA PRICES

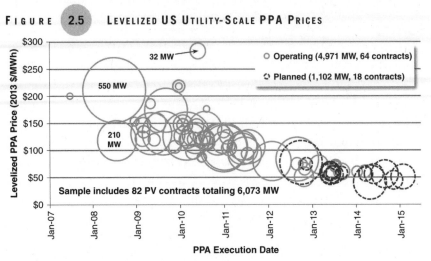

Source: emp.lbl.gov/sites/all/files/lbnl-183129_0.pdf.

actual delivery point is located on the transmission, or high side, of the transformer at the project site. In this case, the buyer is responsible for transmitting the purchased electricity from the seller's location.

The price for solar energy keeps hitting new lows. Lower installation costs and better utility-scale project performance are the two big cost-reduction drivers. The current average for PPA pricing is 4¢/kWh.[5] By way of comparison, US wholesale electricity prices ranged from 2–4¢/kWh in 2015.[6] That puts utility-scale solar right in the middle of the wholesale range, making it an increasingly cost-competitive option for utilities. Since 2009, according to a report published by the Lawrence Berkeley National Laboratory, the installed costs for utility-scale projects are down by 85 percent.

The biggest driver of cost reduction is higher panel efficiencies. As panel efficiencies increase, fewer panels are required for a given level of power output. For a small, home system of 10 KW, it may only mean three or four fewer panels. However, for a 50 to 100 MW utility-scale solar farm, the savings can be dramatic. Even a 1 percent increase in panel efficiency can mean hundreds or thousands of fewer panels on a large system. It also means fewer inverters, less wiring, less racking, and lower installation costs.

As a result of utility-scale solar's lower cost, the pipeline of projects in development just continues to increase. At the end of 2017, the utility-scale solar sector added 6,200 MW of additional utility-scale capacity.[7] At the end of 2017, the total installed utility-scale solar stood at roughly 70 GW, or 60 percent of all installed solar capacity.[8] The market is showing signs of spreading outside of California, as much of the new capacity is located in the southeast and Texas.

Figure 2.6 comes from a Lawrence Berkeley National Laboratories study. Like every other industrial product, solar is getting cheaper as production scales upward. Figure 2.6 shows a trend in time. In the case of solar PV modules, history has shown that doubling manufacturing capacity has reduced costs by 20 percent. When we look at electricity generated from utility-scale solar systems, we get Figure 2.6.

As we can see from Figure 2.6, every doubling of utility-scale solar generating capacity results in a 16 percent reduction in electricity costs produced by the newest solar installations. I expect that if this study were repeated today (the original was undertaken in May 2015), the rate would be higher than 16 percent. The main takeaway from the Lawrence Berkeley National Laboratories study is that scaling up production of panels and solar generating plants is the key factor in reducing both the costs of solar panels and the electricity they produce.

FIGURE 2.6 SOLAR ELECTRICITY PRICES DECLINE AT 16 PERCENT FOR EVERY DOUBLING OF INSTALLED CAPACITY

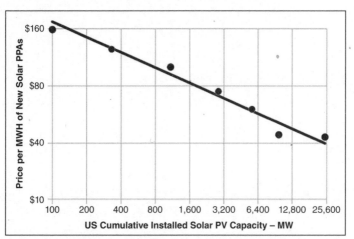

Source: rameznaam.com/wp-content/uploads/2015/08/Solar-Full-PPA-and-LCOE-Learning-Curve.jpg.

We'll cover the bright future of solar (pun intended) in Chapter 5. We'll also look at other promising solar cell technologies in that section. In Chapter 3, I'll outline the information you need to determine if solar is right for you and how to calculate the size of the system. Many installations, because of their location, will be stand-alone systems. For the typical homeowner, economics and storage will play a part as to whether tying to the grid makes sense. I'll cover the pluses and minuses.

NOTES

1. www.solarreviews.com/blog/what-are-the-most-efficient-solar-panels-for-2018
2. www.extremetech.com/extreme/215555–0–55-per-watt-from-solarcitys-record-breaking-new-solar-panel
3. cleantechnica.com/2015/01/29/solar-costs-will-fall-40-next-2-years-heres/
4. https://www.pv-magazine.com/2018/05/25/the-path-to-us0-015-kwh-solar-power-and-lower/
5. https://emp.lbl.gov/sites/default/files/lbnl_utility_scale_solar_2018_edition_slides.pdf, slide 24
6. https://emp.lbl.gov/sites/default/files/lbnl_utility_scale_solar_2018_edition_slides.pdf, slide 24
7. https://emp.lbl.gov/sites/default/files/lbnl_utility_scale_solar_2018_edition_slides.pdf, slide 3
8. https://emp.lbl.gov/sites/default/files/lbnl_utility_scale_solar_2018_edition_slides.pdf, slide 3

CHAPTER THREE

Is a Solar System Right for You?

I n this chapter, we'll look at whether a solar energy system makes sense for your home or small business. Large commercial installations require many engineering consultations and onsite visitations by professional commercial installers. That is beyond the scope of this book, but there are smaller-scale options available for homes and small businesses.

The answer to this chapter's question depends on a number of factors.

- What are the energy requirements of your house or business?
- What is your daily energy coverage target?
- How much sunlight does your area receive?
- How many panels will meet your energy coverage target?

With solar energy costs approaching those of traditional grid power from your power company, the decision is becoming less and less of an economic one. As solar prices continue to drop, adding solar energy to your home becomes more about deciding what your energy goals are. Perhaps you have a remote cabin or home not served by a local power company. In that case, solar plus storage may be one of your only options.

But for most homeowners or small business owners, the decision to add solar is based on minimizing your carbon footprint, maximizing your return on investment, saving as much as you can on your energy bill, or a combination of all three.

WHAT ARE YOUR ENERGY REQUIREMENTS?

The first step in deciding on a system is determining how much energy you use. I recommend that you take an entire year to review your energy usage. This is particularly important if you live where your energy use varies widely with the seasons. At the end of 2015, Congress passed a three-year extension to the renewable energy 30 percent **investment tax credit.** You now have until the end of 2019 to get your renewable energy system components installed. In 2020, the credit drops to 20 percent and then to 10 percent in 2021 and thereafter. In June 2018, the Department of the Treasury issued IRS Notice 2018-59. It clarifies eligibility for the ITC as any project that begins construction before the end of 2019.[1] Taking an entire year to measure and/or reduce your energy consumption will be extremely useful in determining the size of the system you need to cover your electricity usage.

If you absolutely don't want to wait a year, you can take a shortcut. The easiest way to do this is to look at the past two or three years' worth of electric bills. If you're new to the neighborhood, find a neighbor with a similar home and family size, and ask if you could look at their energy use.

Mind you, every family thinks about and uses energy differently. Some homes seem to have all the lights on all the time. Others appear to be almost dark except for one room. Most of us are somewhere in between. If you're not in a hurry, you may also want to consider taking some time to minimize your energy bill *before* trying to calculate your overall energy use. There are plenty of things to consider here. I'll give you a laundry list of energy saving ideas, starting with the low-hanging fruit first. Before we get to that, let's talk about a few showstoppers.

One of the first things you need to determine is whether you have enough roof area or other ground suitable for solar panels. A south-facing roof is best, although I've seen solar panels installed on every imaginable roof surface and orientation. But the further away you deviate from a true south-facing roof, the less energy your system will produce. Put another way, you will need more panels to produce the same amount of energy the further your installation deviates from true south.

The other option is to mount your panels on the ground with special racking. Trees and local zoning ordinances will generally play a part in your decision when it comes to ground-mounting a system. Figure 3.1 is a photograph of the 10-kW ground-mounted system installed at our farm in Pennsylvania.

It is located across the street, 200 feet away from our home in a field we own. We picked that location due to its wide-open exposure to the sun during the entire day. There are no trees to shade or damage the array. All electrical cables run through underground conduits to the control panel located midway between the array and our home. Many localities prohibit or drastically reduce the size of ground-mounted solar arrays. Some neighborhoods may have local deed restrictions prohibiting ground-mounted arrays, roof-mounted arrays, or both.

FIGURE 3.1   10-KW GROUND-MOUNTED SOLAR ARRAY AT AUTHOR'S FARM

It's important to determine any deed or zoning restrictions before you proceed. Obtaining a variance or written permission to install your system may be necessary.

Let's assume you've gotten the green light from your local government to install a system. Now, let's get back to saving energy. The biggest use of energy in any home is heating and/or cooling, depending on where you live. Adding additional insulation in attic or crawlspaces usually pays off in the short-run. Drafty windows and doors should be weather stripped or replaced. You can hire a professional who will come to your home and measure the biggest perpetrators when it comes to energy loss from the structure itself. This will help to make the decision on what to do about more insulation, weather stripping, and window or door replacement.

The next biggest use of energy inside the home is electric hot water heating. If you have an electric hot water heater, consider wrapping it with one or even two of the pre-sized insulation kits available at a big-box retailer like Lowe's or Home Depot. Also, if your electric utility offers peak and off-peak electric rates, sign up for this service if you don't already have it. In most cases, it's a simple replacement of your electric meter. A **dual-rate electric system** means you'll pay more for electricity you use during peak hours (usually 8 a.m. to 8 p.m.) and substantially less for what you use during off-peak hours (8 p.m. to 8 a.m.).

This really works to your advantage if you have a solar energy system. You can schedule most of your heavy electric usage during off-peak hours (dish and clothes washing/drying, hot water heating, electric vehicle charging, etc.). During on-peak hours, you'll produce electricity from your solar energy system. This will offset (at least on a cost basis) your off-peak energy use. To force your electric hot water heater to turn on only during off-peak hours, you will need to have a timer installed between the breaker panel and the heater. If you know what you're doing, this is a relatively easy job. If you have never done electrical work before, this isn't a place to start. In fact, I'm going to make a general disclaimer here. *A licensed and qualified electrician should perform all needed electrical work.* This may actually be a local requirement (it is in most towns and cities). It is especially true when it comes to the installation and connection of your solar system.

Other big energy hogs are refrigerators and freezers. If yours are older than the mid-1990s, consider replacing them. Newer models are far more efficient, and will pay for themselves in six years or less. While this is a relatively big expense, if you are planning to stay in the house for a long time, it's a worthwhile one. You will definitely notice a big drop in energy usage once newer models are installed.

What's left? Remember all those lights that your family leaves on all over the house? Now's the time to go around and replace them all with LED versions. They use about one-sixth of the power that incandescent bulbs use. For example, a 60-watt equivalent LED bulb actually only uses about 9 watts of electricity. Think about which of your lights are on the most and replace them first. Then, work your way through your home. The cost for LED bulbs has come down dramatically since their introduction. Nearly all wattages, base types, and color temperatures are available.

Don't forget your garage and workshop, either. Handymen tend to spend a lot of time there. Believe me, I'm speaking from personal experience on this one. These typically contain lights with four- or eight-foot fluorescent tubes. Besides being a breakage hazard, fluorescent tubes contain small amounts of mercury (they create a disposal hazard similar to CFL bulbs). LED versions are available now, too. They draw one-third to one-quarter of the power, the tubes are plastic (no breakage problems), and they turn on immediately under any temperature conditions. I've found these online for as little as $7.99 for four-foot versions. By the time you read this, they will likely be cheaper. Replacing incandescent and fluorescent bulbs with LED versions will pay for themselves in just a few years. The 25,000- to 50,000-hour lifetimes mean far fewer bulb replacements, too.

WHAT IS YOUR DAILY ENERGY COVERAGE TARGET?

The next decision you have to make is how much of your energy usage you want your solar energy system to supply. Your daily average energy use is going to be quite different from your daily peak energy use. Most homeowners and businesses aim for a percentage of their daily average use, somewhere between 50 and 100 percent. But most experts recommend a cushion of at least 25 percent to cover system inefficiencies.

These inefficiencies are due to a number of factors, the foremost being the weather. If you live in sunny Arizona or California, the amount of solar radiation you receive on a yearly and daily basis is far greater than a homeowner in coastal Oregon, for example. In addition, your solar system generates direct current (DC) electricity. The appliances and lights in your home all use alternating current (AC) electricity. In order to convert the DC electricity produced by your solar array into AC electricity, an **inverter** is required. Inverters are not 100 percent efficient in their conversion of DC to AC. Having a 25 percent cushion should be enough to cover inverter- and weather-related issues. But if your peak loads are greater than 25 percent of your average daily use, you'll want to have a detailed power usage analysis conducted by a licensed professional electrician or engineer. This is especially important if your system is going to be totally off-grid.

HOW MUCH SUNLIGHT DOES YOUR AREA RECEIVE?

As the old saying goes in real estate, the value of one's house is dependent on three factors: location, location, location. That's also true when looking at the amount of sunlight any given area gets. The peak sunlight hours your area receives will directly affect the amount of energy your system can produce. A house in Phoenix, Arizona, is going to have a much higher number of peak sunlight hours than the same house in Seattle, Washington.

That doesn't mean the Seattle home can't enjoy solar energy production. All it means is that the Seattle solar system will need more panels than the Phoenix system. The easiest way to determine the peak sunlight hours your area receives is to look at the U.S. Solar Resource Maps published by the National Renewable Energy Laboratory (NREL).

Figure 3.2 is a sample annual map for solar PV. Monthly maps are also available on the website. These maps provide the amount of solar radiation in kilowatt-hours per square meter per day. This is synonymous with peak sun hours.

The maps use data collected from geostationary weather satellites, daily snow-cover data, the amount of atmospheric aerosols, and monthly averages of atmospheric trace gases and water vapor. The solar resource data are for a panel tilt equal to the latitude of the location.

While the map provides a general idea of peak sun hours, there is a much more detailed data set available, too. The NREL has solar radiation data sets for many major US cities, and it is found in the Solar Radiation Data Manual. Although it is out of print, the entire

FIGURE **3.2**   **PHOTOVOLTAIC SOLAR RESOURCE OF THE UNITED STATES, 1998–2009**

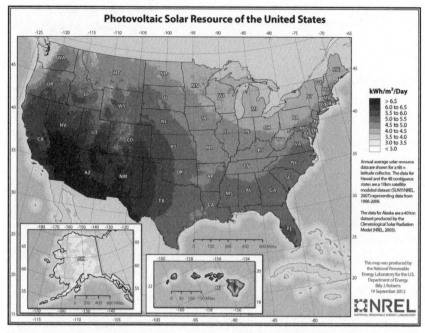

Source: www.nrel.gov/gis/images/eere_pv/national_photovoltaic_2012–01.jpg.

publication is available online on the NREL website. You can download the entire manual, or the data for any individual state (as well as for Puerto Rico and the Pacific Islands), or just the page that has the data for a city close to where you live.

Figure 3.3 is a sample data sheet for Allentown, Pennsylvania, a city near where I live. Each sheet contains data for both **flat-plate** and **concentrating collectors** in various orientations. You'll want the data on the flat-plate collectors. The average monthly climactic conditions are also included.

Most installers recommend installing solar at an angle equal to the latitude of the location. This is a good compromise for maximum solar radiation. There is a formula that you can use to find the best angle of panel tilt.

- Latitude less than 25°, multiply latitude times 0.87
- Latitude above 25°, multiply latitude times 0.76 plus 3.1°

FIGURE 3.3 **NATIONAL RENEWABLE ENERGY LABORATORY SOLAR RADIATION DATA SET**

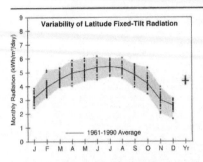

Allentown, PA
WBAN NO. 14737

LATITUDE: 40.65° N
LONGITUDE: 75.43° W
ELEVATION: 117 meters
MEAN PRESSURE: 1003 millibars

STATION TYPE: Secondary

Solar Radiation for Flat-Plate Collectors Facing South at a Fixed Tilt (kWh/m²/day), Uncertainty ±11%

Tilt (°)		Jan	Feb	Mar	Apr	May	June	July	Aug	Sept	Oct	Nov	Dec	Year
0	Average	1.9	2.7	3.7	4.7	5.4	6.0	5.9	5.2	4.2	3.1	2.0	1.6	3.9
	Min/Max	1.6/2.2	2.3/3.4	3.3/4.2	4.0/5.4	4.7/6.3	5.0/6.8	5.2/6.5	4.6/5.9	3.6/4.7	2.6/3.7	1.6/2.3	1.3/1.7	3.7/4.1
Latitude -15	Average	2.8	3.6	4.4	5.1	5.5	5.8	5.8	5.5	4.8	4.0	2.7	2.3	4.4
	Min/Max	2.2/3.4	3.0/4.7	3.9/5.1	4.2/6.0	4.7/6.4	4.8/6.7	5.1/6.5	4.8/6.3	4.0/5.5	3.3/5.0	1.9/3.5	1.6/2.7	4.2/4.7
Latitude	Average	3.1	3.9	4.5	5.0	5.2	5.4	5.4	5.3	4.9	4.2	3.0	2.6	4.4
	Min/Max	2.4/3.9	3.2/5.2	4.0/5.3	4.0/5.9	4.4/6.0	4.5/6.2	4.7/6.0	4.6/6.1	3.9/5.6	3.5/5.3	2.0/4.0	1.6/3.1	4.2/4.7
Latitude +15	Average	3.3	4.0	4.4	4.6	4.6	4.7	4.8	4.8	4.6	4.2	3.1	2.8	4.2
	Min/Max	2.5/4.2	3.3/5.4	3.8/5.2	3.7/5.5	3.9/5.3	3.9/5.3	4.2/5.3	4.2/5.5	3.7/5.4	3.4/5.4	2.0/4.2	1.7/3.3	3.9/4.5
90	Average	3.1	3.6	3.4	3.0	2.6	2.5	2.6	2.9	3.3	3.4	2.8	2.6	3.0
	Min/Max	2.4/4.0	2.8/5.0	2.8/4.0	2.5/3.6	2.3/2.9	2.2/2.7	2.4/2.8	2.6/3.3	2.6/3.8	2.7/4.4	1.7/3.8	1.4/3.2	2.8/3.2

Solar Radiation for 1-Axis Tracking Flat-Plate Collectors with a North-South Axis (kWh/m²/day), Uncertainty ±11%

Axis Tilt (°)		Jan	Feb	Mar	Apr	May	June	July	Aug	Sept	Oct	Nov	Dec	Year
0	Average	2.6	3.7	4.9	6.0	6.8	7.4	7.3	6.7	5.5	4.2	2.6	2.1	5.0
	Min/Max	2.1/3.2	3.0/4.9	4.1/5.8	4.7/7.5	5.6/8.3	5.8/8.7	6.2/8.5	5.8/7.8	4.3/6.4	3.4/5.4	1.8/3.4	1.4/2.5	4.7/5.4
Latitude -15	Average	3.3	4.4	5.4	6.4	6.9	7.4	7.4	6.9	6.0	4.8	3.2	2.7	5.4
	Min/Max	2.5/4.1	3.5/5.9	4.6/6.6	4.9/7.9	5.6/8.5	5.8/8.7	6.2/8.6	5.9/8.2	4.6/7.1	3.9/6.3	2.1/4.3	1.6/3.2	5.0/5.9
Latitude	Average	3.6	4.6	5.5	6.3	6.7	7.1	7.1	6.8	6.0	5.0	3.4	2.9	5.4
	Min/Max	2.7/4.5	3.7/6.3	4.6/6.7	4.8/7.9	5.4/8.3	5.5/8.4	5.9/8.3	5.8/8.0	4.6/7.1	4.0/6.6	2.2/4.7	1.7/3.6	5.0/5.9
Latitude +15	Average	3.8	4.7	5.4	6.0	6.2	6.6	6.6	6.5	5.9	5.1	3.5	3.1	5.3
	Min/Max	2.8/4.8	3.7/6.4	4.5/6.7	4.6/7.6	5.1/7.8	5.1/7.8	5.5/7.7	5.5/7.6	4.5/7.0	4.0/6.7	2.2/4.8	1.8/3.8	4.9/5.8

Solar Radiation for 2-Axis Tracking Flat-Plate Collectors (kWh/m²/day), Uncertainty ±11%

Tracker		Jan	Feb	Mar	Apr	May	June	July	Aug	Sept	Oct	Nov	Dec	Year
2-Axis	Average	3.8	4.7	5.6	6.4	7.0	7.5	7.5	7.0	6.0	5.1	3.6	3.1	5.6
	Min/Max	2.9/4.8	3.7/6.4	4.6/6.8	4.9/8.0	5.7/8.6	5.9/8.9	6.3/8.7	6.0/8.2	4.7/7.2	4.0/6.7	2.2/4.9	1.8/3.8	5.2/6.1

Direct Beam Solar Radiation for Concentrating Collectors (kWh/m²/day), Uncertainty ±11%

Tracker		Jan	Feb	Mar	Apr	May	June	July	Aug	Sept	Oct	Nov	Dec	Year
1-Axis, E-W Horiz Axis	Average	2.0	2.4	2.5	2.7	2.9	3.2	3.2	3.0	2.7	2.6	1.9	1.7	2.6
	Min/Max	1.4/2.8	1.5/3.6	1.9/3.6	1.6/3.8	2.0/4.2	1.9/4.4	2.2/4.1	2.2/3.9	1.7/3.5	1.7/3.9	0.8/3.0	0.6/2.4	2.2/3.0
1-Axis, N-S Horiz Axis	Average	1.5	2.1	2.8	3.5	3.8	4.2	4.2	3.9	3.2	2.5	1.4	1.1	2.5
	Min/Max	1.0/2.0	1.4/3.2	2.1/4.0	2.1/5.0	2.6/5.5	2.5/5.7	2.8/5.4	2.9/5.0	2.0/4.2	1.6/3.8	0.6/2.3	0.4/1.6	2.5/3.3
1-Axis, N-S Tilt=Latitude	Average	2.2	2.8	3.4	3.7	3.7	3.9	4.0	4.0	3.7	3.3	2.1	1.8	3.2
	Min/Max	1.5/3.0	1.8/4.3	2.5/4.7	2.2/5.3	2.5/5.4	2.4/5.3	2.7/5.2	3.0/5.2	2.3/4.8	2.1/4.9	0.9/3.3	0.7/2.5	2.8/3.7
2-Axis	Average	2.4	2.9	3.4	3.8	3.9	4.3	4.3	4.1	3.7	3.3	2.2	2.0	3.4
	Min/Max	1.6/3.2	1.9/4.4	2.5/4.7	2.3/5.4	2.7/5.7	2.6/5.8	2.9/5.6	3.1/5.3	2.3/4.8	2.1/5.0	1.0/3.5	0.7/2.7	2.9/3.8

Average Climatic Conditions

Element	Jan	Feb	Mar	Apr	May	June	July	Aug	Sept	Oct	Nov	Dec	Year
Temperature (°C)	-3.0	-1.5	4.1	9.8	15.7	20.8	23.4	22.3	18.2	11.8	6.2	-0.1	10.7
Daily Minimum Temp	-7.3	-6.2	-1.2	3.8	9.6	14.9	17.6	16.7	12.3	5.8	1.2	-4.2	5.3
Daily Maximum Temp	1.3	3.2	9.3	15.8	21.8	26.7	29.2	27.9	23.9	17.7	11.0	4.0	16.0
Record Minimum Temp	-24.4	-21.7	-18.3	-8.9	-2.2	3.9	8.9	5.0	-1.1	-6.1	-11.7	-22.2	-24.4
Record Maximum Temp	22.2	24.4	30.0	33.9	36.1	37.8	40.6	37.2	32.2	27.2	22.2		40.6
HDD, Base 18.3°C	661	556	441	255	102	6	0	4	46	207	365	572	3214
CDD, Base 18.3°C	0	0	0	0	21	79	157	128	41	4	0	0	429
Relative Humidity (%)	69	67	62	61	66	68	69	72	74	72	70	71	68
Wind Speed (m/s)	4.6	4.6	4.9	4.8	4.1	3.7	3.2	3.2	3.3	3.6	4.3	4.4	4.1

181

Source: rredc.nrel.gov/solar/pubs/redbook/#maps.

Single-axis adjusting mechanisms will adjust panel tilt to latitude plus 15° in winter and minus 15° in summer. Two-axis adjusters will also track the movement of the sun throughout the day. But in most cases the added cost of adding tracking to the panel mounts is not cost-effective.

CALCULATING YOUR SYSTEM SIZE

Okay, let's assume you've completed your calculations and you're ready to figure out how big of a system you need. If you have a grid connection, you will want to calculate your *average* daily energy use. (I'll discuss the requirements for an off-grid system separately later in this chapter.) The easiest way to do this is to look at one to three years' worth of electricity bills. Add up the total number of kilowatt-hours (kWh) used – a kWh is a composite unit of energy equivalent to 1 kW of power sustained for an hour – and divide by the appropriate number of days.

Next, you'll need to come up with an efficiency factor for the overall system. We'll base it on the following assumptions (you can change yours based on the inverter and panels you use and your own site parameters):

- Average solar access (shading derating factor, if you have no trees, yours could be 100%): 95%
- Inverter efficiency: 96%
- Solar module temperature derating factor: 88%
- DC wiring derating factor: 98%
- AC wiring derating factor: 99%
- Module soiling derating factor (dirt and dust on the panels): 95%
- Module mismatch derating factor: 98%
- System availability derating factor: 99%

If we multiply all of the above derating factors together (95% × 96% × 88% × 98% × 99% × 95% × 98% × 99%), we get 72% (rounded). That is the overall system efficiency. Now we have enough information to calculate the system's array size. I'm going to base the following set of calculations on my site location and energy use, so some numbers will more than likely be different from yours. My farm's energy use (including recharging our electric vehicle) is just under 26,000 kWh per year. Using annual solar data for flat-plate collectors with a fixed tilt (from the black box in Figure 3.3), I find that the average peak sun hours for our area is 4.4.

To calculate the size of an array needed to meet my total annual energy use, I divide my annual kWh consumption (25,942 kWh) by 365. This provides the average daily use in kWh. I then divide this amount by the average daily peak sun hours (4.4) and I get the approximate array size in kW. Finally, this value is divided by my system efficiency factor of 72 percent.

$$25,942 \text{ kWh/year} \div 365 \text{ days/year} = 71.1 \text{ kWh/day}$$

$$71.1 \text{ kWh/day} \div 4.4 \text{ sun-hours/day} = 16.2 \text{ kW}$$

$$16.2 \text{ kW} \div 0.72 \text{ system efficiency factor} = 22.5 \text{ kW array}$$

In order to offset 100 percent of my farm and EV electric use, I would have to more than double the size of my current solar array. My energy use is probably a lot higher than yours. I have a small outbuilding with plumbing that needs to be heated in order to keep the pipes from freezing. That probably increases my overall energy use by 20 percent. Our main home, while well insulated, is a 205-year-old stone farmhouse. Our primary heat is wood. However, a stone wall in the middle of the house prevents a lot of the heat from the woodstove from reaching the other side of our home. The balance is made up via electric heat. This adds to our monthly winter bill, and our overall energy use.

BASIC SYSTEM DESIGN

If you plan on installing a system at your home or place of business, you should have a good working knowledge of what each component does. In this section, I'll go over the design of a typical residential, grid-tied solar system. I'll describe the function of each component in the system. I'm going to repeatedly refer to Figure 3.4, which shows the block layout of a typical residential, grid-tied solar system.

Let's briefly cover the solar PV modules, also referred to as the solar panel array. They are shown as one icon in Figure 3.4. But in practice installers may arrange them in two or more groups, depending on how many roof surfaces are available for panel installation and the overall size of the array. Individual panels are electrically connected together to

FIGURE **3.4** GRID-TIED SOLAR SYSTEM

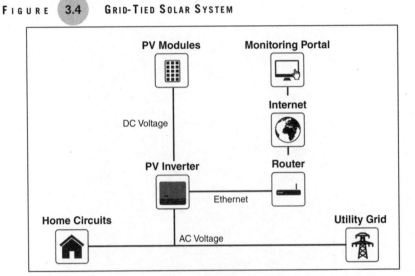

provide the same voltage to one or more inverters. Solar panels generate direct current (DC) voltage. The amount of power is expressed in watts or kilowatts (kW). Power is determined by multiplying the panel voltage by the number of amperes (current) supplied by the array. The more panels an array contains, the higher the amperage (and therefore the power) produced.

All of the wiring from the panel array connects to one or more devices known as inverters (see Figure 3.5). Most panels connect individually to an inverter. Since inverters are rated by the amount of panels and power they can handle, a home system can easily have two or more inverters, depending upon the overall size of the system. My system has two inverters, one rated at 6 kW and a second rated at 4 kW.

An inverter has a number of key roles in any solar energy system. In fact, you can think of the inverter as the system "brain" or controller. This is true if it's a small, 5-kW home system or a large 10-MW **utility-scale solar** farm. The inverter's primary function is to do just what its name says: It "inverts" the direct current (DC) voltage produced by the solar modules into alternating current (AC) voltage compatible with home appliances, lighting, and electronics.

Like any other electronic device, inverter technology has continued to improve significantly over the past decade. In addition to converting the voltage from DC to AC, inverters provide data monitoring to the

FIGURE   3.5   6-KW POWER INVERTER

solar module manufacturer as well as to the owner of the solar energy system (homeowner or business). It provides information such as individual solar module performance, including any modules that are not working properly. This is important in large, utility-scale systems in order to maintain a high-level of performance. However, because of the smaller number of panels in a home system, this type of information is crucial to the system owner.

The system I have requires two inverters because of its size. Both inverters report their status and energy production data to an interface that connects to a router on my wireless data network (see Figure 3.4). From there, the inverters transmit the data to computers located at the panel manufacturer's offices. Using software provided by the panel manufacturer, I can view the power produced by each inverter and the total system at any time, either via computer or smartphone. In addition, I receive an email anytime either inverter has a problem. This function immediately allows the system owner to contact a technician to fix the problem.

Another important and necessary function of every inverter used in a grid-tied solar system is monitoring the grid itself. If the grid goes down, inverters will disconnect themselves from the grid and the homeowner's electrical circuits. While this may seem to defeat the purpose of having solar in the first place, it is a necessary safety feature that protects utility workers dispatched to fix the utility's grid outage. If a customer's solar energy system were to remain active, it would continue to feed power into the grid. It would energize the portion of the grid that utility workers think is dead. This could endanger the life of the utility worker. Every utility requires all grid-connected solar PV systems to have an automatic disconnect feature as a protection mechanism for its workers.

OFF THE GRID

This is a perfect lead-in to begin the discussion of off-grid systems. Incredibly, over 1.3 billion people around the world still don't have access to or use of electricity. Most live in third-world countries with no power grid. However, some are in small isolated communities where extending the existing grid would be cost-prohibitive. Still others live in small island communities. In all three cases, having access to electricity means operating noisy, fuel-guzzling diesel generators. Generators are expensive to run and maintain. As a result, electricity costs are extremely high.

However, in today's world, electricity has almost become one of humanity's basic needs. Economic development just isn't possible without electricity. Our health, clean drinking water, and education all are dependent on electricity. This is especially true in small isolated communities. Residents make products and use services locally. Having electricity makes any community more prosperous. And in today's information age, not having electricity generally means being isolated from the rest of the world's news.

The good news is solar power is giving many of the world's isolated islands and communities energy independence. Solar PV-powered, off-grid energy systems provide a reliable, simple, and low-cost solution for decentralized energy supplies. These isolated communities can build small, stable, decentralized grids in remote locations to serve all the residents and businesses.

Just like wireless cellular telephones bypass the need for landline telephone systems, off-grid solar power systems help developing countries skip the era of fossil fuel-powered electricity generation. The cost to build and maintain fossil fuel-fired power plants, a large central transmission grid and associated substations, and other equipment is huge compared to distributed, decentralized solar PV. These systems are efficient, inexpensive, and quiet. Even better, they require almost no maintenance.

Components of a Simple Off-Grid Configuration

Let's start with the simplest of off-grid configurations (Figure 3.6). This system can provide enough power for a small, solar home or cabin, completely off the grid. Components include some number of PV modules (depending on daytime loads) and a battery storage unit sized to handle evening loads (lights, computer, TV, and possibly heating, although most off-grid homes or cabins use wood stoves for heating). Both the PV modules and the battery storage unit feed into the inverter/system controller. Since both the solar modules and batteries generate DC power, the system must invert the voltage of both to provide AC power to the home loads.

The system controller automatically switches between the solar PV modules and the battery storage system depending on time of day and

F I G U R E   3.6   S I M P L E O F F - G R I D S Y S T E M W I T H B A T T E R Y B A C K U P

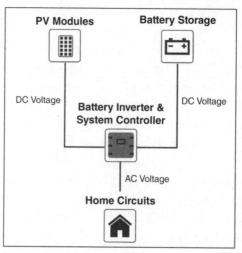

home circuit loads. In addition, it handles the recharging of the battery storage unit during daytime hours. Until recently, remote cabins requiring evening power used a bank of lead-acid batteries similar to automotive batteries. The only difference is these batteries are designed for repeated deep cycling. The disadvantage of lead-acid batteries is they can give off toxic fumes. Keeping them outside in a small shed is an option. However, their performance degrades significantly as temperatures drop.

Today, a number of companies, including Tesla, offer home energy storage systems based on lithium-ion battery technology. They are compact, and can be wall-mounted inside the home since they don't give off any toxic fumes. They also have roughly double the life of lead-acid batteries, which generally don't last more than four to five years.

Off-Grid and Grid-Tied System with Battery Storage and Generator Backup

A slightly more complex off-grid and/or grid-tied configuration uses a more sophisticated system controller (see Figure 3.7). It supports all types of power generation including solar PV, wind, hydropower, and back-up generators. It can also accommodate battery storage to

FIGURE **3.7** GRID-TIED / OFF-GRID SYSTEM WITH BATTERIES AND GENERATOR

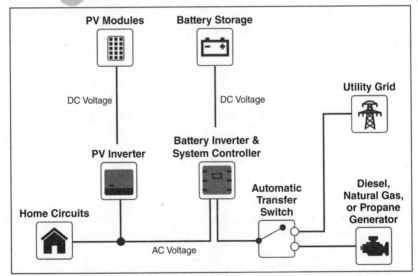

operate nighttime loads. Finally, the system controller can also tie the owner's system to the grid, if available. In this case, the grid would only be used when there is no power (or not enough power) available from other sources. In other words, the grid would be the ultimate back-up. While these types of systems are appropriate for residences, engineers can scale them up to supply entire buildings, factories, and even small villages or towns.

In the case of a stand-alone or off-grid system, an inverter is still required, but several additional units are required as well. I'll go over each in detail. The inverter works the same as described previously, with one exception. It is no longer monitoring the grid. The system controller handles that function if necessary. It's not required if the system is in a remote location where no power is available.

The system controller does monitor the grid in the event that the owner's system goes down, or can't supply enough power to meet overall load requirements. If the system designer sizes it properly, the grid should only be needed in the event of a system failure. As in the standalone off-grid system, we have solar modules and a battery storage unit. Both produce DC power, which the inverter transforms into AC for the home loads. In the event of a sustained period of cloudy weather, the system controller may request the generator to provide additional power to run the loads and/or recharge the battery storage unit. Nearly every generator in production today generates AC power. Some are large enough to run entire homes, businesses, and even factories. The system controller is also capable of switching over to the grid, if available. In the system depicted in Figure 3.7, it would only do this in the event of the failure of the generator.

DETERMINING IF SOLAR MAKES SENSE FOR YOU

Once you have determined the size of the array (in kW) you need, it's time to contact several installers and get a quote from each one for the system size you need. You definitely need to compare apples to apples. Make sure the quotation includes everything: the panels, mounting hardware, inverters, and installation. Make sure any additional wiring (as will be needed in the case of a ground-mount system) and its installation is included in the quote. Only then will you be able to determine the size of the system you want to install based on your budget. Remember, you will receive a 30 percent federal tax credit on any system you begin to install on or before December 31, 2019. This includes any additional wiring, as long as it is part of the system. If the system you're installing is for an off-grid home or cabin, cost may not be an issue if you want to have all the comforts of a grid-tied home.

Homeowners also have the option of leasing solar energy systems or signing power purchase agreements (PPAs) for the power produced. When thinking about buying versus leasing or PPAs, the overall goals of the homeowner come into play. When buying a system, you own it and all the power produced from it. When you lease a system or sign a PPA, someone else owns the solar system. It's a simple distinction, but it impacts the cost, financing terms, system maintenance, and the overall return on investment of the system. Whether you buy or lease a system, your energy costs will be lower. Let's look at the pluses and minuses of all three options.

The plus side of purchasing and beginning to install the system (by 2019) is receiving the 30 percent ITC. Customers may also purchase the system with a home equity loan and still obtain the ITC. In addition, if a customer knows they will be selling the home in a few years' time, it generally pays to buy solar. It will certainly increase the value of the home.

On the minus side, owning a solar energy system means you are responsible for maintaining it. Many installers offer maintenance and insurance plans for those who purchase a system. Most modern panels come with a 20- to 25-year warranty against defects, and as such require almost no maintenance or even none at all.

Customers who may not have the cash on hand, or who are simply interested in clean renewable energy, are candidates for a lease. There are no upfront costs, and customers enjoy the cost savings as soon as installers finish and energize the system. The hassle of financing and maintenance are also not an issue with a leased system, as the maintenance costs are borne by the installer. Generally, when you lease a system, your new, lower monthly electric bill plus the cost of the solar system lease payment are less than what you previously paid for electricity alone. Some companies will allow you to partially or fully prepay your lease for additional savings.

On the minus side of leasing, you don't get to take advantage of the 30 percent ITC. If you decide to move, you must transfer your lease to the new homeowner. This could be a problem if you are in a hurry to move or the new owner isn't interested in undertaking the lease.

Whether you buy or lease a solar system, as electricity rates increase, so do your savings. If you have an electric vehicle, as I do, having solar plus storage is like having your own refueling station. Standing in line waiting for gas or diesel as a result of some geopolitical event becomes a thing of the past.

The third option for many, but not all, homeowners is signing a PPA. This is similar to leasing the system. You pay little-or-no money down. There are no ITCs or rebates available (they belong to the owner of the system). However, unlike a lease where you pay to "rent" the system, in a solar PPA, you agree to purchase all of the power generated at a preset per-kWh price. Similar to leases, PPAs are structured with terms ranging from 7 to 20 years.

At this point, you may be wondering what the potential cost savings and the return on investment is for ownership, lease, or PPA. Savings vary depending on incentives, whether or not the system qualifies for an ITC, interest rates, and other factors. But a general rule of thumb is that homeowners who purchase a system will save between 40 and 70 percent on electricity costs over the lifetime of the system. Once the system is paid for, electricity is free for the entire life of the system, which is anywhere from 25 to 30 years.

If you choose to lease your system or sign a PPA, you'll likely save between 10 and 30 percent off of the prices you currently pay for electricity. If you are serious about solar and you're not a do-it-yourself person, my recommendation is to visit several of the numerous online solar pricing websites. Get plenty of quotes from highly recommended (and preferably local) installers. Make sure you compare apples to apples when comparing quotes. Lastly, if the solar system is a roof install (most are), make sure your contract includes a warranty against any roof leaks. Once the panels are installed, it's a lot of work to remove them to fix a leaky roof. Reputable installers will include this without asking.

CAN YOU DO IT YOURSELF?

Are you a do-it-yourself person? Are you comfortable working on a slanted roof, 20 or more feet off the ground? Do you know your way around an electrical circuit and the National Electrical Code? Does your township or municipality permit you to do this on your own?

If you answered "yes" to ALL of the above questions, then yes, you can install your own solar electric system. I'll make an assumption that you've already gone through the exercise earlier in this chapter that details how to size your system, both to your roof size and budget. Now that you've done that, here are a few more questions you need answers to before you go any further.

- Do any shadows from structures or trees fall on your roof or property area (in the case of a ground-mounted system) during daylight hours?
- Is your roof capable of holding the additional weight of mounting racks and the number of panels you need?
- Can the panels be mounted in such a fashion so that the winter sun hits them as close to perpendicular as possible at noon?
- Have you done all you can to lower your electricity use already? Remember, every dollar you spend on energy efficiency will save you at least $5 in solar system costs.
- Make sure you check out your state and local incentives, rebates, grants, and subsidies. Every state is different, and you may be surprised how much more you can save. Once you've done this, refigure your budget.
- Make sure you are permitted to do the system wiring yourself. Many municipalities require a licensed electrician do the wiring or at least the final hook-up. In any event, you should plan that you or someone else installs the wiring to meet National Electrical Code standards.
- Subscribe to a publication like *Home Power Magazine*. You'll see plenty of articles and advertisements from suppliers of do-it-yourself solar, wind, and hydro systems for the home.

Lastly, there are plenty of online companies willing to sell you everything from the solar panels down to the last nut and bolt you'll need to complete your installation. Visit as many as you can, and make sure to look at customer ratings for each site. But remember, the more you buy from them, the more money they make. Plenty of what you'll need (nuts, bolts, electrical conduit, wire, electrical panels, etc.), you can purchase for less money at one of the big-box home centers or your local hardware store. Make sure you're not overspending when purchasing everything you need.

NOTE

1. https://www.jdsupra.com/legalnews/irs-notice-2018-59-clarifies-rules-on-37668/

CHAPTER FOUR

Utility-Scale Solar Takes Off

There are few, if any, other industries that are undergoing a transformation as rapid and as large as that of the electric power industry. One of the biggest influences and changes has come from the solar power industry, both residential and utility-scale solar. In this chapter I am going to focus on the transformation the power industry is undergoing as a result of the rise of utility-scale solar.

What exactly is utility-scale solar? I'll get into that in greater detail further on in this chapter, but generally speaking, it's any installation greater than 1 MW in size that supplies power to the grid at the utility level, rather than at the distribution level. Utility-scale installations are also known as solar parks, solar ranches, or solar farms. Like any other large power plant, a utility-scale solar plant is designed to feed the power it produces directly into the electrical grid. The connection is generally at a higher voltage than a residential solar installation.

A few decades ago, no one would have predicted that by 2016, more people would be working in the US solar industry than in the oil and natural gas sectors, but it's true. As you can see from Figure 4.1, employment in the solar energy sector overtook that of the oil, gas, and coal sectors during 2015.

And it's no wonder: 95 percent of all the solar PV installations in the United States have come online since 2010.[1] Worldwide, the number of people employed in "green" jobs rose to 10.3 million in 2017, an

FIGURE 4.1   ANNUAL SOLAR JOB ADDITIONS COMPARED TO OIL, GAS,
                AND COAL

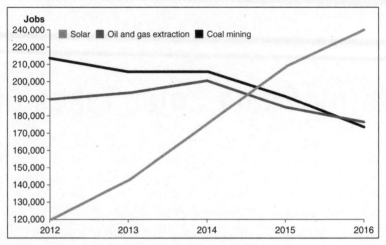

Source: www.nrel.gov/gis/images/eere_pv/national_photovoltaic_2012–01.jpg.

increase of 5.3 percent compared to 9.8 million in 2016. The solar PV industry is by far the world's largest renewable energy employer, with 3.4 million jobs during 2017, a 9 percent rise over 2016.[2] As of November 2017, according to the Solar Energy Industry Association (SEIA), the US solar industry employed 250,271 people. That's more than twice the number employed in 2010. They work at over 8,000 companies in every state in the Union. By 2022, that number is expected to double to over 420,000.[3] Contrast that to the oil and gas producers that cut 351,410 jobs worldwide since mid-2014. Employment in US solar companies during 2015 grew 12 times as fast as overall job growth. During 2015, the solar industry created 1.2 percent of all the jobs in the United States. During 2016, the solar industry increased by another 51,000 workers, to a total of 260,077, according to the National Solar Jobs Census. That's an increase of 168 percent since the first census back in 2010. During 2017, industry employers surveyed by The Solar Foundation expected employment to increase another 10 percent to 286,355 workers.[4] But the reality was that 2017 solar employment dropped to 250,271, which was largely a result of projects being pulled forward into 2016.

The solar industry added one out of every 50 new jobs created in 2016, or 2 percent of all new jobs created in the United States that year.

One of the big reasons was the extension of the 30 percent federal Investment Tax Credit (ITC) for renewables that was originally set to expire at the end of 2016. In late 2015, Republicans in Congress were looking to lift the ban on crude oil exports. Democrats wanted an extension of the **Production Tax Credit** (PTC) for wind producers and the ITC for solar. And the government was running out of money. It desperately needed a $1.1 trillion lift to the debt ceiling to keep the federal government running for the next year.

On December 18, 2015, Congress's very last scheduled work day of the year, the House and Senate each passed a bill. In a rare display of bipartisan compromise, legislators consolidated the two bills into one titled the "Consolidated Appropriations Act," and passed a 2,009-page bill extending both the PTC and the ITC. The bill extended the 2.3 cents per kWh PTC for wind at that rate through the end of 2016. Projects that started construction in 2017 incurred a 20 percent reduction in the PTC. It will continue to drop 20 percent annually through 2020.

Additional 2018 legislation also extended the solar ITC at the current 30 percent rate until the end of 2019, as long as projects begin construction before the end of 2019. It will then drop to 26 percent in 2020, 22 percent in 2021, and 10 percent in 2022. An additional clause will extend the 10 percent credit to any project that was in development and commences construction before the end of 2024.

On the surface, this three-year extension of the US solar ITC may not seem like much. But it's actually a huge deal for the industry here and will keep it on a path of sustained growth. In the United States, during the first half of 2018, installers completed 4.7 gigawatts (GW) of solar. Full-year 2018 growth is expected to be flat versus 2017, with 10.9 GW of total installations.[5] By 2020, when the ITC starts to decline, solar will be deploying over 20 GW every year. As I mentioned earlier, industry employment will be over 420,000. By 2019, the additional power produced from solar will more than compensate for any additional carbon emissions created by lifting the US ban on crude exports.

The extension of the solar ITC will likely go down as one of the most significant policy changes for the US solar industry since its inception and soon it will have passed a significant tipping point. By 2020, solar will be the cheapest form of energy generation on the planet. As its costs continue to drop, wide-scale adoption will continue to ramp up. Let's take a closer look at the drop in the price of solar.

THE COST OF SOLAR PLUMMETS

The real reason solar has taken off like a rocket is its plummeting price. As you can see from Figure 4.2, the cost of solar has undergone a dramatic drop since the year 2000. And that drop is going to continue through 2020.

The average installed price per watt for residential solar dropped from $11.30 in 2000 to $3.00 in 2016.[6] That's a 73.5 percent drop. GTM Research expects residential system prices to drop 33 percent by 2020. The drop in utility scale solar is even more dramatic, decreasing from $9.56 per installed watt to $1.26 in the first half of 2016. That's a drop of 86.8 percent. GTM Research predicts that the installed cost of utility-scale solar will drop to $0.99 by 2020.[7]

Between 2016 and 2020, and as a result of the ITC extension, SEIA predicts over 72 GW of new solar installations will occur. That means

FIGURE 4.2   INSTALLED COST FOR RESIDENTIAL AND UTILITY SCALE SOLAR VERSUS TOTAL US INSTALLED PV

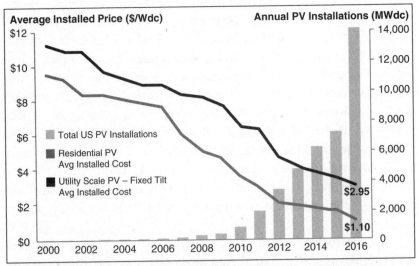

Source: votesolar.org/files/7014/6369/1060/Honeyman-Vote-Solar-Webinar-April-2016.pdf and www.greentechmedia.com/articles/read/solar-pv-prices-to-fall-below-1.00-per-watt-by-2020 (with additional data from author).

by 2020, the United States will have more than 98 GW of solar PV and 2 GW of concentrating solar power (CSP). That's enough generating capacity to power over 20 million homes in the United States. By 2020, the solar industry will be adding more than 20 GW of new generating capacity every year. Incredibly, 20 GW is equal to the entire amount of solar in place at the end of 2014. That is an impressive rate of growth. How impressive? Consider this: In 2010, US solar installations provided just 0.1 percent of all the electricity generated in the country. In 2020, just one decade later, solar is expected to provide 3.5 percent of all US electricity. That's an increase of more than 3,000 percent in just 10 years' time.[8]

Remember my second law of technology: "When it comes to technology, changes happen much faster than anyone expects they will." That's certainly been the case with solar energy up until this point. And it's just going to ramp up even faster from here. A big part of that is going to be utility-scale projects. Let's look into what utility scale really means.

WHAT IS UTILITY-SCALE SOLAR?

The most simplistic definition of a utility-scale solar project is one that generates electric power from solar, feeds it into the grid, and supplies the connected utility with energy. Nearly every utility-scale project has an associated power purchase agreement (PPA) with a utility or other entity. The PPA is a contract guaranteeing that the facility has a market for all of its energy for some fixed period (usually 20 to 25 years).

But that's where similarities among different definitions end. Other than what I described above, there is no one set definition that defines a solar energy project as "utility-scale." Therefore, determining if a given project qualifies as "utility-scale" can be somewhat of a challenge. This is especially true as utilities are increasingly turning their focus to solar energy generation on the distributed side of their grids. The problem is made even worse due to the lack of differentiation of solar modules used for residential or utility-scale solar.

That's not the case with wind power, where a clear difference between a residential-size wind turbine and one used for a utility-scale installation exists. But the very same solar panel or module may be used in a 10-kW residential system and a 20-MW utility-scale project. So, it all comes down to where one draws the size line that defines a utility-scale project. Below are four different definitions of what constitutes a utility-scale project:

1. The Energy Information Administration (EIA) considers a utility-scale project to be any installation larger than 1 MW in size. It makes this determination regardless of ownership and whether the project is connected in front of or behind an electric meter.
2. Greentech Media and the SEIA have a different definition for utility-scale that has nothing to do with the size of the project. They define it as, "any project owned by or that sells electricity directly to a utility (rather than consuming it on site) is considered a 'utility-scale' project."
3. A third definition comes from banks and others who finance and/or invest in large solar installations. For solar PV, that number seems to be about 20 MW (equivalent to an investment of $50 million).
4. Finally, there is a one last definition that considers utility-scale to be any ground-mounted solar project larger than 5 MW in size. This avoids counting smaller projects that are likely commercial in nature.

It's not too surprising that there are variations in the definition of utility-scale solar. Different bodies have different perspectives in what a utility-scale solar system looks like. For purposes of this book, I'm defining a system to be "utility-scale" in size if it is greater than 1 MW in size, is grid-connected, and has a power purchase agreement (PPA) associated with it.

Most utility-scale PV power plants are owned and operated via independent power producers. However, a number of communities, schools, utilities, and other entities with the physical room for a solar park are building and owning them, too. To date and through 2019 in the United States, nearly every utility-scale project is the beneficiary of the renewable energy solar investment tax credit. Over the past decade, the levelized cost of solar power has dropped significantly, and is already at **grid parity** in 20 states today, and could be in most states by 2020.[9] By the time the tax credit fully expires, solar power will be a grid parity everywhere and incentives to deploy it will no longer be needed.

The siting for utility-scale solar is important, especially when it comes to large installations. The ultimate power output will depend on the slope of the site, the mounting type (fixed, one-axis tilt, or two-axis tilt), and panel efficiency. The current efficiency for crystalline silicon panels is over 20 percent. If we assume a fixed, ground-mounted system using panels with 20 percent efficiency, we can expect to use around two acres per MWp in the tropics and just under four acres in the United States and Europe. Power produced will be about 10 percent higher for a single-axis tracker and 20 percent higher for two-axis trackers. The additional installation costs for moveable mounting systems is generally not cost-effective.

In the United States, especially in the eastern part of the country, many brownfield sites are being reborn as solar parks, since the land has no other valuable use.

THE HISTORY OF UTILITY-SCALE

The world's oldest utility-scale **concentrated solar power (CSP)** plants are located in the Mojave Desert in California. They do not employ solar PV modules. Instead, they use solar thermal technology. The nine separate solar thermal energy plants are owned by NextEra Energy, and were constructed between 1984 and 1990. The systems use 936,384 parabolic trough solar collectors covering 1,600 acres. In total, the nine plants have a 354 MW generating capacity. The systems make use of parabolic trough collectors that focus the sun's energy on an absorber tube (see Figure 4.3).

FIGURE 4.3 PARABOLIC TROUGH COLLECTOR

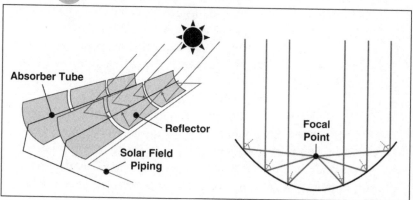

Absorber Tube

Reflector

Solar Field Piping

Focal Point

The parabolic mirrors are in the shape of a quarter-pipe. Whereas regular mirrors are 70 percent reflective, the glass mirrors used in the solar thermal generating systems are 94 percent reflective. Motors automatically move the mirrors to track the sun all day. The mirrors are kept clean via an automated washing system.

The central collector tube is filled with a special synthetic oil. The concentrated rays of the sun are 71 to 80 times stronger than regular sunlight. They heat the oil to more than 750°F (400°C). The super-heated oil passes through a heat exchanger that transfers the heat energy to water. The transferred heat quickly turns the water to steam that powers a steam turbine. The turbine connects to a generator that produces electricity. The reason the collector pipes use oil instead of water is to allow lower pressures in the collector pipes.

The nine systems together produce anywhere from 530 to 664 GWh of electricity per year depending on maintenance and other downtime issues. Southern California Edison, the main electric utility for Southern California, purchases the power produced by the nine generators. The turbines can also be used at night by heating the water with natural gas. This is done if Southern California Edison's power demand warrants it.

While utility-scale CSP systems are great for remote areas of the southwestern United States, where solar insolation is high, utility-scale solar PV systems outnumber CSP systems by more than 40 to 1.

WHAT IS "NAMEPLATE CAPACITY"?

The **nameplate capacity** of a photovoltaic solar power station is rated in one of three ways. The first is in megawatt-peak (MWp). This refers to the total DC power output of the solar array. The second, commonly used in Japan, Canada, Spain, and some areas of the United States, use megawatts-AC (MW_{ac}). This is a measure of the AC power output of the array after the DC power runs through inverters to convert it to AC. This number will be lower than the MWp power due to efficiency losses in the inverters and other system components. The third but much less common rating is megavolt-amperes (MVA). This power-rating format is more often used for transformer ratings, not power station output. That being the case, I won't be mentioning it again in this book. You will see both MWp and MW_{ac} used, and it is important to understand the difference between the two.

The world's oldest PV solar park is located near Hesperia, California. Arco Solar constructed the 1-MWp (megawatt-peak) plant in 1982. A second and larger 5.2-MWp installation took place in California's Carrizo Plain National Monument in 1984. Both of these sites have since been turned off due to their antiquated panels.

CARRIZO PLAIN

The Carrizo Plain site has since become the Topaz Solar Farm, one of the largest solar farms in the world. This $2.5 billion project uses nine million cadmium telluride (CdTe) thin-film solar panels manufactured by First Solar. The power from this 550-MW installation is being purchased by Pacific Gas and Electric under a 25-year power purchase agreement (PPA). During its installation, the 9.5-square-mile site created over 400 construction jobs. Construction started in 2011 and the site was commissioned in 2014.

California has always been at the forefront of positive environmental change. And while that can also be said for the adoption of renewables here in the United States, it's the Germans who must be credited for initiating the widespread adoption of wind power and PV solar. On January 1, 1991, the Germans passed the Electricity Feed-in Act. This law was the very first "green electricity" remuneration scheme in the world. The result of its passage was a very rapid adoption of both wind power and solar PV systems in Germany. In retrospect, it is heralded both nationally and internationally as a successful and innovative renewable energy policy measure.

The next stage in the development of utility-scale solar (and residential, as well) also occurred in Germany at the turn of the century. It all started with the country's passage of the **Renewable Energy Sources Act** (Erneuerbare-Energien-Gesetz, or EEG). The original version of the EEG was passed on April 1, 2000, and has been revised a number of times since. The EEG guaranteed solar energy customers a connection to the power grid and a remuneration for power produced for 20 years. The EEG was funded by surcharging *all* electric customers.

It could be argued that the Germans are responsible for initiating the wide-scale use of renewables, in particular, PV solar. It all started with their introduction of **feed-in tariffs** (FiTs). A feed-in tariff is a government policy mechanism, the purpose of which is to attract and

FIGURE 4.4   GERMAN FEED-IN TARIFF RATES 2001–2016

Development of the Feed-in Tariff (FiT) for Small Rooftop Systems (< 10 KW)

Year	2001	2002	2003	2004	2005	2006	2007	2008
EURcents/kWh	50.6	48.1	45.7	57.4	54.5	51.8	49.2	46.75
	2009	2010	2011	2012	2013	2014	2015	2016
	49.03	39.14	28.74	24.43	17.02	13.68	12.56	12.31

Source: www.iea-pvps.org/index.php?id=6&eID=dam_frontend_push&docID=3195.

accelerate investment in renewable energy. It accomplishes this by providing a remuneration to the energy producer or system owner that is more than the wholesale or retail electric rate currently in force.

FiTs give renewable energy system owners or producers long-term security. The FiT rate is determined by the cost of generation for a specific technology. For example, solar PV FiT rates are higher than those for wind power reflecting higher system installation costs for solar. Figure 4.4 depicts the FiT remuneration for small rooftop solar systems, smaller than 10 kW in size. You can see that as the price of solar has come down, so have the FiT rates.

On August 1, 2014, the EEG had a significant revision take effect. It essentially eliminated the FiT for renewable energy systems. Remuneration rates for system owners are no longer determined by the government, but are set by auction.

CORPORATE AMERICA GOES ALL-IN ON SOLAR DEPLOYMENT

The country's largest corporate adopter of solar isn't Walmart, as you might guess. It's Target. So far, it has solar PV operating on 436 of its 1,800 buildings. In 2017, the retailer added 43 MW of solar PV. It now has a total of 203.5 MW of solar installed.[10]

As of October 2018, Walmart, America's largest brick-and-mortar retailer, had a total of 5,358 locations in the US. In an effort toward sustainable operation, Walmart is in the beginning stages of equipping its rooftops with solar panels. It has solar deployed on 370 of them. In April 2018, it announced it is going to install solar on 130 more. It did not specify the number of megawatts it plans to install, however.[11]

Walmart has a total of 785 million square feet of rooftop space, just in the United States. That's equal to 18,012 square acres, or 28.1 square miles of rooftop. To put that in perspective, Manhattan Island is 22.82 square miles. When Walmart has all of its rooftops covered with solar panels, it will be generating about 3.6 GW of electricity during the day.

And remember, that's just here in the United States. Walmart's 6,377 international stores total another 369.8 million square feet (8,489 acres) of rooftop.[12] Add solar to those and that adds another 1.7 GW of solar power. Walmart eventually plans to equip every one of its stores with solar panels. If it does, it will be one of the largest independent power producers in the United States and the world.

IKEA, a retailer with far fewer stores than either Target or Walmart, is ahead of both of them on a percentage basis. It's installed solar panels on over 90 percent of its stores and warehouses.

Speaking of warehouses, they are going to be another big area of solar power build-out. Once warehouse owners do the math, solar is going to pop up on more and more warehouse rooftops. And the United States has a lot of them. According to Cushman and Wakefield, 67 percent of US industrial space is warehousing. That works out to about 9.1 billion square feet of rooftop. Cap it with solar and we're looking at a whopping 208,907 acres. That turns into 41.8 GW of solar power.

The beauty of using existing rooftops, especially in industrial parks, is it doesn't take up valuable real estate, especially in crowded areas where it's at a premium. Not everyone likes the looks of solar panels, and putting them on flat commercial and industrial rooftops gets them out of sight and out of mind. Most industrial roofs are strong enough to hold the additional weight of solar panels and support racking, or can easily be designed to do so.

What if all of the commercial retail buildings (malls and shopping centers) in the United States sported solar panels, where there is roughly 50 square feet of commercial retail space per capita? That works out to about 16.22 billion square feet of rooftop. That's another 372,360 acres of rooftop, which will produce a massive 74.4 GW of solar energy.

Add our industrial and commercial potential power production together, and solar can easily add 116.2 GW of additional electrical production. And most people would be none the wiser that it happened, because they wouldn't see the panels. So how does 116.2 GW compare to the 2015 (latest available) overall US generating capacity? It's a little more than the amount of nuclear power generating capacity (103.8 GW). It's five times the amount of total solar installed (23.4 GW) and 10 times the amount of utility-scale solar (11.9 GW).[13]

Here's the point I'm trying to make: Even without using any additional land, the United States can increase its utility-scale solar capacity by an order of magnitude. And right now, there is a scarcity of industrial warehouse space in the country. According to the Jones Lang LaSalle 2016 Industrial Outlook,[14] demand outpaced supply last year. Vacancy rates are at 14-year lows. In the third quarter of 2016, new rentals totaled 164 million square feet. Under construction activity was an additional 170 million square feet. Jones Lang LaSalle estimates that current and future demand from active tenants is approximately two times the current space under construction. In terms of additional solar power generating capacity, the new warehouse roof space (164 million square feet per quarter) equals 0.75 GW of potential new generating space every three months.

Organizations like the Solar Energy Industry Association are actively marketing to the above organizations to adopt rooftop solar. With grid parity in over half the states at the utility-scale level (and even more by the time you read this), adding commercial and/or utility-scale rooftop solar is a no-brainer for building owners. The good news is, utility-scale solar adoption rates are continuing to increase annually. In 2015, companies installed 1,686 systems totaling 907 MW. That was a 59 percent increase over 2014. Today's solar installed capacity is 30 times more than just one decade ago.

THE CURRENT STATE OF UTILITY-SCALE

2017's year-over-year drop in utility-scale installations was due to the surge of installations that pulled forward into 2016. This was due to the anticipated expiration of the solar 30 percent federal Investment Tax Credit (ITC). In February 2018, the credit was extended through the end of 2019. But the 2017 slowdown was also affected by uncertainties surrounding the Section 201 tariffs. These affected solar cells and modules. As a result, a number of utility-scale projects were shelved, especially toward the end of 2017.

In the first half of 2018, 8.5 GW_{dc} of new utility-scale solar PV projects were announced. That's more than was installed in 2014 and

2015 *combined*. The current pipeline for utility-scale stands at 23.9 GW$_{dc}$.[15] That's the highest it's ever been in the history of the industry. Tariffs on modules had little effect on solar's pent-up demand. In 2018, utility-scale PV is being procured *primarily* based on its economic competitiveness with both wind and natural gas. Yes, solar is no longer an "alternative" energy source. It's quickly becoming the cheapest way to generate electricity.

UTILITY-SCALE'S FUTURE

By 2020, US utilities will have spent over $300 billion to upgrade a key aspect of US infrastructure: its electric grid. Suffering from age, and lack of capacity and security, the grid has been woefully inadequate to support our growing thirst for energy. A good portion of that $300 billion is going toward utility-scale solar. As of October 2018, there are over 6,000 solar projects of 1 MW or greater either in operation or in development in the United States. More than 26 GW of utility-scale solar are under development.[16] Let's look at where the solar sector is headed, and more importantly, where it's not.

There's no question that US solar has had fantastic growth. But solar is at a crossroads of sorts. Three trends started emerging in 2016 in the solar sector, each raising issues that will determine how residential, utility-scale, and nonresidential solar markets are going to fare in the coming years. Let's look at each trend.

Residential Solar Growth Is Slowing

The first trend is the drop in adoption rates in the top solar markets. That's because third-party financing (introduced in 2010 and made popular by Solar City) lost favor with some customers in the top solar markets. Let's look at the top distributed solar PV markets, as shown in Figure 4.5. Over 47 percent of all residential solar lies in California. That market is reaching saturation.

Customer fatigue is setting in. Customers in the top solar markets are tired of residential solar installers hounding them. After California, the next nine states are responsible for 44 percent of the residential market. The remaining 16 percent is spread across the other 40 states and Washington, DC.

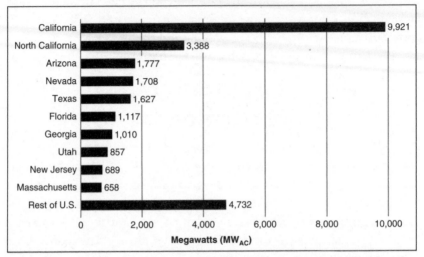

Source: www.eia.gov/electricity/monthly/epm_table_grapher.cfm?t=epmt_6_02_b

California's installed base is high for several reasons. First, it's home to more people than any other state. Second, it has some of the highest electric rates in the country. Lastly, it has lots of sun, and incentives and policies that promote solar.

Starting in 2010, residential solar grew 55 percent annually through 2015. Early adopters (like my wife and me) were responsible for that rapid growth. So customer fatigue isn't that surprising at this point in the top markets. With the continuation of the investment tax credit, residential solar installs will continue, but at a slower pace. Future growth will come from states where solar penetration is not as deep as California's. There are many other states with incentives to install residential solar.

Another issue plaguing the residential market is the struggling publicly traded residential solar companies. Many continue to struggle balancing profitability with growth. As the price of solar continues to drop, the residential market is becoming a low margin business. The relative lack of consumer loans available for solar is another problem plaguing the residential sector.

It continues to be attractive to install, especially on rooftops. Tesla's new building integrated photovoltaic (BIPV) roof shingles will certainly find buyers, especially if the price is right. As of October 2018, Tesla is still not shipping tiles in any meaningful quantity. The company claims it has 250 houses in California with installed tiles as an initial test group. But deliveries of tiles outside of California won't start until 2019.

Utility-Scale Solar Is Booming

A utility-scale solar energy system is capable of producing 1 MW or more of power. Unlike the residential market, utility-scale solar is on fire. That's primarily due to the increasing number of states (29 as of the end of 2016) that have been adopting or increasing **renewable portfolio standards (RPS)**.

These standards require specific percentages of electricity that utilities sell to come from renewable sources. Some states only apply RPS to investor-owned utilities (IOUs). However, some states' RPS include electric cooperatives and municipality-owned power plants. In addition to the 29 states with RPS, eight more states have renewable energy goals.

Utilities, driven by state RPS mandates and goals, are investing in solar like never before (see Figure 4.6). In 2017, a full 70 percent of solar installs will be utility-scale. Some utilities contract to have solar power plants built for them. But most prefer to purchase the power they produce. A utility generally contracts for a minimum amount of power, as stated in a power purchase agreement (PPA). PPA terms are generally 15 to 20 years in length.

Currently there is 19.4 GW of utility-scale solar projects in the sector's pipeline. But many of the new projects are going to be smaller than before. That's because economies of scale have continued to drive down the cost of solar. PPA prices are now between $35 and $50 per MWh. This is below the avoided cost (the cost utilities would pay another utility for power) of many utilities. As a result, many utilities are now interested in PPAs from smaller systems.

Utilities are also viewing long-term solar PPAs as hedges against large swings in the price of natural gas. This allows them to use solar energy systems for peak power needs instead of natural gas-fired plants.

What's in store for 2018 and beyond? In Q1 2018, a total of 1.4 GW_{dc} came online, representing 57 percent of all US solar installed

FIGURE **4.6** ANNUAL US SOLAR PV INSTALLATIONS, 2010-2016

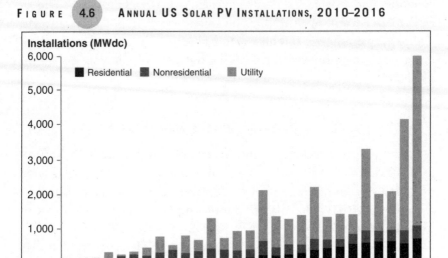

Source: www.seia.org/sites/default/files/H7D82HD9F238SMI2016Q4.pdf (plus additional data supplied by author).

that quarter. By the end of 2018, I believe we'll see 7 GW_{dc} installed. As of October 2018, there are more than 50 GW_{dc} of new projects in the utility-scale pipeline.[17]

I expect the utility-scale solar market will be bigger in 2019, but the mix of projects will change somewhat. Anchoring utility-scale will be utilities procuring solar PV to meet their RPS requirements.

Old Tool, New Energy

Many utilities are beginning to procure new solar PV projects via one of the oldest tools in their energy toolbox: the **Public Utility Regulatory Policies Act** (PURPA). PURPA was enacted November 1978 as part of the larger National Energy Act. It was created in response to the 1973 energy crisis, and its purpose was to reduce energy's demand on fossil fuels via conservation, use of domestic energy sources, and renewable energy. At the time, renewable energy consisted largely of hydroelectric power.

Under PURPA, utilities must purchase energy from efficient cogeneration, solar, and wind projects if their costs are equal to or less than the cost of constructing a new fossil fuel–fired power plant. With the advent of cheap solar, PURPA has driven over 16 GW of new generating capacity from qualified cogeneration, wind, and solar PV projects.

But today, cheap solar installations are undercutting some utilities' ability to make money with new fossil fuel plants. A perfect example is Duke Energy, the largest utility in North Carolina. The Tar Heel State has more PURPA-driven solar PV installations than any other state. That's over 90 percent of the solar PV connected to the state's electric grid (1.271 GW).

All those PURPA-driven installations mean that North Carolina is now second only to California in utility-scale solar capacity. Duke now believes that PURPA is causing too much solar installation in its service area. The utility claims that demand for electricity is slowing. I'm sure that's true (and isn't that the whole point anyway?).

But Duke doesn't see it that way and doesn't want to enter into any more PURPA contracts. So it has proposed additional interconnection requirements that ultimately make it more difficult for smaller solar project developers. By introducing these new requirements, Duke is making it more difficult for its competition. It argues that when generation capacity outstrips demand, its avoided cost will be the operational costs of its existing power plants. At that point, state officials might demand that those plants be retired.

Here's the bottom line: PURPA is helping to replace old, dirty, less efficient (and now) more expensive power plants with clean and efficient utility-scale solar. But other utilities like Duke are beginning to try to weaken or skirt PURPA requirements as utility-scale solar takes an increasing bite of their energy pie. Since PURPA is a federal law, utilities would have to lobby their congresspersons and senators to repeal or replace it. But I don't see that happening any time soon. Utility-scale solar is on a roll, getting cheaper all the time, and becoming more popular with constituents of both parties.

In the next chapter, we'll look at the future of the solar industry, and the impact it will have on the global energy supply, the reduction of fossil fuel use, and the benefit of lower greenhouse gas emissions.

NOTES

1. votesolar.org/files/7014/6369/1060/Honeyman-Vote-Solar-Webinar-April-2016.pdf
2. http://irena.org/publications/2018/May/Renewable-Energy-and-Jobs-Annual-Review-2018

3. www.seia.org/research-resources/solar-industry-data
4. www.thesolarfoundation.org/national/
5. www.seia.org/research-resources/solar-market-insight-report-2018-q3
6. www.pv-magazine.com/news/details/beitrag/gtm-research--utility-scale-solar-pv-prices-will-fall-below-1-per-watt-by-2020_100024811/#axzz4QZvOFNJu
7. www.pv-magazine.com/news/details/beitrag/gtm-research--utility-scale-solar-pv-prices-will-fall-below-1-per-watt-by-2020_100024811/#axzz4QZvOFNJu
8. www.seia.org/research-resources/impacts-solar-investment-tax-credit-extension
9. cleantechnica.com/2018/01/15/will-reach-grid-parity/
10. https://pv-magazine-usa.com/2018/04/19/target-remains-the-largest-adopter-of-on-site-corporate-solar-power/
11. https://pv-magazine-usa.com/2018/04/23/walmart-to-host-solar-power-on-130-more-sites/
12. http://stock.walmart.com/investors/financial-information/unit-counts-and-square-footage/default.aspx
13. Data from the EIA: www.eia.gov/electricity/annual/html/epa_04_03.html
14. www.joc.com/international-logistics/distribution-centers/us-industrial-demand-forecast-exceed-space-2016_20151218.html
15. https://www.greentechmedia.com/articles/read/despite-tariffs-utility-solar-picking-up-steam#gs.iWKiMt4
16. https://www.seia.org/initiatives/utility-scale-solar-power
17. https://www.seia.org/research-resources/major-solar-projects-list

CHAPTER FIVE

What's Ahead for Solar Energy

So far, we've looked at the history of solar energy, how modern solar energy systems produce electricity, whether or not a solar energy system makes sense for the reader, and the rise in utility-scale solar. In this final chapter on solar, we're going to cover what's ahead for what is quickly becoming the world's most ubiquitous energy source.

SOLAR GROWTH, SMASHING RECORDS

In 2016 solar energy in the United States nearly doubled the previous year's installation record, adding 14,626 megawatts (MW) of solar PV. That's a 95 percent increase over 2015's 7,493 MW[1] (see Figure 5.1).

On an annual basis, US solar PV was the top source of new capacity additions for electric generation. This is the first time in history solar ranked as number one. It was 39 percent of all new generating capacity in 2016.

Abigail Ross Hopper, the president and CEO of the Solar Energy Industry Association (SEIA), put solar's record rise into the proper perspective: "What these numbers tell you is that the solar industry is a force to be reckoned with. Solar's economically winning hand is generating strong growth across all market segments nationwide, leading to

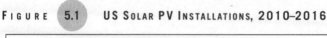

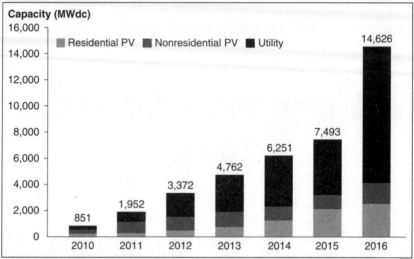

Data source: www.greentechmedia.com/articles/read/us-solar-market-grows-95-in-2016-smashes-records.

more than 260,000 Americans now employed in solar."[2] The US solar industry now employs more than twice as many people as it did just five years ago. These workers are at over 9,000 companies located in every state. By 2021, the SEIA expects the US solar sector will employ more than 360,000 Americans.[3]

THE GRAND COMPROMISE

At the end of 2015, the future for renewable energy was in doubt. The Production Tax Credit (PTC), which benefited wind, expired at the end of 2014. The Investment Tax Credit (ITC), which benefited solar, was set to expire at the end of 2016. That would have been a huge blow to what was a great start to renewable energy. Over the previous decade, wind and solar attracted investments of more than $400 billion.

Analysts and industry experts predicted that wind and solar would reach "grid parity" pricing by 2020. By that time, they'll be at or below the price of other forms of power generation. A financial incentive was clearly needed, one that would bridge the five-year gap. Without it, investment in renewables would slow down significantly, and grid parity would take much longer.

But in a late December 2015 "grand compromise," as it is now referred to, Congress agreed to reinstate the PTC and extend the ITC in exchange for lifting the 40-year ban on the export of American crude oil dating back to the oil embargo crisis of the 1970s, thus avoiding the potential "valley of death" that would have resulted if the ITC and PTC were not renewed.

Congress voted to extend the solar ITC at its current 30 percent rate through the end of 2019. Any project that is under construction before the end of 2019 qualifies. The ITC drops to 26 percent in 2020, 22 percent in 2021 and 10 percent in 2022. Any project that is under development before 2024 will receive the 10 percent credit. The PTC for wind was applied retroactively to any project under development or constructed in 2015 and 2016. After 2016, it declines each year until it completely expires in 2020.

Extending the ITC and renewing the PTC ensures renewable energy development will continue along its rapidly declining cost curve. It's great news for the big corporations that are adding significant renewable generation capacity in the United States. In 2017 alone, they've signed deals with energy providers to construct 2.78 GW of large, utility-scale renewable capacity.[4]

Perhaps the best thing to come from the extension of the ITC and PTC is the ability for all the companies in the renewable energy business to plan for and forecast their future business levels accurately. They'll be able to secure financing, cut costs, and prepare project pipelines. In another few years, when the subsidies expire, costs will be low enough so that solar and wind will be the go to energy sources. It's a watershed moment for solar.

How far away from grid parity are renewables? Wind is already past grid parity, which explains why wind farms now appear in all 50 states in favorable locations. Utility-scale solar is also on par or below natural gas–fired generation. Community solar gardens and rooftop installations on commercial and industrial buildings are also on par with natural gas–generating plants. Residential rooftop solar must still come down in price to be at or below grid parity.

The utility-scale segment of solar was the big growth driver for 2017 and 2018. During Q2 2018 the US installed 2.3 GW of solar capacity.[5] Some of those projects moved forward in anticipation of the end of the federal ITC for solar which was set to expire at the end of 2016.

Congress then extended it through the end of 2019, as long as the project construction starts before the end of 2019.

But the growth in utility-scale solar can also be contributed to its cost-competitiveness with natural gas–fired power plants. For instance, the average generation rate in dollars per Megawatt-hour (MWh) for Boston is $126. That compares to $51 per MWh for thin-film utility-scale solar. A natural gas–fired **peaker plant** can cost as much as $191 per MWh depending on the cost of natural gas at the plant's location.[6] As a result of 2017's remarkable growth in solar PV, the United States now boasts over 1.8 million solar PV installations. The total cumulative capacity is more than 58 GWs.[7] As we'll soon see, the growth in utility-scale solar is just getting started, with the addition of new, smaller installations complementing the large, 100 MW-plus solar farms.

SOLAR ENERGY UNDER TRUMP

As I write in 2018, the cost of solar power continues to drop, and more US electric utilities are installing solar. But they are doing it just when our president, Donald Trump, wants to boost coal, oil, and natural gas. Trump's full-on support of fossil fuels and his disbelief in climate change have raised concerns of supporters of renewable energy in the United States.

In his 2015 book *Crippled America*, Trump made it clear that he thinks investing in renewable energy is a bad idea. He even thinks the development of alternative forms of energy using renewable resources is "a big mistake."

In his book he writes: "To begin with, the whole push for renewable energy is being driven by the wrong motivation, the mistaken belief that global climate change is being caused by carbon emissions. If you don't buy that—and I don't—then what we have is really just an expensive way of making the tree-huggers feel good about themselves."

Since becoming president, Trump hasn't said much at all regarding solar energy. The White House website has a link to the "America First Energy Plan," the Trump administration's plan for US energy. It won't take you long to read it. It's a paltry 361 words long. The words, "solar," "wind," and "renewable" are not mentioned at all.

However, the administration provided a list of 50 infrastructure projects, totaling more than $137 billion, to the National Governor's Association. These are projects that would presumably get funded first if and when the president gets his infrastructure-spending plan through Congress. The document, first obtained by the *Kansas City Star* and the *News Tribune,* is titled, "Priority List – Emergency & National Security Projects."

While the federal spending is $137 billion, Trump is looking for private-sector investments of that much or more in order to fund the projects. The document lists the number of "job years" that would be created. Direct job years would be 193,350 and there would be an additional 241,700 indirect job years created. Interestingly, the number of long-term jobs created is there, but is blank.

The list of projects is impressive, and covers US infrastructure from A to Z, including 12 road and bridge replacement projects. Of the 50 projects, 7 are electrical power grid upgrade and expansion projects. Many are necessary to deliver clean, renewable wind energy from the Midwest to load centers in California, Nevada, and the Southeast. There's even an energy storage project underway in California. Concerned over power blackouts, the California Public Utilities Commission is expediting the construction of energy storage systems in critical locations.

But the president isn't the only one with an infrastructure-improvement plan. The Senate Democrats, led by Chuck Schumer, have their own infrastructure plan. The "Blueprint to Rebuild America's Infrastructure" touts it will create over 15 million jobs. It will also spend $1 trillion, but that would all come out of the federal treasury (taxpayer pockets). The Democrat's plan addresses everything the Trump plan does, and a lot more.

Like the Trump plan, the Democrats want to invest $100 billion in upgrades to the power grid in the United States. In addition, their plan would create a permanent incentive for renewable energy generation, biofuels, and improvements in energy efficiency. Energy tax credits would reward the use and generation of clean energy and promote investment and inventiveness in both energy conservation and renewable energy.

The Democrats believe that this new certainty in the US tax code will enable viable, large investments that support next generation energy and energy infrastructure. These will bring down energy costs for consumers, protect the environment, and increase energy efficiency.

Trump has talked about axing the Obama administration's Clean Power Plan. That would be unfortunate, but it wasn't supposed to take effect until 2020. But even if he does manage to kill it, it won't matter. Whether he likes it or not, the solar energy train has already left the station.

Even though the word "solar" doesn't appear in Trump's America First Energy Plan, the solar industry is racking up some dramatic job growth numbers. The Solar Foundation, a nonprofit industry support group, indicated that 2016 saw the creation of over 51,000 new solar industry jobs. That's a 24.5 percent jump over 2015. The report states that the solar sector now employs over 260,000 workers at more than 9,000 companies in every US state.[8] And 2016 was the fourth consecutive year of 20 percent-plus job growth for the solar industry.[9] In 2017, the solar sector pumped $17 billion into the US economy.[10] The growth in large part is a direct reflection of the increasing number of American businesses and families that are installing solar.

Solar has another thing going for it. That is the unstoppable force of technological innovation. And all the technologies surrounding solar are clean, very reliable and getting more affordable every day. The price of solar panels in dollars per watt in 2018 ranges from $0.28 to $0.45.[11] That's more than competitive with every other form of generation. That's Fessler's First Law of Technology, "Technology marches on," in action. The pace of improvements in technology, and solar in particular, happens independently of what's going on in politics or who is directing policy. If it makes good common sense, it's going to happen no matter what any one person thinks about it or says in public.

SAN FRANCISCO BREAKS NEW GROUND

I've mentioned in previous chapters that California has led the US adoption of renewables, in everything from geothermal to wind. But nowhere has it been more evident than with solar. And in 2016, San Francisco was the first city in the nation to have an ordinance requiring all new buildings to install solar panels on their roofs.

San Francisco's Board of Supervisors passed this ordinance unanimously and it went into effect at the beginning of 2017. The law is applicable to all commercial and residential buildings that are 10 stories or fewer in height. Before this ordinance, builders had to make buildings "solar-ready," which meant that 15 percent of the roof had to be clear and unshaded. The new ordinance means builders actually have to install either thermal or electrical solar panels that produce either heated water or electricity. The city has a long-term goal of meeting its electrical demand with all renewable sources by 2025.

I've always maintained that there is so much wasted and available roof space that could be used for solar panels. In a statement announcing the ordinance, Scott Weiner, the city supervisor who introduced the legislation, apparently agrees, "Activating underutilized roof space is a smart and efficient way to promote the use of solar energy and improve our environment. We need to continue to pursue aggressive renewable energy policies to ensure a sustainable future for our city and our region."[12] Since San Francisco adopted its new legislation, the cities of Lancaster and Sebastopol, California, have passed similar laws.

It's another great example of cities and states moving faster than Washington, DC. I expect that will continue to be the case with renewables. Local and state governments are not as gridlocked as Washington is. And if you ask the average person about solar, most have no issue with it and generally feel it is good for the environment. No wonder solar is fast becoming a mainstream source of power.

YOU CAN'T PUT THE SOLAR GENIE BACK IN THE BOTTLE

Implied in all of this is more investment in solar. Even if the Trump energy "plan" is the one we end up living with, very little is going to change concerning solar. That's because renewable energy adoption has become popular with many Americans. In addition, many states have renewable portfolio standards that encourage the adoption of solar. This is happening with increasing frequency, as the cost for wind and solar continue to fall.

As of this writing, 29 states and the District of Columbia have renewable portfolio standards (see Figure 5.2). But Washington and the White House in particular have little or no influence on state and local policies, regulations, and incentives regarding renewable energy. So I expect the rollout of solar to continue at a robust pace. Even with the flurry of new installations, solar power generates only a little over 1 percent of all the power in the United States right now.

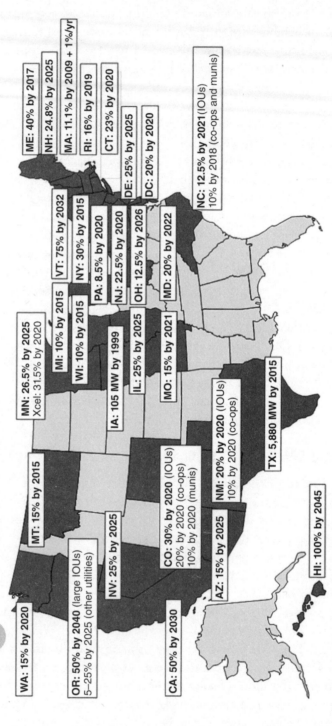

FIGURE 5.2 RENEWABLE PORTFOLIO STANDARDS

ME: 40% by 2017

NH: 24.8% by 2025

MA: 11.1% by 2009 + 1%/yr

RI: 16% by 2019

CT: 23% by 2020

DE: 25% by 2025

DC: 20% by 2020

NC: 12.5% by 2021 (IOUs)
10% by 2018 (co-ops and munis)

VT: 75% by 2032

NY: 30% by 2015

PA: 8.5% by 2020

NJ: 22.5% by 2020

OH: 12.5% by 2026

MD: 20% by 2022

MN: 26.5% by 2025
Xcel: 31.5% by 2020

MI: 10% by 2015

WI: 10% by 2015

IA: 105 MW by 1999

IL: 25% by 2025

MO: 15% by 2021

MT: 15% by 2015

NV: 25% by 2025

CO: 30% by 2020 (IOUs)
20% by 2020 (co-ops)
10% by 2020 (munis)

NM: 20% by 2020 (IOUs)
10% by 2020 (co-ops)

TX: 5,880 MW by 2015

AZ: 15% by 2025

HI: 100% by 2045

WA: 15% by 2020

OR: 50% by 2040 (large IOUs)
5–25% by 2025 (other utilities)

CA: 50% by 2030

Source: emp.lbl.gov/projects/renewables-portfolio.

I expect this will grow rapidly, however, as utilities move from large utility-scale installations into smaller solar installations. Known as solar farms, many of these are under development by nonprofit organizations and local cooperatives. Why are utilities going smaller? To combat homeowners installing their own systems.

Solar energy systems have become so inexpensive, so fast, that utilities are scrambling to preserve their core business: generating and selling power. The more competition they have from homeowners, the fewer dollars available to recoup their plant and grid maintenance costs.

But even a president who "digs coal" can't stop the trend as utilities move away from dirty, coal-fired power plants. Even if federal policies manage to lower or even scrap current greenhouse gas emissions levels, utilities are moving in the direction of natural gas, wind, and solar. Lazard, a financial advisory firm, undertook an apples-to-apples study that compared the cost of all generation types without any of their federal subsidies. They found that the average lifetime cost of utility-scale solar and wind is now cheaper than nuclear and coal, and about the same as natural gas.

Not only that, the study found solar's costs are continuing to decline. Utility-scale solar's median levelized cost of energy (LCOE) is down 11 percent from 2015 to 2016. Rooftop solar PV technology dropped 26 percent during the same timeframe. But it's not quite cost-competitive without government subsidies.

In 2016 wind and solar accounted for roughly 66 percent of new generation capacity in the United States. That was more than fossil fuels for the third year in a row, according to the Department of Energy (see Figure 5.3).

As I mentioned earlier, utilities are concerned that too many homeowners installing rooftop solar could impede their ability to finance and maintain their grids and power plants. That's why they've taken such an interest in "shared solar," also called community solar.

THE COMMUNITY SOLAR GARDEN MODEL

Under this model, a utility has a large solar array built for itself. It then gets customers to sign up and lease some number of panels from the array or agree to buy the power that they produce. The utility then credits this electricity to customers' bills. Utilities typically get customers to

F I G U R E   **5.3**   RENEWABLE GENERATION CAPACITY ADDITIONS, 2010–2016

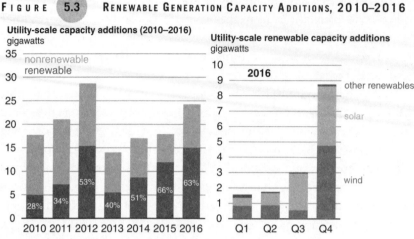

Source: www.eia.gov/todayinenergy/detail.php?id=29492.

sign contracts that lock in rates for 10 to 20 years. Electricity from utility-run solar plants feeds into the utility's grid, not directly to an individual homeowner or business owner.

In many cases, utility-run shared solar is the only option for roughly half of the US households and businesses. A study done by the National Renewable Energy Laboratory found that 48 percent of businesses and 49 percent of all US households aren't able to install a solar PV system.[13] That's because the homeowner or business doesn't own the structure, lacks good credit, doesn't have enough roof space, or the roof is facing the wrong direction.

Up until recently, small nonprofit groups, membership-based electric co-ops, and small municipal utilities came together and ran many of the shared solar "gardens" or "parks."

But now, having been pushed into them by state renewable portfolio standards, utilities are now quickly adopting the shared solar model. In early 2017 about 20 percent of all US community solar programs in 32 states were owned by utilities. These investor-owned utility solar farms represent about 70 percent of the total power output of all of the nation's solar farms.

The state with the largest number of community solar project applications is Minnesota. Xcel Energy is the largest utility in the state and had nearly 2,000 applications totaling 2 GW worth of power for community solar garden projects. At the beginning of 2017, roughly 318 MW worth of applications were in the design phase. Another 178 MW across 49 sites were under construction.

A total of 17 community solar gardens were up and running with 57 MWs of capacity. The projects were installed by Geronimo Energy and financed by BHE Renewables, a division of Berkshire Hathaway. Xcel Energy had about 700 MWs of utility-scale solar projects and roughly 700 MW of community and residential solar up and running by the end of 2017.[14] Xcel Energy plans to have almost 10 percent of its energy produced from solar by 2030. Minnesota's community solar program is off to a good start, and several other states are getting into the community solar program as well.

New York calls its program Community Distributed Generation (CDG). It has almost 2 GW worth of project applications among its participating utilities. New York's CDG program is available to home-owners, renters, businesses, and even entire municipalities.[15] Maryland has a new three-year pilot community solar program. The state expects it will result in the development of 192 MW of community solar.[16]

In Colorado, utilities have a state mandate to obtain 30 percent of their electrical generation from renewables by 2020. While Colorado has a lot of wind generation, it's now focusing on community solar. It already has 28 community solar gardens up and running, thus gener-ating over 16 MW. Another 26 are under construction and will generate an additional 31 MW when completed.[17]

A common thread running through all of the state community solar programs is the accessibility by low- and moderate-income customers and renters. These are groups of customers who in all likelihood would not have access to solar energy via any other means. Participating in a community solar project gives these individuals an immediate reduc-tion in their electricity bills.

The big question is how much of a credit can a typical homeowner expect to receive by participating in a community solar program? The answer varies, depending on the state and the utility involved in the community solar program where the homeowner lives.

In Minnesota, the rates were initially based on the retail electric rate. Credits ranged from $0.12 per kilowatt-hour (kWh) to $0.15 per kWh, depending on the class of the subscriber and a number of other factors. However, Minnesota switched over to a **value of solar (VOS)** rate at the beginning of 2017. The VOS rate attempts to total all of the benefits and costs of distributed solar and assign a true cost. In Minnesota, the initial VOS rate for community solar programs run by Xcel Energy was established at slightly more than $0.10 per kWh. It will be adjusted every year for inflation.

In Maryland and New York, community solar project subscriber reimbursement rates vary by contract. The membership terms, bill credit rates, and any provisions for exiting membership are included in the contract between the sponsor and the subscriber. In Maryland, any individual subscriber cannot receive credit for over 200 percent of their average annual usage.

As of this writing, 25 states have at least one community solar garden. Twelve states and the District of Columbia have policies and programs in place encouraging the growth of community solar projects. It looks like utilities, municipalities, and businesses are all currently focused on the community solar garden model as a means of advancing solar energy in particular and renewables in general. State renewable portfolio requirements will continue to drive solar energy demand at the utility level.

I expect community solar projects will be one of the big drivers of solar adoption, especially in the United States. As more states adopt community solar models and more projects begin operating, it will become readily apparent that solar has definitely arrived as a mainstream energy source.

THE GLOBAL GROWTH OF SOLAR

While it's clear that solar is on a growth tear here in the United States, the global demand for solar is greater than any time during the past seven years. In 2017, 73 percent of all solar PV installations will be in the top four markets (the US, India, China, and Japan). In 2017, India, the world's fastest growing economy increased its solar installations by 9.5 GW. The country is aiming for 28 GW of installed solar by the end of 2018.[18] Overall, the global solar PV market grew nearly 30 percent in 2017. The total global installed solar PV is now 405 GW. Fully 89 percent of that was installed since 2010.[19]

The global demand driver is no different than what it is here in the United States: Solar is dropping PV module prices. A glut of Chinese modules flooded the market in late 2016 and early 2017. The result? Module prices are being quoted between $0.28 and $0.45 per watt. That is very competitive with any other traditional power source. And remember, solar power price agreements (PPAs) lock in electricity pricing for 20 to 30 years. Except for wind power, there is no similar pricing lock-in for any other form of electrical generation. That makes solar look increasingly competitive when thinking long-term.

According to the industry research firm SolarPower Europe, 2017 marked the 11th year of global demand growth for solar PV. In 2017, installers added 98.9 GW of new capacity around the world, a 30 percent year-over-year growth from 2016.[20]

The United States grew at record rates in 2016 (95 percent year-over-year). But India was the top growth market in 2017, with the US market coming in second. Following them will be Africa, the Middle East, China, and finally Mexico. On the other hand, UK, Japanese, Australian, and German markets, viewed by analysts as more mature, are expected to remain flat or contract slightly.

The world saw an additional 95 GW of solar capacity installations during 2017. Interestingly, IHS Markit expects 2018's growth will slow to a mere 8 percent. We should see a much stronger recovery in 2019.

Around the globe, solar project developers are thinking big. More than 67 percent of the global project pipeline for solar PV consists of projects larger than 50 MW in size. Developers in China and the United States are taking advantage of abundant land in areas where solar radiation is the greatest. In the states, that's the Southwest. According to IHS, there are over 45,000 PV projects around the world in pipeline, under construction, or completed.[21]

From a financial standpoint, solar is in great shape. Over half of the largest infrastructure funds poured money into renewable energy in the first quarter of 2017. Roughly 69 percent invested in energy and 52 percent invested strictly in renewables. That translates to over $100 billion that is waiting to be put to work. I'll bet a good portion of that is ultimately going to be put to work on renewable projects.

Another major kick to renewable energy generation is coming from the corporate sector. There is an increasing trend toward investing in renewable energy. Google hit its 100 percent renewable energy target by the end of 2017.[22] The RE100, a list of companies committing to go "100 percent renewable," now has 152 members. The list is impressive in its scope and size. It's rapidly growing, too, with 13 new companies joining in September 2018.[23] Of course, the easiest way for most of these companies to go 100 percent renewable is to cover their roofs with solar panels. Going 100 percent renewable is now viewed as good corporate environmental stewardship. I expect we'll see this list continue to rapidly grow annually.

A NEW LOOK FOR SOLAR: BUILDING-INTEGRATED PHOTOVOLTAICS

While the big solar manufacturers continue to make panels by the millions, there are new products on the horizon that are making their debut. I'm talking about building-integrated photovoltaic (BIPV) products. Roofing tiles, building siding, and even solar PV glass windows are all either on the drawing boards or available today.

Perhaps the most innovative product to hit the market in 2017 is Tesla, Inc.'s new solar PV roofing tiles. Tesla isn't the first company to market solar shingle products. Other companies including Dow, PowerLight, AstroPower, UniSolar, Atlantis, BP Solar, CertainTeed, and Suntegra have all introduced solar shingle products. As of this writing, only Atlantis, CertainTeed, and Suntegra solar roof shingles are still on the market. Solar shingles have not taken off as much as manufacturers would like. This has been primarily due to the high costs of the shingles themselves as well as steep installation costs.

Tesla believes its shingles are far better than what's been offered so far. Every shingle has a 6-inch, high efficiency solar cell behind a colored louver film and a coating of protective, tempered glass. The tempered glass layer makes Tesla's cells extremely durable. From below, Tesla's cells are not visible to the naked eye. The roof looks just like any other roof in the neighborhood. As of 2018, Tesla offered four different styles of roofing tiles: Smooth Glass, Slate Glass, Textured Glass, and Tuscan Glass (see Figure 5.4).

The big difference between other roofing tiles and what Tesla offers is simple. Competitive tiles are still installed over an existing roof. Tesla's roofing tiles *are* the roof. Tesla's initial problem is that roofers aren't trained to work with electrical wires and connectors and solar installers aren't roofers. Anyone installing Tesla's products has to be trained by Tesla on installation procedures.

Beyond solar roof tiles, manufacturers have yet to make home siding or building glass that is able to turn the sun's rays into usable

F I G U R E   5.4   TESLA SOLAR ROOF TILES

Source: Tesla, Inc. Reproduced with permission.

electricity. I believe that's in our future, but is in all likelihood at least a decade away. Remember, not all technologies that work in a laboratory or on a small scale are able to be manufactured at a scale that brings profitability.

THE FUTURE OF SOLAR CELL TECHNOLOGY

There are many emerging photovoltaic technologies. It's an exciting time in the field of solar energy. Not all of the emerging technologies I'll review below will become "photovoltaic blockbusters." Silicon photovoltaics are still being used in many of the panels sold today. But some of the emerging cell technologies could be used in niche applications or create other offshoot cell technologies.

Before I review existing and new solar cell technologies, a paragraph or two about cell **conversion efficiency** is in order. Conversion efficiency is a measure of how well a solar cell converts the sun's energy into electricity. It does this by converting photons into electrons. The majority of solar panels produced today use polycrystalline silicon solar cells. Silicon, often referred to as the "first generation" solar cell technology, is still the solar module material of choice, and has been for some time. The theoretical conversion efficiency for a traditional single-junction silicon solar cell is about 30 percent. That's because the bulk of the sun's energy that strikes the solar cell passes through it without being absorbed, or it changes into heat energy that simply heats up the cell and the surrounding material.

In universities around the world, however, engineers are experimenting with new solar cell designs that will raise the current limitation on conversion efficiency. They are doing this by creating silicon solar cells with multiple junctions. Having multiple junctions that are sensitive to more bands of light beyond visible (infrared and ultraviolet, to name a few), means more of the sun's energy hitting the cell can be converted into electricity. The current world record for conversion efficiency for a single-junction solar cell is 46 percent. A Japanese research team led by Professor Kita Takashi at the Kobe University Graduate School of Engineering designed and created the cell. The team leapfrogged the theoretical 30 percent limit for a single-junction cell by using two photons instead of one. This new mechanism is unique to the team's cell design. Takashi's team demonstrated theoretical efficiencies of 63 percent using the two-photon design.[24] The team continues to work on new solar cell designs with an eye toward creating low-cost, high-efficiency silicon solar cells. Aside from advances in conversion efficiency in silicon solar cells, there are "second generation" solar cell technologies that could soon supplant polycrystalline silicon. I'll review some of the most promising ones here.

Today's solar panels are a collection of interconnected silicon wafers (solar cells). However, there are three other technologies, collectively called "thin-film" technologies, that eliminate silicon wafers. They are copper-indium-gallium-diselenide (CIGS), cadmium-telluride (CdTe), and amorphous thin-film silicon (a-Si, TF-Si). These present a huge opportunity for a reduction in material costs.

The film thickness is as thin as a few nanometers to tens of micrometers. That's much thinner than conventional silicon solar cells that are about 200 micrometers thick. Thin-film's advantage allows cells and modules to be flexible, semi-transparent and much lighter than conventional first-generation cells. As a result, building-integrated photovoltaic (BIPV) product manufacturers use thin-film cells. Some semi-transparent films are laminated onto glass windows. Thin-film solar panels are constructed by sandwiching the film between two panes of glass.

While thin-film solar panels have always cost less than their first-generation silicon-cell counterparts, they have always lagged conventional cells in conversion efficiency. The nonprofit foundation, Centre for Solar Energy and Hydrogen Research Baden-Württemberg (ZSW), holds the current efficiency record for a CIGS thin-film cell. Based in Stuttgart and Ulm, Germany, ZSW is a pioneer of solar research. Its goal is to transfer technology research results to practical applications for use by German companies. The head of the Photovoltaics division is Professor Michael Powalla. Powalla believes CIGS efficiencies of 25 percent will be achievable "in the next few years."[25]

Some of the world's largest solar PV power stations (the Topaz Solar Farm) use cadmium telluride (CdTe) photovoltaic solar panels because CdTe technology is extremely cost-competitive, even when pitted against low-cost Chinese silicon solar panels. CdTe panels being made and sold today have efficiencies of 17 percent. First Solar is a large US manufacturer of CdTe solar panels. It currently holds the world record for conversion efficiency of a CdTe panel at 22.1 percent. According to First Solar, "The achievement validates CdTe's continuing competitive advantage over traditional crystalline silicon technology." Right now, most CdTe panels are used in large, utility-scale installations. However, a real possibility exists that CdTe solar panels may supplant silicon solar panels in the not too distant future.

Amorphous silicon (a-Si, TF-Si), the third of thin-film technologies discussed here, has the lowest efficiency compared to CIGS and CdTe cells. Its lower efficiency has relegated its use for devices that require small amounts of power. Solar pocket calculators are an example of a-Si use. Energy Conversion Devices, the only manufacturer of a-Si solar panels and a-Si BIPV products filed for Chapter 11 bankruptcy in February 2012. The company simply could not compete with the continuing drop in the cost of conventional silicon solar panels.

Another emerging solar cell technology is dye-sensitized solar cells (DSSC). So far, the National Renewable Energy Laboratory (NREL)

FIGURE 5.5   DYE-SENSITIZED SOLAR CELL ARCHITECTURE

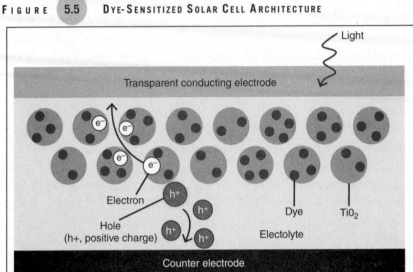

has certified the maximum efficiency of DSSCs at 11.9 percent. DSSCs work differently than conventional silicon cells (see Figure 5.5).

Light (photons) transmitted through a transparent conducting electrode is absorbed by light-harvesting red dye molecules that are coating titanium dioxide (TiO_2) nanoparticles. Electron-hole pairs (e^-/h^+) are formed. Electrons are injected into the TiO_2 particles and are transported to the top-conducting electrode. Positive charges (holes) migrate through the electrolyte to the lower counter electrode. This generates an electrical current.

DSSCs, while lower in efficiency that silicon cells, can be manufactured in very thin films that are low in weight, extremely thin, and translucent. This allows DSSCs to be used in BIPV applications like window glazing. A DSSC film can be sandwiched between two panes of glass. This effectively turns every south-facing window into a solar panel. Dongjin Semichem, a South Korean company, has been manufacturing glass-based DSSC modules since 2010. The company markets its glass panels to architects, window manufacturers and construction materials companies.

The quantum dot solar cell (QDSC) is another cell technology that a number of academic researchers believe holds promise. In QDSCs,

FIGURE 5.6 QUANTUM DOT SOLAR CELL ARCHITECTURE

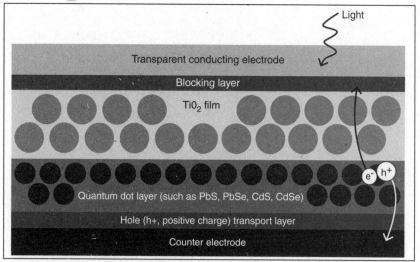

nanocrystals of semiconducting metal (lead sulfide, cadmium sulfide, cadmium selenide, or lead selenide) is the light-absorbing layer (see Figure 5.6).

Similar to a DSSC, light shines through a transparent conducting electrode onto the photosensitive layer of nanocrystals. This creates electron-hole pairs (e^-/h^+), and the charged particles flow to their respective electrodes as in a DSSC. The maximum NREL certified efficiency of QDSCs is 11.3 percent. As of this writing, there are no commercial products based on QDSC technology. However, Solterra Renewable Technologies in San Marcos, Texas, is working on a prototype QDSC. It hopes to demonstrate a multi-cell module by 2018. It is also working to improve its manufacturing process to be able to produce QDSC film in high volumes.

Organic photovoltaic modules are quite different from other photovoltaic technologies. In an **organic photovoltaic device**, a combination of light-sensitive polymers mixed together absorb light, setting their electricity generating abilities in motion (see Figure 5.7).

When the sun shines on an organic solar cell, photons pass through a transparent protective coating and a transparent conducting electrode. The photons stimulate electron-hole pairs (e^-/h^+) in the photoactive

FIGURE 5.7 ORGANIC SOLAR CELL ARCHITECTURE

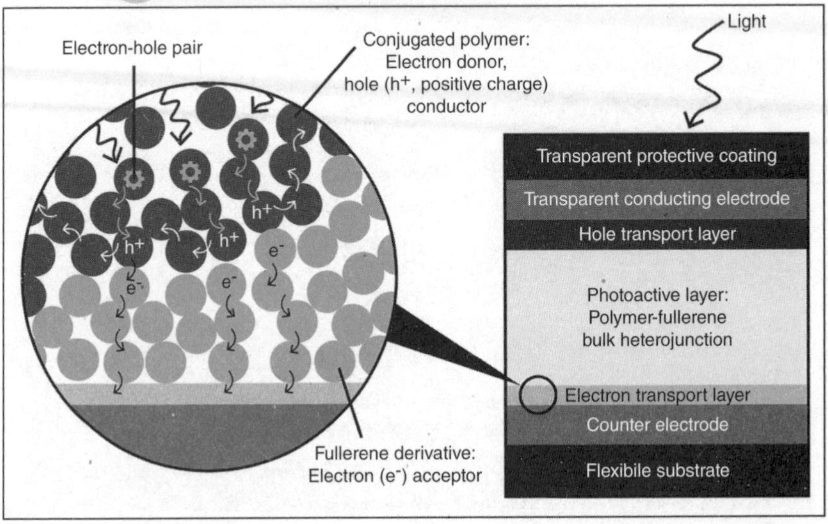

layer (see enlarged area in Figure 5.7). Once the pairs reach the interface between the conductive polymer (dark dots) and a fullerene (light dots) the pair splits. Electrons migrate down to the counter electrode while holes migrate up through the hole transport layer to the upper conducting electrode, generating an electrical current.

As of today, the NREL certified maximum efficiency for an organic photovoltaic device is 11.5 percent. Organic photovoltaic modules are also thin, flexible, and lightweight. Companies have placed them on building exteriors and integrated them into fabrics for use on tents and even backpacks. One of the world's leading producers of organic photovoltaic modules is Heliatek. Based in Dresden, Germany, Heliatek holds the world efficiency record for an organic photovoltaic device of 13.2 percent.[26] Currently, the company is ramping up production. It expects to eventually manufacture solar films in high volume.

Gallium arsenide (GaAs) solar cells have a history dating back to the early 1970s. That's when GaAs solar cells were first developed. GaAs has a number of advantages that are unique to this technology. It has a strong resistance to both UV radiation and moisture, making cells and panels extremely durable. The cell design allows for high output power density and very efficient photon absorption. So, it's not surprising that GaAs solar cells (built by Alta Devices) hold both the single and dual junction conversion efficiency records at 28.8 percent and 31.6 percent, respectively. It also performs well in low temperatures and low light. This allows more solar energy to be captured on the front and back ends of the solar day.

Instead of a silicon wafer, a GaAs solar cell is built on a GaAs wafer. In the cell design pictured in Figure 5.8, some photons bounce off the back of the solar cell. This allows the creation of more electron-hole pairs (e^-/h^+) in the photoactive layer. This is why GaAs solar cells have achieved much higher conversion efficiencies.

The final solar cell technology I want to review may indeed be the face of the future when it comes to solar cell design. I'm talking about the perovskite solar cell. Most emerging solar cell technologies have taken years for manufacturers to increase their conversion efficiencies. But perovskite solar cell conversion efficiencies have skyrocketed in just a few years' time to over 27.3 percent.[27] It's all because perovskite materials have a special type of crystalline structure. What are perovskite crystals? The one used most for solar applications has the chemical compound $(CH_3NH_3)PbI_3$. Interestingly, scientists don't know why or how the positive and negative charges generated by photoexcitation in perovskite crystals reach their respective destination electrodes as efficiently as they do. This is why many researchers have dropped research activities on other solar technologies in favor of studying perovskite solar cells.

FIGURE   5.8   GALLIUM ARSENIDE SOLAR CELL ARCHITECTURE

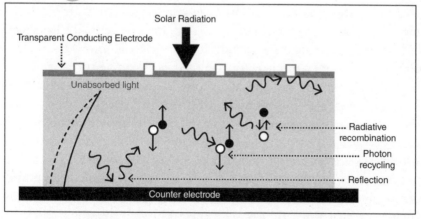

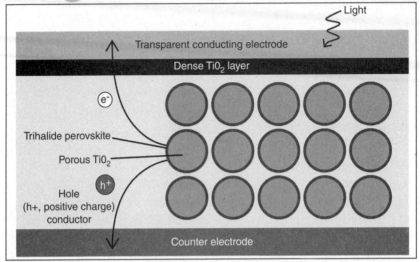

The structure of a perovskite solar cell is deceptively simple (see Figure 5.9).

In operation, photons pass through the transparent conducting electrode and a dense layer of titanium dioxide (TiO_2) and land on the photosensitive perovskite material. That creates electron-hole pairs (e^-/h^+). How and why that happens is the mysterious part of the process. In the end, electrons migrate through the dense TiO_2 layer to the upper conducting electrode and holes migrate to the bottom counter electrode. This generates an electrical current. Presently, the NREL-certified conversion efficiency for a perovskite solar cell is 22.1 percent.

There are no perovskite cells in commercial production now, although I would expect to see commercialization of this technology in the next several years. Perovskite crystals are translucent and convert solar radiation into electricity at a different wavelength than silicon solar cells. For this reason, perovskite solar cell technology could potentially be layered on top of today's high efficiency silicon solar cells. This would drastically increase the overall efficiency of the hybrid solar cell.

As you can see, there are plenty of emerging solar technologies that are being researched by academia and existing solar module manufacturers. It tells me that the future of solar is bright indeed.

SOLAR ENERGY: DISRUPTING HOW WE GENERATE ELECTRICITY

While it's still relatively in its "early days," solar energy is already well on its way to achieving disruptor status in the electrical generation sector. Solar was the largest source of new generating capacity additions (36 percent) during 2016.[28] In 20 years' time, Elon Musk predicts we'll be getting 50 percent of our electricity from solar. Known futurist Ray Kurzweil believes we'll be getting 100 percent of our energy from solar by then. Even if both are off by 50 percent, that means solar will provide somewhere between 25 and 50 percent of our energy needs. That compares to about 1.3 percent from solar as of October 2018.[29] So, you might think that Musk and Kurzweil are off their collective rockers. But consider this: Over the past decade, solar energy has achieved a **compound annual growth rate (CAGR)** of more than 60 percent.[30]

But let's take a very pessimistic view and assume solar energy only grows at a CAGR of 30 percent over the next 20 years. That means it will double seven times, which equals a 128-fold increase. So, solar's current 0.9 percent share of energy production will grow to 115.2 percent, or more than enough to meet all of America's energy needs. So you see, solar's future looks extremely bright. Its costs continue to drop (67 percent since 2011 and 29 percent in 2016 alone), and its adoption continues to increase. Adoption by Fortune 500 companies (like Apple, Target, and Walmart) is happening at breakneck speeds. The largest 25 corporate solar users in the United States have installed more than 1.1 GW of capacity. They've done it at more than 2,000 different locations around the United States.[31]

But solar is about to undergo an even more radical change than it has already. Solar energy systems are being paired with a capability that makes solar even more attractive. I'm talking about energy storage. Adding energy storage to a solar energy system allows the energy that's captured during the solar day to be time-shifted into the solar night. Up until now, cheap battery storage didn't exist. But the drop in the cost of battery storage has been just as dramatic as the rise in solar energy adoption. Cheap battery storage is driving the electric vehicle (EV) boom as well as the solar-plus-storage market. Both EVs and solar plus storage are in their infancy. I examine EVs from the early days to the present in Section 2. You'll see how they will ultimately play a big part in meeting America's energy storage needs.

By the time you get to the end of this book, you'll see how solar, EVs, and energy storage are going to totally disrupt how we generate, use, and store energy. Billions of people will have access to inexpensive, carbon-free energy. Energy production will, in effect, undergo democratization. Everyone will be able to participate in generating their own energy.

NOTES

1. www.greentechmedia.com/articles/read/us-solar-market-grows-95-in-2016-smashes-records
2. www.seia.org/news/us-solar-market-grows-95-2016-smashes-records
3. Ibid.
4. https://www.nytimes.com/2018/06/01/climate/companies-renewable-energy.html
5. https://www.seia.org/solar-industry-research-data
6. www.lazard.com/media/438038/levelized-cost-of-energy-v100.pdf
7. https://www.seia.org/solar-industry-research-data
8. https://www.seia.org/solar-industry-research-data
9. www.lazard.com/media/438038/levelized-cost-of-energy-v100.pdf
10. https://www.seia.org/solar-industry-research-data
11. https://www.seia.org/solar-industry-research-data
12. medium.com/@Scott_Wiener/press-release-board-of-supervisors-unanimously-passes-supervisor-wiener-s-legislation-to-require-693deb9c2369
13. www.colorado.gov/pacific/energyoffice/community-solar
14. http://investors.xcelenergy.com/Presentations
15. www.nyserda.ny.gov/All-Programs/Programs/NY-Sun/Communities/Shared-Solar
16. pv-magazine-usa.com/2017/02/17/maryland-greenlights-192-1-mw-in-community-solar-projects/
17. www.colorado.gov/pacific/energyoffice/community-solar
18. https://www.ft.com/content/a42e23be-8900-11e8-affd-da9960227309
19. https://e360.yale.edu/digest/the-world-added-nearly-30-percent-more-solar-energy-capacity-in-2017
20. https://e360.yale.edu/digest/the-world-added-nearly-30-percent-more-solar-energy-capacity-in-2017
21. www.pv-magazine.com/2016/02/09/ihs-global-solar-pv-pipeline-surpasses-200-gw_100023117/
22. https://www.greentechmedia.com/articles/read/google-officially-hits-100-renewable-energy-target#gs.CUL=Avo
23. http://there100.org/news/14282487/
24. www.sciencedaily.com/releases/2017/04/170424093942.htm

25. www.pv-tech.org/news/zsw-takes-cigs-thin-film-cell-to-22-conversion-efficiency

26. https://www.heliatek.com/en/solar-films/technology

27. https://www.greentechmedia.com/articles/read/a-new-efficiency-world-record-for-a-perovskite-solar-cell-can-oxford-pv-hit#gs.VqBqMnA

28. www.seia.org/research-resources/solar-industry-data

29. https://www.eia.gov/tools/faqs/faq.php?id=427&t=3

30. www.seia.org/research-resources/solar-industry-data

31. www.seia.org/research-resources/solar-industry-data

Electric Vehicles: Disrupting Transportation

CHAPTER SIX

The History of Electric Vehicles

L ong before I started working as a writer and financial analyst, I was
an electrical engineer. I spent nearly 25 years in the semiconductor industry. Even now, I love puttering around with new technologies
and gizmos. Back in December 2011, we installed a 10-kilowatt (kW)
ground-mounted solar array at our farm in Pennsylvania.

So getting an electric vehicle (EV) wasn't much of a stretch. It was
the waiting game we had to play. When Nissan Motors announced it
was developing an electric vehicle in 2009, I was all ears. After some
research, I determined I had to have one. And why not? Nissan was
having a bit of a problem moving its LEAFs out of inventory. So they
offered a two-year lease that was $50 less a month than my wife was
spending on gasoline to drive her Acura MDX back and forth to work.
She was initially concerned with the 80 to 90 mile range, but it's only
15 miles from our house to the school where she teaches.

So we went to the Nissan dealer and ordered a LEAF. We took delivery of it in June 2013. When our lease was up, we called Nissan and
asked if we could extend it for another year at the same price. They were
happy to agree. For the three years we had the car, all we did was replace
the wiper blades. That's it. No oil changes, brake jobs, muffler replacements, or any of the other dozens of things you have to worry about

in a car with an **internal combustion engine** (ICE). And charging the LEAF's battery cost us between \$20 and \$30 per month. That's about half of what it cost to fill the MDX's tank. All my wife did was plug the car into its charging port on the garage wall. The car was programmed to do its charging between 11 p.m. and 5 a.m. We have a dual-rate meter and our electricity is cheaper at night. Fifteen minutes before my wife would leave for work, the car's temperature control system would turn on. It would heat or cool the car as necessary to get the interior temperature to 75°F. Doing this while still connected to the charging system avoided using any battery power.

Fast-forward to June 2016. We returned the LEAF to Nissan and took delivery of a brand new Tesla Model X SUV. Rather than lease the Model X, we decided to purchase the car. As of this writing, the car has performed flawlessly. It was back to the Tesla Service Center once to replace a faulty door sensor. The difference between the LEAF and the Model X is like the difference between a Cessna two-seat plane and an F-18 fighter jet. I could go on and on about the Tesla (and in a later chapter, I will).

But here's the point. It's not just my family hopping on the EV bandwagon. According to *Bloomberg*, EVs will account for 35 percent of all new vehicle sales by 2040.[1] I think that could happen a decade earlier, by 2030. Remember, Fessler's Second Law of Technology states: "When it comes to technology, changes happen much faster than anyone expects." EVs are clearly at a tipping point. They are poised to send ICE vehicles the way of the horse and buggy. Speaking of horse and buggies, let's take a look at the long, colorful history of the EV.

THE HISTORY OF SELF-PROPELLED VEHICLES

Throughout history, humans have been fascinated with speed. Before vehicles, a galloping horse was top-speed when it came to fast transportation. Historians believe that somewhere around the third millennium BCE, ancient Egyptian sailors harnessed the power of wind to sail their papyrus ships upstream against the Nile's current. Several millennia later, the Chinese followed the Egyptians with wind-propelled chariots in the sixth century AD.

Fast-forward 1,000 years and we have a vehicle of similar design, constructed by Flemish mathematician Simon Stevin (1548–1620)[2]

FIGURE 6.1   WIND CHARIOT OR LAND YACHT (ZEILWAGEN)

Data source: upload.wikimedia.org/wikipedia/commons/9/96/Simon_Stevins_zeilwagen_voor_
Prins_Maurits_1649.jpg.

(see Figure 6.1). Stevin's wind chariot or land yacht (Zeilwagen) was built for the amusement of his friend Prince Maurice of Orange, in what is now the Netherlands. Maurice used it for racing along the sandy beaches between the villages of Petten and Scheveningen. Propelled only by the wind, Stevin's Zeilwagen reportedly could outrun horses.

Even before Stevin constructed his land yacht, other Europeans were designing self-propelled vehicles. The Italians have a long history of car designs. An Italian physician, inventor, and engineer, Guido von Vigevano (1280–1349), designed windmill-powered battle cars, battle wagons, and siege engines[3] such as the one seen in Figure 6.2.

The battle car used wind power that relayed wind force through gears to the vehicle's wheels. It was designed for King Phillip VI of France. He was planning a crusade using the vehicle, but it never happened. Some historians view this as the first self-propelled vehicle, or certainly the predecessor of it.

FIGURE 6.2   GUIDO VON VIGEVANO BATTLE CAR

Source: Courtesy of Ulrich Alertz.

Fast-forward now to the 1440s, and we find the development of wound springs to power portable clocks. In 1478, Leonardo da Vinci (1452–1519) scaled up wound springs and used them in the design of a self-moving car or automobile for use on stages[4] (see Figure 6.3). It is the first self-propelled, stored energy vehicle.

Historians believe that Leonardo never constructed the vehicle during his lifetime. Perhaps others considered it too dangerous to operate, or the materials just weren't readily available to build it. Since then, engineers (your author among them) have constructed a number of working models. However, like many of Leonardo's inventions, his automobile was far ahead of its time and went nowhere else.

FIGURE 6.3   LEONARDO DA VINCI'S SPRING-POWERED STAGE CAR

Yet another Italian engineer, Giovanni Branca (1571–1645), designed a steam turbine in 1624.[5] That design was incorporated into a toy car designed by Ferdinand Verbiest (1623–1688), a Flemish Jesuit Missionary. Verbiest's design dates from 1672 while he was stationed in China.[6] This was well before Thomas Newcomen (1664–1729) and James Watt (1736–1819) designed and built steam engines in 1712 and 1774, respectively.[7]

Not surprisingly, technological advancements in steam engines soon provided versions that could generate sufficient mechanical power. Engineers being who they are, steam-powered vehicles soon followed. A French army engineer officer, Nicholas-Joseph Cugnot (1725–1804), built a 7.25-meter long tricycle.[8] This was used as a cannon transporter. The braking system was under-designed and the vehicle had stability issues. Higher performance was obtained by British engineer Richard Trevithick (1771–1833) in 1784.[9] Trevithick's design used a high-pressure boiler that took advantage of recent developments in steam and steel technologies.

The first real internal combustion engine (ICE) was designed by Leonardo da Vinci. But it was the French-Swiss inventor François Isaac de Rivaz (1752–1828) who actually built one in 1807.[10] The engine ran on a mixture of hydrogen and oxygen. In 1808, de Rivaz used it to power what would be the first ICE automobile. However, commercial success of de Rivaz's engine was not in the cards. The engine and his automobile remained one-of-a-kind inventions for decades.

How Ørsted's Big Discovery Changed the World

In 1820, an experiment undertaken by Danish chemist and physicist Hans Christian Ørsted (1777–1851) changed the world. It was the discovery of electromagnetism.[11] Ørsted's experiment consisted of the simple deflection of a compass needle in the presence of an electrical current. It was the first time anyone observed the interaction of a magnetic and electrical field. As with steam, soon after Ørsted's discovery inventors and engineers of the time attempted to build electrically powered cars. The first rotating device powered by electricity was designed in 1822 by the English physicist and mathematician Peter Barlow (1776–1862).[12] Known as Barlow's wheel, it was a crudely built, spiked disc that rotated in the presence of a magnetic field and an electrical current. His design was not suitable for translating motion of the disc into useful mechanical action. Stronger electrodynamic forces would be needed in order to build the first EV.

Enter German physicist Johann S. C. Schweigger (1779–1857). In 1820, Schweigger developed the first electric coil. The effect of a coil is to intensify or multiply electromagnetic forces. Five years later, English inventor and physicist William Sturgeon (1783–1850) wound the coil wire around an iron core, creating the first electromagnet. It was able to lift nine pounds. In 1828, Joseph Henry (1797–1878), an American scientist, was able to improve upon Sturgeon's coil by insulating the coil wires with silk and winding them tightly around the iron core. Henry's electromagnets could lift iron and steel bodies weighing up to one ton. Engineers and inventors finally had electromotive forces strong enough to make EVs.

The heart of any EV is its electric motor. It's what replaces the ICE in a conventional car. It also eliminates the need for a transmission, drive shaft, differential, and exhaust system components. As a result, modern EVs have a perfectly flat floor. The unsung designer of the first electric motor was a Slovak-Hungarian priest, Ányos Jedlik (1800–1895). In 1827, Jedlik began experiments with

F I G U R E   **6.4**   THE WORLD'S FIRST ELECTRIC MOTOR: ÁNYOS JEDLIK'S
"LIGHTNING-MAGNETIC SELF-ROTOR"

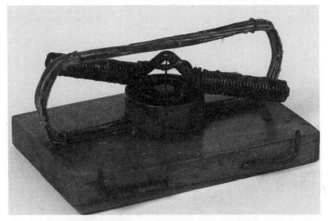

Source: en.wikipedia.org/wiki/%C3%81nyos_Jedlik#/media/File:Jedlik_motor.jpg.

rudimentary motors. He called them *lightning-magnetic self-rotors.*
In 1828, he constructed and demonstrated the very first electric motor
(see Figure 6.4).

This direct current (DC) motor had a stator coil, a rotor, and com-
mutator. The wire leads sticking out of the wood connect to the power
source. Just one year later, Jedlik redesigned his motor to power a small
toy electric car (see Figure 6.5).

In 1835, Professor Sibrandus Stratingh (1785–1841) of the University of Groningen in the Netherlands built a different version of a
small-scale electric car[13] (see Figure 6.6).

Finally, Robert Anderson of Scotland constructed a very crude electric carriage between 1832 and 1839.[14]

During the same period, inventors were experimenting with EVs
on rails. The first toy electric locomotive was built by an American
blacksmith and inventor. In 1831, Thomas Davenport (1802–1851)
used a primitive electric motor he designed himself to power the toy.[15]
A Scottish inventor and entrepreneur, Robert Davidson (1804–1894),
started his own experiments with electric motors in 1827. In 1842,
Davidson took the wraps off the first, life-size electric locomotive, called
the Galvani.[16] The Edinburgh to Glasgow rail line tested it the same
year. It reached a speed of four miles per hour with no passengers or

FIGURE 6.5   JEDLIK'S ELECTRIC TOY CAR

Source: http://www.electricvehiclesnews.com/History/historyearlyII.htm.

freight on board. Like all other EVs of the time, the Galvani used disposable batteries. These batteries could only be used once before throwing them away.

Americans were experimenting during this period as well. Charles Grafton Page (1812–1868) made an electrically powered locomotive in 1851.[17] Inventors soon realized that making the rails themselves conductive would allow the batteries to be housed in a stationary location. This technique was patented in 1840 in Great Britain and in 1847 in the United States.

Problems and Limitations

The electric vehicles I described above had several problems. The first was their motors. They weren't efficient or powerful enough to put in locomotives or cars for use in practical applications. Besides having motors with very primitive parts, the batteries of the time were one of three different electrochemical cell designs. The first was a depolarized cell developed in 1829 by Antoine-César Becquerel (1788–1878).[18] The second was a zinc-platinum cell developed a year later by the Welsh

FIGURE **6.6**   STRATINGH'S SMALL-SCALE ELECTRIC CAR

Source: Courtesy of University Museum Groningen. Reproduced with permission.

chemist William R. Grove (1811–1896).[19] In 1836, an English chemist and physicist, John Daniell (1790–1845), developed an improved double electrolyte depolarized cell.[20] In 1841 a German chemist, Robert W. E. Bunsen (1811–1899), developed a cell in which he replaced the platinum electrode with one made of carbon.[21]

The problem with these cell designs was once their charge was exhausted, they had to be disposed of. This made for expensive energy sources. Calculations of the day showed the consumption of zinc batteries was 40 times more expensive (and a lot less convenient) than burning coal in steam engines. Remember, at this time in history steam railways were expanding like wildfire.

As a result of battery and electric motor power limitations, those early EVs never achieved commercial success. But they did run, and they were developed prior to ICE vehicles that made a dubious appearance in 1826. That's when the American inventor Samuel Morey (1762–1843) introduced the first ICE-powered car.[22] They wouldn't see any further significant advances until 1863, with new motors designed by the Belgian engineer Étienne Lenoir (1822–1900).[23]

THE NINETEENTH-CENTURY EV DISRUPTION

In the second half of the nineteenth century, a number of achievements took place in Europe in both battery technology and dynamos (electromechanical generators). A number of additional technological advancements contributed to the development of a viable dynamo. One of the most notable was the creation of a solid iron rotor, developed in 1856 by Werner Siemens (1816–1892). This allowed for an increased excitation field that vastly increased the power produced.[24] There were five or six other developments during the next decade. All of them, including Siemens's iron rotor, were merged together in 1869 by a Belgian electrician, Zénobe Gramme (1826–1901).[25] The resulting generators were capable of producing virtually unlimited electrical power when driven by steam engines.

In parallel with the development of steam-powered generators, the French physicist Gaston Planté (1834–1889) developed the first rechargeable lead-acid battery in 1859.[26] In 1881, the French chemist Camille Alphonse Faure (1840–1898) developed an improved version suitable for commercial use.[27] Direct current (DC) motors were under development at the same time as generators. In 1873, Gramme demonstrated a reversible DC motor. Finally, all the pieces were in place to produce a practical, commercial EV.

In 1873, 31 years after Davidson constructed his electric locomotive, he built what is generally considered to be the first working EV. The problem was his design still used disposable iron/zinc batteries, making it unsuitable for large-scale production. The next attempt at an EV was in 1882, in the form of a light electric-powered tricycle. William E. Ayrton (1847–1908) and John Perry's (1850–1920) design used a 0.5 horsepower motor and 10 lead-acid cells designed by Planté.[28] While it was operational, the excessive weight of the batteries limited its speed and made it commercially unviable. Two years later in 1884, a prominent British inventor, electrical engineer, and industrialist by the

Source: https://commons.wikimedia.org/wiki/File:Thomas_Parker_Electric_car.jpg.

name of Thomas Parker (1843–1915) built the first successful EV[29] (see Figure 6.7).

Parker's company, Elwell-Parker Limited, not only manufactured his EV, it also produced the rechargeable batteries. Parker's interest in electricity wasn't just limited to EVs. In 1890, Elwell-Parker Limited electrified the London Underground. It also installed overhead tramways on the line between Liverpool and Birmingham. In 1896, his company produced an electric bus.

After Parker's EV made its debut, a number of other vehicles followed in quick succession. In 1886, the Ward Electric Car Company, started by Radcliffe Ward (1859–?) developed an EV powered by 28 cells.[30] It had a reasonable operating speed of 13 km/h. Ward's company went on to produce an electric bus and a van for the London Postal Service.

Just two years later, another British engineer, Magnus Volk (1851–1937) manufactured an electric tricycle, called Volk's Electrically Propelled Dog Cart[31] (see Figure 6.8).

FIGURE 6.8 **MAGNUS VOLK'S THREE-WHEELED EV**

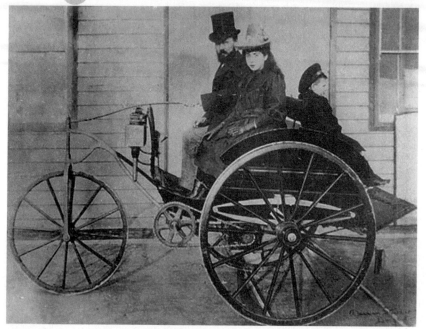

Source: https://commons.wikimedia.org/wiki/File:Magnus_Volk_on_his_electric_dog_cart,_
1897.jpg.

Six batteries under the seats powered a motor that could drive the
tricycle for six hours. Volk's Dog Cart could hit speeds of 8.7 mph on
level terrain. Volk later became famous for building the very first electric
railway. The Volks Electric Railway opened in August 1883, and today
it still runs between Brighton and Hove. It is the oldest electric railroad
in the world still in operation.

Also in 1888, Immisch and Company of London built a
four-passenger dogcart. This was belt-driven by a motor designed by
the company's founder, Moritz Immisch (1838–1903).[32] Immisch
entered into business with Volk to start the London Electric Cab
Company in 1889. The cars had a fast exchange design for their
40 cells. However, the company only lasted two years, due once again
to excessive battery weight and other technical issues.

England wasn't the only place that inventors and engineers were
experimenting with early EVs. In 1881, at the first Paris Exposition
Internationale d'Électricité, a French electrician named Gustave

Trouvé (1839–1902) presented his electric tricycle powered by a Faure battery.[33] At the same exposition, Charles Jeantaud (1843–1906) demonstrated an EV also using a Faure battery powering a Gramme motor.[34] Jeantaud went on to produce EVs from 1893 to 1906.

In 1889, the Belgian gun maker Henri Pieper (1840–1898) constructed an electric carriage.[35] Following in his father's footsteps, Henri's son Nicholas Pieper (1870–1933) built the very first hybrid-electric vehicle called the Auto-Mixte.[36] The small gasoline motor was directly connected to a dynamo that could power the car or recharge the cells.

In 1893, the French inventor Paul Pouchain developed an electric carriage capable of transporting six passengers at speeds of 10 mph for distances of nearly 44 miles.[37] Like most other EVs of the day, it was very heavy. Its 54 lead-acid cells helped the car attain a curb weight of 2,970 pounds.

In 1894, another Frenchman, Louis Antoine Kriéger (1868–1951), began to design and build EVs.[38] Over the next four years, interest in EVs continued to grow in France. So Kriéger formed the Kriéger Company of Electric Vehicles. The company produced three models: the Brougham, the Electrolette, and the Landaulet pictured in Figure 6.9.

Kriéger's company produced 43 EVs in 1901 and 65 the following year. Not exactly mind-blowing volumes, but remember these vehicles were primarily being purchased by upper-class citizenry of means. One thing that's standard on today's EVs was a Kriéger invention: **regenerative braking.** That's when the car's electric motor is turned into a generator that recovers energy from the slowing down of the vehicle. This energy is transferred back into the battery cells.

Not surprisingly, once a number of different manufacturers started making EVs, companies agreed to race their vehicles to promote new models and features. This was particularly popular among French manufacturers. The first official land speed record was set by the French aristocrat Count Gaston de Chasseloup-Laubat (1867–1903).[39] His blistering 39.23 mph record was on December 18, 1898, in an EV built by Jeantaud Duc. Not to be outdone, Gaston's rival, the Belgian driver Camille Jenatzy (1868–1913), broke Gaston's record just four months later.[40] On April 29, 1899, Jenatzy drove a missile-shaped EV named Jamais Contente (Never Satisfied). His top speed was 65.79 mph. At the time, this was faster than even the

FIGURE **6.9** **1905 KRIÉGER ELECTRIC LANDAULET**

Source: Library of Congress, Harris & Ewing Photographs (rights and restrictions information: www.loc.gov/rr/print/res/140_harr.html); picture source: cdn.loc.gov/master/pnp/hec/16500/16598u.tif.

fastest **steam locomotive.** The French elite's EV purchases soon made France the world's largest automobile maker. It would take until 1904 before the United States would surpass France.

The leading German electric company, Siemens & Halske, initially focused on electric public transportation. It presented the first electric, six-passenger tramway in 1879 at the Berlin Industrial Exhibition. It had DC motors designed in 1872 that received power from the rails. The company built the Gross-Lichterfelde Tramway, the first commercial application of its design in southwestern Berlin in 1881.[41]

As for late nineteenth-century automobiles, German engineers focused on ICE-powered versions. The first ICE prototype car was constructed by Siegfried Marcus (1831–1898) in 1870.[42] Fifteen years later, Karl Friedrich Benz (1844–1929) built a car that was designed to use an ICE motor from the start.[43] Benz's first effort was a three-wheel tricycle. A year later, Gottlieb Daimler (1834–1900) designed an ICE-powered bike. He then followed that with a four-wheel automobile in 1886.[44]

It wasn't until June 1898 that an Austrian engineer by the name of Ferdinand Porsche (1875–1951) built the first German EV.[45] His car was code-named P1. Like many early EVs, it was a glorified carriage that developed three horsepower. It had 12 different speed ranges, a cruising speed of 15 mph and a maximum speed of 21 mph. Its overall range was up to 49 miles on a single charge. The P1 participated in a 24-mile, all-electric race in Berlin in September 1899. Ferdinand, with three passengers aboard the P1, won by a gap of 18 minutes. Ferdinand's second EV was called the Lohner-Porsche, and it turned heads when it was exhibited at the 1900 Paris World Exhibition. The car had front wheel hub motors, an innovation designed by Porsche. Porsche went on to design a gasoline/electric hybrid EV in 1900. The Semper Vivus combined his hub motors with two gasoline combustion engines.

US EVs appeared later than their European counterparts. The first American to develop an EV was Andrew L. Riker (1868–1930).[46] In 1884, at the ripe old age of 16, he made an electric bike by adding a battery and electric motor to a bicycle. He formed the Riker Electric Motor Company in 1888 and a year later, he started the Riker Motor Vehicle Company in Elizabeth, New Jersey, to build electric cars.

The Electric Vehicle Company was founded on September 27, 1897, by Isaac Rice (1850–1915).[47] Rice formed it as a holding company of early battery-powered EV manufacturers. Rice's first acquisition was in May 1897 when he acquired the Electric Carriage and Wagon Company in New York. Rice then acquired Riker's company in 1901.

The Electric Carriage and Wagon Company's EV was designed in 1894 by Henry G. Morris, a mechanical engineer, and Pedro G. Salom, a chemist. Both had previous experience building battery streetcars. When that business started to decline, they decided to design an EV. They patented the Electrobat on August 31, 1894.[48] The vehicle had steel wheels. These were necessary to support the weight of the 1,600-pound lead-acid battery. They started production of the Electrobat in 1895. A year later, the two inventors founded the Morris and Salom Electric Carriage and Wagon Company.

Later versions of the Electrobat had **pneumatic** tires and lighter 900-pound batteries. The Electrobat had rear wheel steering and two 1.5 horsepower motors. The Electrobat could travel up to 25 miles on a single charge at an average speed of 20 mph. In 1897, Morris and Salom had a fleet of 13 Electrobats in use in Manhattan as taxicabs. It was the first fleet of taxis in the United States. Once Rice acquired the company, he built an additional 87 Electrobats to serve the Manhattan public. The cabs were a sensation. When the Electrobat's battery charge started to run low, the driver could pull into any one of 10 service stations located around Manhattan. A hydraulic lift removed the spent battery assembly and quickly replaced it with a fresh one. Cabs were back out on the street in a few minutes.

Another early EV, able to seat four, was developed in 1888 by William Morrison (1850–1927).[49] Morrison developed the car in secret in Des Moines, Iowa. It amazed thousands at its first appearance during the Seni Om Sed Parade in fall 1888. The car had a 4-horsepower motor, used front wheel drive, and had steel-rimmed wagon-wheel-like tires. It had a top speed of 20 mph. Morrison then went on to develop a six-passenger EV (see Figure 6.10).

This EV used 24 battery cells that were under the front seat. The batteries were designed and produced by Morrison and each cell

FIGURE 6.10   1890 MORRISON ELECTRIC CARRIAGE

Source: Iowa Department of Cultural Affairs, Special Collections Department.

weighed 32 pounds. Connected together, they produced 112 amperes of current at 58 volts. They were rechargeable, but took 10 hours to recharge. The US Patent Office issued Morrison's company more than 20 patents associated with electric storage batteries. This car had a 100-mile range, not bad for its time. Morrison patented his EV in 1891. He relocated to Chicago where he sold his company to the American Battery Company. The EV made an appearance at the 1893 World's Columbian Exposition in Chicago to much acclaim.

The 1880s saw the spread of Thomas Edison's electricity networks. This early electrical infrastructure was vital to EV owners who had to be able to recharge their battery cells. The Exposition in Chicago marked the success of the EV and of electricity in the United States. The next two decades saw the early EV market start to take off. One of the leading bicycle manufacturers, the Pope Manufacturing Company, was founded by Albert Augustus Pope (1843–1909) in 1876 and developed and marketed an EV in 1896.[50] By 1899, Pope had produced more than 500 EVs. That year the Electric Vehicle division was spun-off into an independent company called the Columbia Automobile Company, which by the end of 1899 was also acquired by the aforementioned Electric Vehicle Company. By this time, the EV market was heating up. Many EV companies formed in order to participate in the market. These included: Waverly; Rauch & Lang; Bailey; Woods; Chapman; Columbia; Detroit; Anderson; and Studebaker.

EVs eventually caught the interest of Thomas Edison (1847–1931). In 1899, he started using EVs to test new storage battery designs.[51] Between 1900 and 1910, Edison developed and perfected the nickel-iron alkaline storage battery. Edison's battery was far more rugged than the lead-acid batteries of the day. Another big advantage of Edison's batteries was their ability to handle more charge/discharge cycles than lead-acid versions. What's more, the repeated cycling of the battery didn't degrade its performance. Edison claimed his batteries would last 100 years, and recent testing of some of his original batteries have validated his claims.[52] He formed the Edison Storage Battery Company in New Jersey on May 27, 1901. It produced batteries for EVs, mining lamps, submarines, and other uses.

Edison was no stranger to EVs, and owned some of the top-of-the-line models in production.[53] Figure 6.11 shows Edison holding up the hood of a Baker and Detroit Electric EV in order to

FIGURE **6.11**   EDISON SHOWING OFF HIS NICKEL-IRON BATTERIES

Source: https://en.wikipedia.org/wiki/File:EdisonElectricCar1913.jpg#filehistory.

show off its new Edison nickel-iron battery cells. In 1903, Edison decided to employ electric motors and his new batteries in the conversion of four large touring cars to EVs. That same year, Henry Ford (1863–1947) founded the Ford Motor Company. His sole intention was to mass-produce a gasoline-powered automobile.[54] His engineers even developed a flywheel magneto system avoiding the need for a battery.

By 1910, there were three established types of automobiles in the United States. Steam-powered cars accounted for about 40 percent of the market. They were fast and powerful, but had lengthy startup times of 25 to 45 minutes. A fire had to be lit in order to boil water to make steam. They were limited to short-range driving, as they required frequent water tank refills. In addition, they were difficult to operate, and usually had a dedicated driver. Gasoline-powered cars had reached 22 percent of the market. Initial models were noisy, difficult to operate, and notoriously unreliable.

EVs held a comfortable 38 percent of the market. Like today's EVs, they were easy to start, anyone could drive them, and they were odorless and silent. Many EV manufacturers marketed them to women. Their drawbacks were cost. They were more expensive than gasoline-powered cars, in some cases costing twice as much. In addition, they were slow, with average speeds of 20 or so mph. Finally, most had a limited range of 50 miles or less before their cells needed recharging or replacing.

By the turn of the twentieth century, streets were starting to be paved in major cities in continental Europe. Great Britain had started paving 30 years earlier, as had the United States. Most early EVs ended up in the driveways of well-to-do city dwellers. They could afford to pay the higher prices for the luxuriously appointed EVs. Even Henry Ford owned three Detroit Electric EVs for himself and his family. His wife, Clara Ford, drove a 1914 model.[55] John Davison Rockefeller was another famous EV owner. By 1912, the production of early EVs had hit its peak.

What caused their demise? Several factors. While Thomas Edison's nickel-iron cell worked well in early EVs, it was still limited in range. Gasoline-powered cars were far less expensive (one-third to one-sixth the cost of an EV) and they were manufactured on assembly lines, which greatly improved their reliability. What's more, paved highways between cities started to appear in the early 1920s. Gasoline-powered cars had the extended range to be able to make longer drives. Finally, the discovery of large reserves of crude oil in California, Texas, and Oklahoma sent gasoline prices plunging. That brought the operating cost of gasoline-powered cars well below that of EVs. While initial gasoline-powered cars had to be hand-cranked to start, electric starters found their way into the American car market in 1912. By the mid-1920s early EVs had all but disappeared from American and European roads and streets. They would remain on the sideline of American transportation for about half a century.

NOTES

1. about.bnef.com/blog/electric-vehicles-to-be-35-of-global-new-car-sales-by-2040/
2. en.wikipedia.org/wiki/Land_sailing
3. www.notechmagazine.com/2009/07/guido-vigevanos-wind-car-1335.html
4. auto.howstuffworks.com/da-vinci-car1.htm
5. en.wikipedia.org/wiki/Giovanni_Branca
6. en.wikipedia.org/wiki/Ferdinand_Verbiest#cite_note-CuriousExp-17

7. en.wikipedia.org/wiki/Thomas_Newcomen and en.wikipedia.org/wiki/James_Watt

8. en.wikipedia.org/wiki/Nicolas-Joseph_Cugnot

9. en.wikipedia.org/wiki/Richard_Trevithick

10. en.wikipedia.org/wiki/Fran%C3%A7ois_Isaac_de_Rivaz

11. en.wikipedia.org/wiki/Hans_Christian_%C3%98rsted

12. en.wikipedia.org/wiki/Peter_Barlow_(mathematician)

13. nl.wikipedia.org/wiki/Sibrandus_Stratingh

14. en.wikipedia.org/wiki/Robert_Anderson_(inventor)

15. en.wikipedia.org/wiki/Thomas_Davenport_(inventor)

16. en.wikipedia.org/wiki/Robert_Davidson_(inventor)

17. en.wikipedia.org/wiki/Charles_Grafton_Page

18. en.wikipedia.org/wiki/Antoine_C%C3%A9sar_Becquerel

19. en.wikipedia.org/wiki/William_Robert_Grove

20. en.wikipedia.org/wiki/John_Frederic_Daniell

21. en.wikipedia.org/wiki/Robert_Bunsen

22. en.wikipedia.org/wiki/Samuel_Morey

23. en.wikipedia.org/wiki/%C3%89tienne_Lenoir

24. en.wikipedia.org/wiki/Werner_von_Siemens

25. en.wikipedia.org/wiki/Z%C3%A9nobe_Gramme

26. en.wikipedia.org/wiki/Gaston_Plant%C3%A9

27. en.wikipedia.org/wiki/Camille_Alphonse_Faure

28. en.wikipedia.org/wiki/William_Edward_Ayrton and en.wikipedia.org/wiki/John_Perry_(engineer)

29. en.wikipedia.org/wiki/Thomas_Parker_(inventor)

30. www.gracesguide.co.uk/Ward_Electric_Car_Co

31. en.wikipedia.org/wiki/Magnus_Volk

32. en.wikipedia.org/wiki/Moritz_Immisch

33. en.wikipedia.org/wiki/Gustave_Trouv%C3%A9

34. en.wikipedia.org/wiki/Jeantaud

35. en.wikipedia.org/wiki/Pieper

36. www.forgottenweapons.com/biography-henri-nicolas-pieper/

37. www.autocyber.fr/article/POUCHAIN-Pouchain-1893

38. en.wikipedia.org/wiki/Krieger_Company_of_Electric_Vehicles

39. en.wikipedia.org/wiki/Gaston_de_Chasseloup-Laubat

40. en.wikipedia.org/wiki/Camille_Jenatzy

41. en.wikipedia.org/wiki/Siemens_%26_Halske

42. en.wikipedia.org/wiki/Siegfried_Marcus

43. en.wikipedia.org/wiki/Karl_Benz

44. en.wikipedia.org/wiki/Gottlieb_Daimler

45. en.wikipedia.org/wiki/Ferdinand_Porsche

46. en.wikipedia.org/wiki/Andrew_L._Riker

47. en.wikipedia.org/wiki/Isaac_Rice

48. en.wikipedia.org/wiki/Electrobat

49. ir.uiowa.edu/cgi/viewcontent.cgi?article=7666&context=annals-of-iowa
50. en.wikipedia.org/wiki/Albert_Augustus_Pope
51. en.wikipedia.org/wiki/Thomas_Edison
52. www.thetruthaboutcars.com/2015/12/ford-motor-co-invests-4-5b-evs-century-henry-ford-gave-electric-cars/
53. www.wired.com/2010/06/henry-ford-thomas-edison-ev/
54. en.wikipedia.org/wiki/Henry_Ford
55. content.time.com/time/specials/2007/article/0,28804,1669723_1669725_1669734,00.html

CHAPTER SEVEN

Henney's Kilowatt and GM's EV1: Ahead of Their Time

The next chapter in the history of EVs (electric vehicles) opens nearly half a century after the early EVs succumbed to cars with internal combustion engines (ICEs). In 1959, the Henney Kilowatt was introduced as "The New *Electric* Powered Automobile." The Kilowatt was the brainchild of American businessman C. Russell Feldmann (1898–1973). Feldmann's first company, the Winton Engine Company, eventually became the Diesel Engine Division of General Motors. Feldmann had been president of the Eureka Williams Company and the National Union Electric Company, a producer of automobile radios.

Eureka Williams started out as the Eureka Vacuum Cleaner Company in 1909. In 1945, it merged with the Williams Oil-O-Matic Company, a manufacturer of oil-based refrigerators and heaters for home use. The name of the company was then changed to Eureka Williams. The company expanded its product line to include school furniture, air conditioners, and heaters. The Henney Motor Company, located in Freeport, Illinois, purchased Eureka Williams in 1953. It subsequently became a division of the National Union Electric Corporation in 1959.

To design the body of the Kilowatt, Feldmann used the coachwork division of the Henney Motor Company, located in Canastota, New York. It turns out Henney was a long-time coach maker, having been in the business since 1868. It was affiliated with Ford Motor Company and the Packard Automobile Company, having built hearses, ambulances, and limousines on Lincoln and Packard chassis.

In addition to car radios, the National Union Electric Company was the manufacturer of **Exide batteries**. Because of this, it wanted to see American automobile manufacturing shifted toward EVs. Exide batteries were high-quality lead-acid batteries. For the drivetrain of the Kilowatt, Feldmann consulted with Victor Wouk, an electrical engineer, best known for being a hybrid-electric vehicle (HEV) pioneer.[1]

Wouk designed the speed control electronics for the Kilowatt. He recruited his friend Lee DuBridge, who was the president of Cal Tech at the time. In addition, he contracted the services of Linus Pauling (1901–1994) to investigate better performing batteries. In order to get the Kilowatt to market as quickly as possible, Henney cut a deal with Renault to use its Dauphine chassis and running gear. It bought the cars without motors, exhausts, or gas tanks.

The 1959 model used a 36-volt electrical system that used 6-volt, deep-cycle batteries. These cars could reach 40 mph and had a range of about 40 miles. The 1960 and 1961 models had a redesigned 72-volt electrical system; they used the same 6-volt batteries, but had 12 of them. The 1959 model could almost reach 60 mph and had a range of more than 60 miles on one charge. The accelerator pedal contacted relays in six different configurations, giving the car six speeds. A total of 24 of the 36-volt models were produced and 23 of the 72-volt models. Today, less than 10 of these cars still exist. Figure 7.1 shows one of the few cars in private hands.

Some sources describe the Kilowatt as "the first transistor-based electric car." However, that is not true. The speed controller has no transistors in it. In fact, it has diodes and relays that control the voltage and current sent to the motor. While the Kilowatt has also been referred to as the world's first mass-produced EV, we know that's not true. Just look back to Chapter 6 and we can find plenty of "mass-produced" EVs that were made in higher quantities than the Henney Kilowatt. Still, it is an important part in the history of EVs and deserves a mention.

F IGURE 7.1   HENNEY KILOWATT

Source: https://commons.wikimedia.org/wiki/File:Kilowatt.jpg.

GENERAL MOTORS GETS IN THE ACT

Fast-forward to 1987 and the inaugural World Solar Challenge. This biennial, solar-powered automobile race is still held in the Australian Outback. The total distance is 1,878 miles from Darwin, Northern Territory, to Adelaide, South Australia. General Motors worked with engineers at AeroVironment to build the "Sunraycer." It won the race, but more impressively it had an *average* speed of 42 mph. Excited and emboldened by the success of the Sunraycer, GM CEO Roger Smith challenged the Sunraycer design team to come up with a practical EV. Initial versions were designed by Alan Cocconi. If that name sounds familiar to you, it's because he's an EV drivetrain guru. He's worked on projects at GM and Tesla. It all started with his interest in building a 100,000-watt stereo amplifier. That project morphed into an AC drivetrain controller for an EV.

At the 1990 Los Angeles Auto Show, with much fanfare, Roger Smith introduced the GM concept EV, the Impact. He said, "This is going to represent a great step forward in commuting if you don't have to drive more than 120 miles a day." Like the Sunraycer, the Impact was designed by AeroVironment, a military subcontractor. Thanks to the work of Cocconi, the Impact had an electronic drive controller.

As a side note, Cocconi later formed his own company, still in existence today, called AC Propulsion. He'll take a current model year Scion xB and replace the internal combustion engine with his EV drivetrain. Of course you need to provide the basic Scion and pony up another $55,000 for him to convert it. But a newer version of Cocconi's original drivetrain can be found in the Tesla Roadster. Yes, the EV world is a small one.

Roger Smith was so impressed with the Impact that in April 1990 he announced that GM would turn it into a production vehicle. At the same time, California was looking for any possible means to curb vehicle-produced air pollution. California's smog problem was especially bad in the Los Angeles area, where temperature inversions are commonplace. A temperature inversion results in a stagnant air mass that stays in one spot and close to ground level. When this happens, air pollution rises to unhealthy levels. Respiratory problems and burning eyes are common problems during an inversion.

From 1991 to 1993, Jananne Sharpless was chairwoman of the California Air Resources Board (CARB). In an interview in the documentary *Who Killed the Electric Car*, she said, "California has the worst air quality in the nation and it impacts some of our largest population centers." Alan S. Lowenthal was a California state senator (2004–2013) for the 27th State Senate district, encompassing most of western Los Angeles's suburbs. He had a name for the smog covering the port area of Los Angeles and surrounding neighborhoods, the "black cloud of death." He wasn't far from the truth. California saw climbing asthma rates, cancer rates, and abnormal lung development in children. A 1989 study found that one in four 15-year-olds in Los Angeles County had severe lung lesions.[2]

CARB got wind of GM's Impact (and their intention to produce it) and saw it as the answer to California's growing air pollution problems. Said Sharpless, "The electric vehicle is the technology of greatest promise." As a result, CARB passed a huge environmental initiative, called the Zero Emissions Mandate. It required the seven major automakers at the time, and GM was the largest, to make 2 percent of their California cars zero emission vehicles (ZEVs) by 1998, 5 percent by 2001, and 10 percent by 2003. This was not an option if the automakers wanted to continue to market cars with internal combustion engines in California. The mandate had nothing to do with wanting EVs. All California wanted to do was reduce air pollution from vehicles any way it could. The vehicle manufacturers only had two choices, they could comply with California's mandate or they could fight it. When all the dust settled, it became apparent that they would eventually do both.

In the beginning, it looked like they were all going to comply. All the members of the American Automobile Manufacturers Association plus Honda, Toyota, and Nissan, developed a zero-emissions prototype vehicle. General Motors had a head start. In 1994, GM started a program called "PrEView" under which it would lend 50 hand-built Impact EVs to willing drivers for one- to two-week intervals. The goal was to have the cars rotate through 1,000 households across the country. The only catch was drivers had to write about their experience with the car. They also had to have a place where the local utility could install the battery charging system. The company expected less than a hundred volunteers in the Los Angeles area. However, it had to shut down the phone line after it received over 10,000 calls. Even the automotive press gave the car good reviews.

So GM decided to introduce the EV1, largely based on the design of the Impact concept car (see Figure 7.2). There was a catch, though. The cars could only be leased to customers through select Saturn dealerships. Further, the lessee had to be a resident of the city of LA, or of Phoenix and Tucson, Arizona. The entire program was administered by GM's Advanced Technology Vehicles group. The same Saturn dealerships that sold the cars would service them. After the first year, GM also made cars available in San Francisco and Sacramento, California, and a limited state-wide leasing program in Georgia.

EV1 customers loved their cars. Most wanted to renew their leases. Celebrities like Tom Hanks and Mel Gibson wanted to keep their EV1s. Nevertheless, it was an extremely unprofitable venture for GM. It was only able to lease about 800 vehicles in a four-year time. Production and development costs amounted to $1 billion over the same period.

FIGURE 7.2 GM EV1

Data source: en.wikipedia.org/wiki/General_Motors_EV1#/media/File:EV1A014_(1)_cropped .jpg.

None of the other six major manufacturers was interested in spending billions to develop production lines to make ZEVs in high volumes. So in January 2002, GM, Daimler Chrysler, and several car dealerships teamed up with the George W. Bush administration's Justice Department and sued the California Air Resources Board over its ZEV mandate.

In essence, the auto industry was challenging California's long-standing right under the federal Clean Air Act to set its own standards for clean air. This included vehicle pollution standards. Now it was going to court to kill the only nationwide program requiring automakers to build ZEVs. The amendments the feds attacked were ironically ones that gave carmakers credit for building hybrid vehicles like the Toyota Prius. After all, it was California's ZEV program that drove Toyota to develop the Prius in the first place.

What were carmakers really afraid of? Having to spend billions of dollars tooling up to make and sell EVs when it appeared that customers really had little interest in purchasing them. They knew that anything that would be mandated in California would eventually be applied to the rest of the country. California has always been a leader in reducing air pollution. It had to be because of its unique climate conditions.

The National Resources Defense Council (NRDC) and a number of other environmental groups all filed friend of the court briefs siding with the state of California. They claimed the automakers' suit had no merit. CARB's ZEV mandate was not intended to regulate fuel economy but was solely intended to reduce air pollution on California's highways. Cleaner running vehicles are part of CARB's efforts to clean up California's air.

After a loosening of the ZEV requirements occurred, GM canceled the EV1 leasing program in 2002. It immediately started a massive recall of its EV1 automobiles. There was just one problem: EV1 lessees loved their cars. But because of the expense of the program (GM claimed service, parts, and liability expenses), it wanted out. So except for donating about 40 disabled EV1s to car museums and educational institutions, it recalled nearly all of them. As 2002 came to a close, GM had successfully removed all of the EV1s from America's highways. It then systematically hauled them out to its proving grounds site in the Arizona desert and unceremoniously put them through a car crusher (Figure 7.3).

EV1 owners were absolutely livid that GM was crushing all the EV1s. Many wanted to buy them and continue driving them. But GM wouldn't hear of it. It even went so far as to guard car carriers heading to the desert to keep the cars from getting hijacked.

The discontinuation of the EV1 was a controversial decision that is still discussed among former EV1 lessees and car enthusiast groups. They accused the company of self-sabotaging the EV1 to avoid having to sell spare parts at a potential loss (due to government regulations). GM claimed that the EV1 program wasn't a failure. They claimed that advances in battery technology enabling higher ranges just weren't there. It also said CARB's ultimate elimination of its zero-emissions mandate was another reason for the cancelation of the EV1 program. GM was ultimately accused of fighting CARB's mandate in order to sabotage the EV1 program. Critics claim it was all about saving money.

FIGURE 7.3   CRUSHED GM EV1s

Data source: en.wikipedia.org/wiki/General_Motors_EV1#/media/File:Ev1_crush5.jpg.

Ironically, in 2006, former GM CEO Rick Wagoner claimed that the worst decision of his career at GM was "axing the EV1 electric-car program and not putting the right resources into hybrids. It didn't affect profitability, but it did affect image."[3] As a result of GM's repossession of its EV1s, a working model is one of the most rare automobiles from the 1990s. Film director Francis Ford Coppola had an EV1 in his personal car collection, allowing it to appear on the TV show *Jay Leno's Garage* in 2016. The only other intact EV1 resides in the Smithsonian Institution.

It would be almost a decade later, in late 2010, when GM introduced the Chevrolet Volt, its first plug-in hybrid EV. It would follow up the Volt with the Chevrolet Spark EV in June 2013. The Spark was the very first all-electric EV introduced by GM since it discontinued production of the EV1 in 1999. I'll discuss these in more detail in Chapter 8.

NOTES

1. www.physics.ohio-state.edu/~kagan/phy596/Articles/HybridElectric/HybridElectricVehicles.pdf
2. Info from the movie *Who Killed the Electric Car?*, a 2006 documentary produced by Jessie Deeter.
3. *Motor Trend*, June 2006, p. 94.

CHAPTER EIGHT

The Vision of Elon Musk

He's been compared to Apple founder Steve Jobs. He's been called the Thomas Edison of the twenty-first century. He's disrupting the transportation industry, solar energy, and space travel. "He" is Elon Musk.

MUSK: THE EARLY DAYS

Elon Musk was born on June 28, 1971, in Pretoria, South Africa. His mother, originally from Canada, was a nutritionist. His father was an engineer, which was likely the reason he was so taken by computers. At the age of 12, he had already written the code for a video game he had designed called "Blastar."[1] He's the founder, CEO, and CTO (chief technology officer) of SpaceX. He is the cofounder and CEO of Tesla, Inc. And he was a cofounder and chairman of SolarCity, his solar energy company. (On November 17, 2016, SolarCity and Tesla Motors merged and became Tesla, Inc.[2]) The goal of his three current ventures is to "change the world and humanity."

SpaceX is Musk's space transportation company. Its mission is to develop reusable rockets and is dramatically lowering the cost of space launches. Tesla is moving the world toward a sustainable energy model. Its products are EVs, energy storage, and solar roofing tiles. SolarCity (which merged with Tesla in 2016) manufactures and installs commercial and residential solar panels. Its products and services are now offered through Tesla.

Musk spent his early childhood in South Africa. In 1989, at the age of 17, he immigrated to Canada. He left Canada in 1992 when he landed a scholarship to study physics and business at the University of Pennsylvania.[3] In 1995, Elon and Kimbal Musk, his brother, started a web software company called Zip2, with $28,000 borrowed from their father.[4] Zip2 developed, hosted, and maintained consumer websites, particularly those of media companies. In February 1999, Compaq purchased Zip2 for $307 million in cash and $34 million in stock options. Elon Musk's share was $22 million.[5]

Not one to waste any time, Musk started an online email payment and financial services company called X.com in March 1999. He used $10 million of his Zip2 proceeds.[6] A year later, during the dot-com boom, X.com merged with Confinity, which had developed a money transfer service by the name of PayPal. In 2001, Confinity changed the company's name to PayPal. Musk owned 11.7 percent of PayPal's shares. In October 2002, eBay acquired PayPal for $1.5 billion. Musk's share from the sale was $165 million.[7] He would go on to fund both SpaceX and Tesla with the money he earned from the PayPal sale.

TESLA: THE EARLY DAYS

As you may recall from the previous chapter, AC Propulsion's EV drivetrain was developed by Alan Cocconi. AC Propulsion built three tZERO prototypes using Cocconi's drivetrain. The fiberglass body was the Piontek Sportech kit car. The car's frame was reinforced steel space frame including double independent wishbone suspension with rack and pinion steering. The drivetrain, dubbed the AC-150, used a single-speed electric motor. The overall gear reduction ratio was 9:1. The tZERO was initially outfitted with 28 lead-acid batteries manufactured by Johnson Controls. They were connected in series, and the 336-volt string produced 150 kW of power, equivalent to about 200 horsepower. The maximum range of this prototype was 80 to 100 miles. The 2,290-pound car accelerated from 0 to 60 mph in 4.07 seconds.

In 2003, that was faster than all but the fastest gasoline-powered racecars. However, Martin Eberhard, a slight, mild-mannered, gray-bearded entrepreneur, had other ideas. The 43-year-old Eberhard was familiar with markets like cellphones and laptop computers – billion-dollar markets created virtually overnight. At the time, those companies were spending fortunes to increase the power density of lithium-ion cells. Eberhard had a eureka moment: convert the tZERO to run on lighter-weight lithium-ion cells. AC Propulsion accomplished it in six months, and by September 2003, the tZERO battery pack consisted of 6,800 lithium-ion laptop batteries, each about the size of an AA cell.

The lithium-ion powered tZERO blew the doors off its predecessor. It was 500 pounds lighter than the one with the lead-acid batteries. Its 0-to-60 time was 3.5 seconds, and it could cruise for about 300 miles on the highway. Eberhard was thrilled. He told Cocconi he would find investors who would fund the production of the tZERO. Cocconi wasn't interested, having been burned by GM on the EV1 project.

But Eberhard just knew the time was right for starting an EV car company. It turns out Eberhard and Elon Musk had a mutual friend. He was a young engineer named J. B. Straubel. Through conversation with Eberhard, Straubel was aware of the lithium-ion powered tZERO. He mentioned it to Musk one day over lunch. Musk told him he'd be very interested in seeing Cocconi's tZERO. A month later, Cocconi drove his tZERO over to SpaceX, Musk's private rocket ship company. Musk proposed to Cocconi that they electrify a high-performance sports car. Cocconi, who was interested in electrifying a Nissan economy car, said no, and recommended that Musk talk to his partner, Martin Eberhard. "He thinks the way you do," Cocconi said.[8]

Meanwhile, Eberhard and his partner, Marc Tarpenning, excited by the prospect of a high-performance EV, incorporated Tesla Motors in Delaware on July 1, 2003. They were interested in building an EV sports car based on the tZERO concept, capable of long-range trips. After driving the lithium-ion powered tZERO, Musk invited Eberhard over to his SpaceX office. Unbeknownst to Eberhard, Musk shared his passion for high-performance sports cars. At the time, the US high-performance car market was about $3 billion annually. Clearly a lithium-ion EV sports car would fit in to that market nicely.

Beginning in 2004, the two founders invited Elon Musk to participate in the company. Musk initially invested $7.5 million, but that would eventually grow to $27 million. Musk's enthusiasm was the reason that Larry Page and Sergey Brin (Google's founders) also jumped on board as passive investors. Then Musk convinced VantagePoint Venture Partners, Michael Dubilier (from Valor Equity Partners), and Draper Fisher Jurvetson to invest in Tesla's future. The company now had all the initial capital it needed. All it had to do was design a brand new EV sports car, manufacture most of the parts, assemble them, make the car work, iron out the bugs, and get it to market.

Tesla's initial plan was to produce a sports car based on AC Propulsion's tZERO concept car. However, now that Musk was involved, that plan would change considerably. The tZERO was too expensive to put into production. Plus, it would never meet National Highway and Safety Administration crash tests. Undaunted, Eberhard commissioned four automotive design teams to produce sketches of possible car designs. He put them up on a wall in his home. At a company Christmas party in December 2004, Tesla employees voted on their favorite. The winning sketch was by Barney Hatt, of Lotus Design. Hatt had based his design on the Lotus Elise. It was the world's lightest production sports car, weighing in at 1,984 pounds. The chassis would be able to be used by Tesla with few modifications. And the body was different enough that most enthusiasts would welcome it as a new design. Tesla contracted Lotus to do final assembly on the first run of the new car. Tesla was off to the races.

TESLA'S 2006 MASTER PLAN

In August 2006, Musk published "The Secret Tesla Motors Master Plan."[9] On the surface, it only had five steps:

1. Build sports car.
2. Use that money to build an affordable car.
3. Use *that* money to build an even more affordable car.
4. While doing above, also provide zero emission electric power generation options.
5. Don't tell anyone.

In Musk's view, emissions from power plants are cleaner than those from individual vehicles. So it's always been his goal to develop a wide range of EV cars and trucks, including affordable family sedans and SUVs. According to Musk, Tesla is not just an EV company. In his

August 2006 master plan he states, "The overarching purpose of Tesla Motors (and the reason I am funding the company) is to help expedite the move from a mine-and-burn hydrocarbon economy towards a solar electric economy, which I believe to be the primary, but not exclusive, sustainable solution."

As with any new technology, initial versions are expensive. Once volume production starts, individual unit costs come down (think back to the introduction of the iPhone). In his Master Plan, Musk noted, "This is no less true for electric cars." He further states, "The strategy of Tesla is to enter at the high end of the market, where customers are prepared to pay a premium, and then drive down the market as fast as possible to higher unit volume and lower prices with each successive model."[10] Initially, analysts, auto industry wonks, and the media looked at Tesla and gave it two chances for success: slim and none. Well, Tesla is in the midst of pulling off one of the greatest feats since Steve Jobs came back to run Apple. Let's review Musk's plan so far.

THE SPORTS CAR

On July 19, 2006, Elon Musk introduced the Tesla Roadster, the very first EV produced by Tesla Motors (now called Tesla, Inc.). It was an invitation-only event held in a hangar at the Santa Monica Airport. In November 2006, Tesla took the Roadster to the San Francisco International Auto Show. The car was also featured in other auto shows including in Detroit, Los Angeles, and internationally in Frankfurt. The Roadster had a range of more than 200 miles. From 2008 through 2012, Tesla sold roughly 2,450 Roadsters to sports car enthusiasts in more than 30 countries (see Figure 8.1). The company produced a right-hand drive model for European export.

The Roadster was a rear-wheel drive, rear mid-motor, two-seat, two-door, all-electric sports car. The very first car off the production line went to its architect and company founder, Elon Musk. During the 2009 model year, Tesla produced 500 Roadsters.

In mid-July 2009, the company began producing the 2010 model year of the Roadster. Known as the Roadster Sport, it contained the second version of the company's proprietary and patented powertrain. The Roadster Sport had a 0 to 60 mph time of 3.7 seconds, two-tenths of a second faster than the standard Roadster. The 2010 Roadster came with

FIGURE **8.1**   TESLA ROADSTER

Source: Tesla, Inc. Reproduced with permission.

an upgraded interior including exposed carbon-fiber, premium leather seats, and Tesla's rectangular video display screen. The suspension was adjustable and the car incorporated a number of design changes that dramatically reduced vibration, noise, and rattles.

A year later, in July 2010, Tesla announced the Roadster 2.5, containing more new features. Tesla swapped the seats for new ones that were larger, more comfortable and contained a lumbar support feature. The front fenders were dual-wall with sound-reducing material to lessen cabin noise even further. Tesla produced this model through January 2012. The company produced a total of 2,500 Roadsters (all models). Even with a base price of $109,000, the Tesla Roadster quickly sold out.

In December 2014, Tesla announced the availability of a new upgrade to all Roadsters, calling it Roadster 3.0. The biggest part of the upgrade was a new battery pack made by LG Chem. The new battery increased capacity by 50 percent to 80 kWh. In addition to a larger capacity battery, the upgrade included a kit of aerodynamic panels to reduce drag, and lower-rolling resistance tires. As part of its future product line, Tesla has plans to introduce a new-generation Roadster in 2018 or 2019.

BUILDING THE MODEL S SEDAN

At least measured by the sell-out of the Roadster, Musk's Secret Tesla Motors Master Plan was off to a roaring start. The next item in the plan was to create an "affordable" car. Tesla codenamed its next-generation sedan "Whitestar." Originally, Tesla was going to build two powertrain options. The first would be an all-electric version with a range of up to 200 miles. The second would an "extended-range vehicle" (REV). The REV version of Whitestar would travel 40 to 50 miles in all-electric mode. Then a small gasoline engine would recharge the batteries and run the vehicle at the same time. The REV was to have an overall range of 400 miles.[11] In September 2008, at the GoingGreen conference, Musk announced that Tesla would only produce all-electric EVs.[12]

In August 2008, Franz von Holzhausen, then Director of Design at Mazda, announced his resignation and accepted the position of Design Director at Tesla Motors. In an interview with *Car Design News*, he commented on his move. "It's going to be an exciting adventure. I'm looking forward to working at a new startup company that doesn't have the confines of a large OEM. Tesla is changing the paradigm. We're going to turn the world on its ear and create high demand through design. There is a new hunger in the air for automotive design and looking to where automobiles are going in the future. Tesla will capture this through good design and engineering."[13]

The Model S prototype was unveiled to the public at a press conference on March 26, 2009. At the time, *Automobile* magazine called the Model S a "cross between a Maserati and an Aston Martin." The Model S, a sedan with seating for up to seven passengers, can travel up to 300 miles on a single charge (see Figure 8.2).

Unlike other EVs, Tesla's Model S carries its battery charger around as part of the vehicle. This allows car charging from any 120V, 240V, or 480V outlet. Charging from 480V outlets takes just 45 minutes. By coordinating meal and overnight stops with charging, a trip from New York to Los Angeles would take the same amount of time as for a gasoline-powered vehicle. The vehicle's powertrain is so compact that the Model S has both a front and rear trunk. The rear passenger seats fold flat. That feature, combined with a hatchback rear window, allows the Model S to stow mountain bikes, surfboards, or even a 50-inch television. The Model S has more trunk space than most SUVs and

FIGURE 8.2   TESLA MODEL S

Source: Tesla, Inc. Reproduced with permission.

every other sedan on the market. When announced, the base price of the low-end Model S was $57,400 before any options or federal and state tax credits.[14]

By early May 2009, Tesla had already received more than 1,000 reservations for the Model S sedan. Each of these customers plunked down a $5,000 deposit to reserve their car. At this point, Tesla had only opened its reservation system to California residents and at its California showrooms. It was clear that demand for the Model S, like the Roadster, was exceeding company expectations. But Musk and Tesla decided a limited rollout in California would make sense in order to correct any defects or make any modifications before rolling out to other markets.

In addition to disrupting the conventional car market, Tesla was also disrupting the way cars were marketed and sold. There was no TV or print advertising. The company issued frequent press releases, and early adopters hung on every word for clues about what the company was doing next. Tesla has an owner referral program, but uses word of mouth advertising to attract buyers. One of the things that became readily apparent was that Tesla didn't need dealerships, so it never contacted any. Instead, prospective customers reserved their cars online, and can choose their options and process their orders without ever talking to a salesperson unless they wanted to. And why not? Who likes haggling with car salespeople and sales managers over prices and options? Tesla knew the answer.

EVs require far less maintenance than a comparably equipped ICE vehicle. There are no oil changes, exhaust system repairs, belts to replace, and other maintenance associated with ICE cars. That's where dealers make most of their profits. Instead, Tesla opened showrooms in shopping malls. Prospective owners can visit the store, sit in the car, and look at its marvelous twenty-first-century features. Tesla showroom employees are there to answer questions about the cars, not sell them, although they can take a reservation deposit. Eventually, Tesla established "delivery centers" where owners take delivery of their vehicles. This differs from the conventional dealership since all employees work for Tesla, not an independent dealership network.

This initially infuriated many dealerships and state car dealer associations. It turns out that in the United States, many states have franchise laws that prohibit vehicle sales directly by manufacturers. As a result, dealership associations and dealerships lodged numerous lawsuits against Tesla, stating they were in violation of local and state franchise laws. Tesla went to court and, generally, was successful in challenging most of these suits. Currently, Tesla has over 200 stores and galleries worldwide. More than 80 are here in the United States, located in 22 states and the District of Columbia. Even the Federal Trade Commission has recommended the allowance of direct selling by manufacturers.[15] Tesla has argued that car dealerships are just one more form of regulation. Who better than the consumer to choose how, what, and where they buy a car? It's no different than anything else they buy. So far, there are nine states that have successfully challenged Tesla, and they have done that mostly by strengthening state franchise laws. Back in 2014, Michigan amended its auto dealer franchise statute to specifically exclude Tesla from the Michigan auto market. And it was passed on the last day before the legislature adjourned. No debate. No committee process. And no input from legislators. In 2016, after numerous attempts to get Michigan legislators and state regulators to cooperate, Tesla sued Michigan for the right to sell its cars there. Tesla claimed Michigan's franchise law was unconstitutional. As of 2018, state officials have yet to respond to the lawsuit. Tesla has opened a "gallery" location in a Nordstrom's department store in Michigan.

However, Michigan residents who want a Tesla must order online and take delivery at a Tesla store in a neighboring state.[16] Interestingly, no other country has laws that protect car dealerships.

It was clear to Musk from the start (and part of The Secret Tesla Motors Master Plan) that Tesla would need more money to bring the Model S into production. After all, we're talking about an entire vehicle assembly plant, a robotic assembly line, and thousands of administrative, design, engineering, and manufacturing employees. So Tesla applied for $465 million in low-interest loans from the US Department of Energy (DOE). The loans were available through the Advanced Technology Vehicle Manufacturing (ATVM) program. The DOE created the program in 2007 and Congress funded it in September 2008. The $25 billion program was to create "green collar" jobs and reduce the amount of foreign oil imports. The DOE built the ATVM program to provide incentives to both established and new automakers to design and build more fuel-efficient vehicles. (The ATVM should not be confused with the stimulus and bailout funds that General Motors and Chrysler received in order to keep from going bankrupt during the 2008–2009 Great Recession.)

Tesla received approval for the $465 million ATVM loans in June 2009. Elon Musk commented about the loan in a press release: "Tesla will use the ATVM loan precisely the way that Congress intended – as the capital needed to build sustainable transport. We are honored that the US government selected Tesla to be among the first companies to participate in this progressive program."[17]

Tesla used $365 million to purchase and fit out the old New United Motors Manufacturing Inc. (NUMMI) plant in Fremont, California. NUMMI was a joint venture between General Motors and Toyota from 1984 through 2009. At its height, it produced 500,000 cars annually. The site has buildings that contain 5.3 million square feet of office and manufacturing space. After Tesla purchased the facility, it added skylights and high-efficiency lighting to brighten the place up. It had the floors, walls, and ceilings painted bright white. This made the space even brighter and gave the manufacturing facility a high-tech, laboratory-like look. The highly automated manufacturing line uses state-of-the-art robots to turn, lift, assemble, and weld the Model S occupant cells and bodies together. The use of robots allows for the holding of extremely high tolerances during the manufacturing process.

The remaining $100 million was used to develop a powertrain manufacturing plant in Palo Alto, California. This 350,000-square-foot facility develops and supplies all-electric powertrains for Tesla vehicles and for other EV manufacturers, including Daimler AG, the manufacturer of Mercedes. This facility employs 650 people.

A month before the announcement of the receipt of the low-interest loan funds, Tesla announced a deepening of its relationship with Daimler AG. Tesla had already agreed to integrate Tesla's lithium-ion battery technology and charging electronics into the first 1,000 units of the German automaker's first electric smart car. In order to deepen the working relationship and presumably to allow Daimler access to Tesla's technology, Daimler agreed to acquire an equity stake of almost 10 percent of Tesla. Daimler's head of Group Research and Mercedes-Benz Cars Development, Dr. Thomas Weber, commented on the purchase: "Our strategic partnership is an important step to accelerate the commercialization of electric drives globally. As a young and dynamic company, Tesla stands for visionary power and pioneering spirit. Together with Daimler's 120 years of experience in the automotive sector, this collaboration is a unique combination of two companies' strengths. This marks another important milestone in Daimler's strategy for sustainable mobility."[18]

Musk had a few comments of his own: "Daimler has set the benchmark for engineering excellence and vehicle quality for more than a century. It is an honor and a powerful endorsement of our technology that Daimler would choose to invest in, and partner with, Tesla. Daimler is also on the leading edge in the field of **sustainable mobility**. Among others, the lithium-ion pouch-cell battery developed by Daimler and especially designed for automotive applications, is of interest to us. We are looking forward to a strategic cooperation in a number of areas including leveraging Daimler's engineering, production and supply chain expertise. This will accelerate bringing our Tesla Model S to production and ensure that it is a superlative vehicle on all levels."[19] In return for the purchase, Professor Herbert Kohler, Vice President E-Drive and Future Mobility at Daimler, now has a seat on Tesla's board of directors.

The Model S manufacturing process is like that of no other car. It is highly (but not completely) automated. Tesla automobile frames and bodies are 100 percent aluminum. Huge rolls of aluminum in various widths and gauges arrive from suppliers and are stored in Tesla's raw material area. From there, individual rolls are picked up and loaded onto spools at the front end of a blanking machine. The aluminum is unrolled and flattened, before it enters the machine. A laser precisely cuts a blank from the sheet. From there, it goes through various stamping dies until a completed piece of the car emerges. The various frame members and body parts travel to separate lines where they are automatically picked up by robots and welded into complete frames and bodies (see Figure 8.3).

These subassemblies travel through automated cleaning, sealing, and painting processes. Interior seats are installed and bolted down by robots. Cars move automatically between stations where both robots and humans connect and install various wiring and other components.

Building a Tesla automobile is more like building a computer than making a car. After all, there is no engine, gas tank, fuel lines, and exhaust system. It doesn't use any gas or generate any exhaust. The battery pack is installed underneath the floor of the vehicle and can be removed in 90 seconds. Having the battery pack less than 18 inches off

FIGURE 8.3 ROBOTS WELDING AND ASSEMBLING MODEL S FRAMES

Source: Tesla, Inc. Reproduced with permission.

the ground gives the car a very low center of gravity and a very low probability of rollover in an accident. The Model S is also one of the safest cars on the road. In August 2013, the National Highway Traffic Safety Administration (NHTSA) awarded the Tesla Model S a 5-star safety rating. It wasn't just an overall 5-star rating. It gave the car a 5-star rating in every subcategory with no exceptions. About 1 percent of all cars tested by the NHTSA achieved a 5-star, across-the-board safety rating. And while NHTSA does not publish a star rating above five, the overall Vehicle Safety Score (VSS) that's provided to the manufacturer does. The Tesla Model S achieved the highest score for any vehicle ever tested: 5.4 stars. The Model S also established a new high score for the lowest probability of injury to its occupants. Even though it's a sedan, the Model S exceeded the score of all minivans and SUVs as well. The score calculates the probability of injury from side, front, rear, and rollover accidents. With no engine block in front, the Model S has a very large crumple zone, adding to its safety in a high-speed, front-end collision.[20]

The Model S is available in rear or all-wheel drive models. The all-wheel drive version has both front and rear drive motors. The Model S is also available with different size battery packs. The current offerings are 75 kWh and 100 kWh. A performance version of the car changes the 0-to-60 mph acceleration time from 4.1 seconds to 2.5 seconds. This is the fastest time of any car in production today.

In its third quarter ending on September 30, 2018, Tesla produced 26,903 Model S and X vehicles and 53,000 Model 3s. Deliveries in Tesla's Q3 totaled 83,500 vehicles. These consisted of 14,470 Model S, 13,190 Model X, and 55,840 Model 3 vehicles. To put that in perspective, Tesla delivered 80 percent more vehicles in Q3 2018 than it delivered in all of 2017. How's that for a production ramp-up?[21]

There are plenty of things that differentiate Tesla from other EV car companies. But the most important one is Tesla's proprietary charging network. It provides prospective Tesla owners with nationwide charging solutions, something that no other car company has done. Tesla realized early on that a nationwide network of charging stations would allow its car owners to roam about the country without worrying about running out of battery charge. It began building its network of fast-charging stations, called Superchargers, in 2012, starting in California and then rolling out across the country into other major metropolitan

F I G U R E   **8.4**   **TESLA SUPERCHARGER STATION, ARLINGTON, TEXAS**

Source: Tesla, Inc. Reproduced with permission.

areas. At the beginning of 2017, Tesla had 830 Supercharging sites in 31 countries with 5,400 individual charging connections at those sites. By June 2018, Tesla had opened its 10,000th charging connector.[22] In order to keep other EV drivers from utilizing Tesla Superchargers, Tesla made the plugs on its charging cords and its vehicle charging ports unique to Tesla vehicles. Also, even with adapters, other EVs are recognized as being "non-Tesla" and the chargers will fail to operate.

Tesla also realized early on that the *location* of its Superchargers was as important as having them in the first place. So it partnered with retailers in every location. The Superchargers are strategically located at points along our nation's interstate highway routes, enabling long-distance travel. Every location has at least 6 charging stations, with busier locations having as many as 24 (see Figure 8.4).

In addition to its Supercharger network, Tesla has created a far more abundant network of "destination chargers." These are available at restaurants, shopping centers, and hotels.

Charging speed is something very important to an EV owner. It only takes ICE vehicle owners 10 minutes to fill their gas tanks. It shouldn't take much more time than that to recharge an EV battery. Tesla realized this early on, and designed its battery pack and charging network to give customers the fastest charging time possible.

Tesla Superchargers charge a Tesla battery pack at 480 volts. This results in charging times of 20 to 30 minutes, important when on a road trip and not unreasonable after a four- to five-hour drive. Average drivers want to get up and stretch their legs after that much time in the seat anyway.

Having a Supercharger network like Tesla's is useless if you can't easily find the chargers. Tesla's onboard navigation system knows the location and status of every Supercharger position in its network. Drivers can simply navigate to a destination. The Tesla navigation software automatically calculates the route the driver needs to take and what Superchargers need to be visited. It dynamically shows the amount of charge that will be left when arriving at the next Supercharger, and how much time they will have to spend charging. It also shows drivers any speed limitations they must heed in order to reach their next Supercharger or their destination. No other EV manufacturer has this kind of network, or has any plans to build one. This gives Tesla a big advantage over other EV manufacturers, at least in the short-term.

THE WORLD'S FIRST ELECTRIC SUV

After a successful introduction of its Model S sedan, Tesla designers, under the tutelage of Tesla's chief designer Franz von Holzhausen went to work designing Tesla's second high-end vehicle. The prototype of the Tesla Model X SUV was unveiled on February 9, 2012, at the company's Hawthorne, California design studios. The Model X is the world's first all-electric SUV (see Figure 8.5).

Using the Model S platform as a starting point, designers ended up with an SUV that shares roughly 30 percent of its content with the Model S. The curb weight of the Model X varies by battery pack size, but is in general about 10 percent more than a similarly equipped Model S. Both cars are produced at Tesla's factory in Freemont, California. Tesla began deliveries of the Model X in September 2015. As of the end of September 2016, global deliveries of the Model X totaled over 25,000 units. By the end of 2017, Tesla had delivered another 46,535 Model X SUVs.[23] This compares to the Tesla Model S deliveries that were over 50,000 during 2016 and 54,777 in 2017.[24]

The Model X is the fastest SUV ever mass-produced. Equipped with the performance "Ludicrous Mode," the Model X will transport you

FIGURE **8.5**   TESLA MODEL X

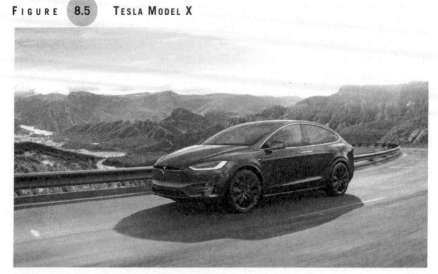

Source: Tesla, Inc. Reproduced with permission.

from 0 to 60 mph in 2.9 seconds.[25] That's faster than any other SUV, and most sports cars. The Model X is also the safest SUV, too. On June 13, 2017, the NHTSA announced that it awarded the Model X a 5-star safety rating in every category and subcategory. That makes it the highest safety-rated SUV that NHTSA has tested. There's only one vehicle that has a lower probability of injury in a crash, and that's Tesla's Model S sedan.[26]

What makes the Model S and X so much safer than other comparable vehicles in production today? Both vehicles have an all-electric powertrain and architecture. The battery pack is extremely rigid and mounted beneath the vehicle's floor. In the Model X, this creates an extremely low center of gravity. So low in fact, that the Model X has the lowest probability of a rollover of any SUV ever produced. The NHTSA calculated a rollover resistance of 9.3 percent for the Model X. In fact, it could not tip its test vehicle in its dynamic rollover test. The Model X is so safe that, in the event of a serious accident, there is 93 percent probability that the vehicle's passengers will walk away from the scene with no serious injury.[27]

In addition to being the safest SUV on the road, the Model X is also one of the most comfortable. Its stylistic rear falcon wing doors allow easy access to both the second and third row of seating. The falcon wing doors and the front doors are two of the most intelligent doors found on any automobile. Both are actuated by simply touching the door handle, which is flush with the surface of the car. Tesla engineers designed the falcon wing doors with a unique double-hinging action. When the doors open, the double hinge allows the door's leading edge to stay tightly close to the car's body. This feature allows the doors to open and close with as little as 12 inches of space between the Model X and adjacent vehicles. A **wideband radar system** mounted in each door detects other cars, people, and other objects. It can see through metal to keep the doors from hitting nearby objects during opening or closing.

The falcon wing doors are a remarkable piece of engineering. Unfortunately, they were a major source of problems in prototype models. Tesla hired a US subsidiary of the Swiss auto parts supplier Hoerbiger to develop the doors. In January 2016, Tesla filed a lawsuit in the US District Court of Northern California against Hoerbiger, accusing them of being unable to come up with a working design for prototype doors delivered to Tesla between February 2014 and May 2015. According to the lawsuit, none of the prototype doors delivered during the aforementioned timeframe were up to Tesla's engineering standards. The doors leaked hydraulic oil and sagged from their open position. In addition, some doors produced excessive amounts of heat during operation causing subsequent malfunctions.[28] The two parties settled the suit in September 2016.[29] Tesla engineers redesigned the complex doors themselves using a Tesla-proprietary electromechanical design. Ultimately, Tesla hired a different supplier to produce the doors. The company has used over-the-air software updates to fine-tune the operation of the falcon wing doors of customer cars. The doors in my Model X have worked flawlessly from delivery onward.

Customers can configure the Model X with either a six-passenger or a seven-passenger seating arrangement. The seven-passenger con-figuration has three seats in the second row. At the touch of a button, all second-row seats collapse and slide forward to allow easy access to third-row seating. All front and rear seats are individually electrically adjustable and heated. The car ventilation system is fitted with a HEPA filter. Tesla claims that this produces cabin air with medical-grade cleanliness. When enabled as part of the "Bioweapon Defense Mode," the system prevents all spores, viruses, and bacteria from entering the passenger cabin. The Model X, like its predecessor the Model S, comes with all the hardware necessary to provide Enhanced Tesla Autopilot. This includes an ultrasonic-based side collision avoidance system and a front radar-based autonomous emergency braking system. Tesla plans to continuously update its autopilot software over the next several years.

The Model X is equipped with a dual-motor, all-wheel-drive powertrain. It has an official EPA-rated range of 289 miles.[30] It's hard to imagine that a luxury SUV with a starting price of $79,000 would receive a lot of attention. But the Model X wasn't just any luxury SUV. It was the very first all-electric SUV, and Tesla made it. Within the first 24 hours after unveiling the Model X on February 10, 2012, Tesla received 500 reservations (at $5,000 each) for the luxury SUV.[31]

By March 2014, Tesla Motors Club members crowdsourced a total of more than 12,000 Model X reservations.[32] By September 2014, that number had ballooned to more than 20,000. All for a car whose deliveries weren't going to start until the second half of 2015.[33] Incredibly, Tesla had yet to disclose the Model X price or its single-charge range.

On September 29, 2015, Tesla delivered the first Model X. By that time, the company had received an estimated 27,000 Model X reservations. That's impressive by any standards, especially given that the price tag ranged anywhere from $90,000 to as much as $150,000 for a high-end, fully optioned model.[34] By the end of 2017, Tesla had sold 46,535 Model X SUVs. The company's Model X run rate was nearly 12,000 per quarter.[35]

A TESLA FOR THE MASSES

With 27,000 reservations representing $2.4 billion in sales, Tesla had enough money to finance its next project. That would be its "make or break," inexpensive EV for the masses, the Model 3 sedan. Musk alluded to it in his original Master Plan. In 2013, some early details about the Model 3 began to surface. Franz von Holzhausen, Tesla's design chief, attended the 2013 Detroit Auto Show. After talking about Tesla's then newest model, the Model X SUV, Holzhausen indicated his excitement over Tesla's as yet unnamed third-generation car. It will "be an Audi A4, BMW 3-Series, Volkswagen Jetta type of vehicle that will offer everything: range, affordability, and performance. We're confident we can do it at a starting price of $30,000, which is the break-in point, where we can bring all this excitement and technology to the average customer."[36]

Tesla gave its employees early access to Model 3 reservations, sight unseen, a few days before the general population. SpaceX employees were also give the opportunity to reserve a Model 3 before its unveiling. Like Tesla's employees, those at SpaceX did so sight unseen as well.[37] The amazing (or maybe not so amazing) thing is, those employees reserved about 13,000 Model 3s.[38] What a vote of confidence in Elon Musk and Tesla. After Tesla and SpaceX, customers who already owned a Tesla Model S or X were given an opportunity to reserve a Model 3, since their purchases helped pay for its development.

On March 31, 2016, Tesla allowed new customers to reserve a Model 3 at its stores or online. A refundable deposit of $1,000 was required to reserve a car. When the dust settled, Tesla ended up with 455,000 Model 3 reservations. At $1,000 per reservation, that represents $455 million worth of confidence in Elon Musk. Big Auto could only look on enviously. Fast-forward to July 29, 2017, when Musk handed over the keys to the lucky, first 30 folks who ordered a Model 3 (see Figure 8.6). From this initial production run, Tesla plans to slowly ramp up to 10,000 cars per *week* by the end of 2018.[39] As of October 14, 2018, Bloomberg reported that Tesla was manufacturing 4,225 Model 3s per week and had made a total of 101,067 Model 3s so far.[40]

FIGURE 8.6   TESLA MODEL 3 INITIAL DELIVERY EVENT

Source: Tesla, Inc. Reproduced with permission.

F I G U R E   **8.7**   **TESLA MODEL 3 INTERIOR**

Source: Tesla, Inc. Reproduced with permission.

That may seem like a tall order. The current Model S and X combined run rate is about 100,000 units per year. But the Model 3 is nothing like the Model S or X. First, there is no driver display (see Figure 8.7).

Drivers handle every function via the central, horizontal touch screen. That means fewer buttons and switches. The same thing goes for side view mirrors and steering wheel positions. According to Musk, "There's nothing in the Model 3 that doesn't need to be there." Turn around and look up and the openness and cleanliness of the car continues. The sweeping glass roof (Figure 8.8) is unlike any other car, regardless of price.

And the price is what is turning heads. There are other $35,000 EVs on the market (I'll review them in Chapter 9). But none are as sleek and stylistic as the Model 3. It has clutter-free, clean lines, not unlike those of its larger stable mate, the Model S. Even car designers believe Tesla's EV models will far outlast those of the competition. Geoff Wardle, a transportation design instructor at the College of Design in Pasadena, California, feels that Tesla's design simplicity gives its models longevity. "I think all of their model range will last well, whereas other vehicles like the Bolt are going to age quickly."[41]

FIGURE 8.8   TESLA MODEL 3 GLASS ROOF

Source: Tesla, Inc. Reproduced with permission.

Tesla is selling two versions of the Model 3. The first one available for delivery is the higher-end, $42,000 model. This includes a larger, 310-mile-per-charge battery pack. Everyone learns from difficulties and problems, and Tesla is no different. The Model X is the most complicated car Tesla has produced to date. As a result, Model 3 engineering was simplified. Unless something had a compelling reason to be included, it wasn't. Even the Model 3 battery pack is simplified. It has just 3 battery modules compared to Model S's 16.[42]

But don't think for a minute that Tesla's "less is more" philosophy carries over to the Model 3's engineering. The car's supercomputer has more processing power than most small businesses. It's loaded with sensors, radar, and front- and rear-facing cameras. When something needs tweaking, Tesla's software engineers can easily push out software updates over the Model 3's WiFi connection, not unlike the way Apple does with its products. This makes the Model 3 and Tesla's other models future-proof. It's the difference between big auto that typically just incorporates new technology into a car and a top technology company that makes cars.

If you go through Tesla's Model 3 ordering process (I have), you will see just how few options are available for the Model 3. This simplifies everything from parts ordering to the speed of the production line. And it allows Tesla to make Model 3s as fast as it possibly can. Musk believes he can build 250,000 Model 3s in the same factory footprint it takes to churn out 50,000 Model Ss.[43] Hey big auto, welcome to the twenty-first century.

"MASTER PLAN, PART DEUX"

By mid-2016, Musk's first Master Plan was in its final stages of completion. The fact that Tesla hadn't yet gone bankrupt was a major accomplishment, in and of itself. Here's how Musk expressed it on the Tesla website: "The list of successful car company startups is short. As of 2016, the number of American car companies that haven't gone bankrupt is a grand total of two: Ford and Tesla. Starting a car company is idiotic and an electric car company is idiocy squared."

So now it was time for what Musk calls "Master Plan, Part Deux." Here it is, in typical Musk simplicity:

1. Create stunning solar roofs with seamlessly integrated battery storage.
2. Expand the electric vehicle product line to address all major segments.
3. Develop a self-driving capability that is 10X safer than manual via massive fleet learning.
4. Enable your car to make money for you when you aren't using it.

Let's look at each of the four plan elements in more detail.

Integrated Energy Generation and Storage

On August 1, 2016, SolarCity Corporation agreed to be acquired by Tesla Motors, Inc. for $2.6 billion. This was part of Musk's Master Plan, Part Deux. He couldn't very well provide an integrated energy generation and storage product if SolarCity was still operating as a standalone company. To many analysts, Musk was doing the acquisition to save his struggling solar company. But from Musk's perspective, he needed Tesla and SolarCity working together. In addition to new vehicles, Tesla was busy developing its energy storage products. Its Powerwall product line would integrate nicely with SolarCity's new solar roofing tiles. Together, they would provide home and vehicle owners with all of the energy they need at home, as well as a "gas station" to fill up their EV.

Beyond the Model 3: The Tesla Semi

The Model 3 marks the introduction of Tesla's fourth EV. What's next for the company? Musk alluded to it in his Master Plan, Part Deux: "In addition to consumer vehicles, there are two other types of electric vehicle needed: heavy-duty trucks and high passenger–density urban transport. Both are in the early stages of development at Tesla and should be ready for unveiling in 2017. We believe the Tesla Semi will deliver a substantial reduction in the cost of cargo transport, while increasing safety and making it really fun to operate."[44]

Although Musk originally expected to unveil Tesla's all-electric semi in September 2017, the unveiling of the Tesla Semi, as it is now referred to, occurred on November 16, 2017. Here's how Musk initially described what could be the biggest disruptor since his previous EVs: "It is a heavy duty, long range, semi-truck. So it has the highest weight capability and with long range. So essentially it's meant to alleviate the heavy duty trucking loads. And this is something that people today do not think is possible. They think the truck doesn't have enough power or it doesn't have enough range. And then with those with the Tesla semi we want to show that no, an electric truck can out-torque any diesel semi. If you had a tug-of-war competition, the Tesla semi would tug the diesel semi uphill."[45]

Jerome Guillen leads the Tesla Semi program. Guillen was the former Model S program director during a tumultuous time for Musk's EV program. Prior to coming onboard Tesla, Guillen was an engineer at Mercedes. There, he led the successful development of Mercedes' Cascadia truck. He also has had a stint at Mercedes' Freightliner division, where he led the development of its newest generation of Class 8 tractors. That ultimately led to Cascadia's development.[46]

Even after the delayed unveiling, it was clear that Musk and Tesla did not disappoint. Musk described the truck as one that would "blow people's minds into an alternate dimension."[47] The Tesla Semi (see Figure 8.9) is a Class 8 semi-trailer, all-electric truck. Initial production

FIGURE **8.9** **TESLA SEMI**

Source: Tesla, Inc. Reproduced with permission.

is slated for 2019. Musk said the Tesla Semi would cost 20 cents per mile less than a diesel truck. In order to compete successfully with diesel trucks, the range has to be there. And it is. The Tesla Semi comes in two versions: a $180,000, 500-mile range, long-haul tractor and a $150,000, 300-mile range, short-haul tractor.

Tesla's Semi uses the same motor that powers the Tesla Model 3. But it uses four of them, one on each of the four drive wheels (two on each drive axle). Like most other EVs, it has no transmission or gears of any kind. That equals less maintenance for owners. It's one of the reasons that Tesla's Semi comes with a 1-million-mile guarantee. The truck is equipped with Tesla's Autopilot as a standard feature. Its dual electronic screens (see Figure 8.10) display everything that Tesla's current EV screens do, plus additional information regarding battery charge and energy use.

The timing of Tesla's Semi introduction couldn't be better. The electrification of the transportation sector is hitting the trucking industry, too. It's being driven by interest in improved driver safety, cleaner energy, and lower costs. And the trucking industry accounts for $30 billion in annual sales.[48] The movement of freight by trucks, ships, planes, and trains is responsible for 16 percent of all greenhouse gas emissions. That's a huge part of the carbon footprint here in the

FIGURE 8.10   TESLA SEMI INTERIOR

Source: Tesla, Inc. Reproduced with permission.

United States. Regarding safety, the Federal Motor Carrier Safety Administration reports that 4,564 people died in large truck and bus accidents in 2016 (most recent statistics available).[49] There's no question that the majority of those accidents could probably have been avoided altogether or would have been less severe if the truck were autonomously in control.

While the Tesla Semi's battery pack will certainly be larger (perhaps as large as one megawatt-hour), charging won't be an issue. Tesla claims it can add 400 miles of charge in 30 minutes. This can happen during drivers' mandatory 30-minute break, scheduled every six or seven hours of driving.[50] In addition, while waiting to unload, drivers have another opportunity to charge. There's no question that Tesla is poised to take a significant portion of the Class 8 truck market. It all depends on a successful Tesla Semi launch.

A number of customers have ponied up reservation fees for the Tesla Semi. Here's the current list, as of this writing:

- A day after its unveiling, Walmart ordered 15 Tesla Semis. In a statement released by the company, it said, "We have a long history of testing new technology – including alternative-fuel trucks – and we are excited to be among the first to pilot this new heavy-duty

electric vehicle. We believe we can learn how this technology performs within our supply chain, as well as how it could help us meet
some of our long-term sustainability goals, such as lowering emissions." Five of the trucks will be tested in the United States and
10 will be evaluated by Walmart Canada.[51] Walmart ordered an
additional 30 trucks in September 2018.[52]

- On November 17, 2017, Loblaw Companies Limited of Montreal,
  Canada announced it had preordered 25 Tesla Semis for delivery
  in 2019. Loblaw is Canada's largest supermarket group. It wants
  to reduce its carbon footprint by fully electrifying its fleet by
  2030. That means replacing all 350 of its trucks with all-electric
  versions.[53]

- On November 17, 2017, J. B. Hunt announced that it had
  reserved "multiple" Tesla Semis. Rumors have the number as
  many as 40. The company plans to use the Semi to support its
  West Coast operations. Specifically, they would operate in J. B.
  Hunt's Dedicated Contract Services and its Intermodal divisions.
  CEO John Roberts, commenting on the company's move, said,
  "Reserving Tesla trucks marks an important step in our efforts
  to implement industry-changing technology. We believe electric
  trucks will be most beneficial on local and dray routes, and we
  look forward to utilizing this new, sustainable technology."[54]

- Also on November 17, 2017, the Michigan-based Meijer supermarket chain ordered four Tesla Semis for evaluation. The company
  will test the vehicles and evaluate their economics and other factors
  before deciding whether or not to complete the purchase.[55]

- On November 21, 2017, JK Moving Services, the largest independently owned mover in the United States ordered four of
  Tesla's short-haul Semis and five of the sleeper cab, long-haul
  models. Chuck Kuhn, JK Moving Services founder and president,
  commented on his tour of Tesla's factory: "It's standard operating
  procedure to get a factory tour, Tesla or diesel, ahead of committing
  to spend what could be well over a million for new trucks. None
  of the other factories compared to what we saw out of Tesla." JK
  Moving could eventually decide to replace all of its 485 trucks
  with Tesla Semis.[56]

- On November 28, 2017, DHL revealed it had preordered 10 of the
  Tesla Semis. It initially plans to use them on same-day customer

deliveries and shuttle runs in a number of major US cities. It also intends to test them on some longer runs and to evaluate driver comfort and safety. Representatives from the DHL Supply Chain division have already test-driven the Semi prototypes in California. Jim Monkmeyer, president of DHL Supply Chain isn't bothered by the long lead time: "Something like this that's new and is as complex as the Semi, I don't know if we can count on specific dates. We understand the challenges that they are facing. This is the future and we want to be in on the ground floor."[57]

- On December 7, 2017, Anheuser-Busch announced it ordered 40 of Tesla's Semi trucks. The company wants to reduce its carbon footprint by 30 percent. If successful, it is likely Anheuser will buy or lease additional units. The company expects to use the trucks to deliver goods to wholesalers that lie 150 to 200 miles from its breweries. The company spends about $120 million annually on fuel costs for its truck fleet.[58]

- Sysco is the largest food distributor in the world. On December 8, 2017, it ordered 50 of Tesla's Semis. The company has a plan to increase efficiencies in its distribution network by adopting new technologies. If successful, Sysco could eventually decide to update its entire fleet of more than 7,000 trucks.[59]

- On December 12, 2017, PepsiCo Inc. reserved 100 of Tesla's Semi trucks. It hopes to reduce both emissions and fuel costs.[60] This could eventually be huge for Tesla, as PepsiCo operates a 10,000-vehicle fleet. Initially, the Tesla Semis would be used for short-haul distribution runs that fall within the 500-mile range of the Semi. PepsiCo plans to reduce its greenhouse gas emissions by 20 percent by 2030.[61]

- On December 19, 2017, UPS said it was purchasing 125 of Tesla's Semi trucks. This is the largest known order for the Semi so far.[62]

As of late 2018, Tesla had at least 680 orders for the Tesla Semi.[63] Tesla expects to start production of its Semi in 2019. From here, it looks as though Tesla will be one of the first US companies able to deliver an all-electric semi-truck.

A big surprise at Tesla's Semi truck debut was the unveiling of Tesla's second-generation Roadster. See Figure 8.11. Named the 2020 Roadster, based on when salivating would-be owners will be able to get their

FIGURE **8.11** **TESLA 2020 ROADSTER**

Source: Tesla, Inc. Reproduced with permission.

hands on one, it is one amazing car. It's a four-seat, all-wheel-drive sports car. It reaches 60 miles an hour from a standing start in a blistering 1.9 seconds. Its top speed is an eyeball-popping 250 miles per hour. Owners will be able to travel 620 miles before recharging. An amazing car with a sticker price to match: If you'd like one of the first 1,000 Founders Series models, the deposit is the entire price of the car, $250,000. Regular Roadster would-be owners have to shell out a deposit of $50,000 to reserve their $200,000 model.[64] As of its unveiling, the 2020 Roadster will be the fastest street-legal, mass-produced car in the world. And it's a bargain compared to the other exotic sports cars that it will leave in its dust.

Tesla is also working on some version of an all-electric bus. The vehicles will be able to be summoned by riders via buttons at bus stops. Thus, it will serve that segment of the population without phones. The design is expected to accommodate bikes, wheelchairs, and strollers. In April 2017, Musk said Tesla plans to unveil an all-electric pickup truck in "18–24 months."[65]

And it doesn't stop there. Tesla plans to add autonomous (or self-driving) technology to the Tesla Semi, too. The company says that "platoons" of trucks will automatically follow a lead truck. In fact, Tesla plans to make all of its vehicles fully autonomous as the technology continues to mature. Even though all Tesla vehicles currently in production come with radar, sonar, cameras, and computing hardware, the algorithmic autonomy software will take much longer to complete.

Even with autonomous-driving-ready software, the capability will only be available when individual jurisdictions approve its use. In the United States the insurance industry and the Department of Transportation have yet to even begin studying the regulatory issues. Tesla believes six billion miles of autonomous driving will be necessary for regulatory approval. The current fleet is "learning" the world's roadways at the rate of just over three million miles daily. Tesla's current partial autonomy is already significantly safer than the average driver. Tesla ultimately wants its self-driving capability in its **autonomous EVs** to be 10 times safer than manual driving.

IS CHINA IN TESLA'S FUTURE?

Tesla has a big jump on EV manufacturing and sales in the United States and Europe. But its biggest future opportunity could lie in the land of the Red Dragon: China. The Chinese auto market is the world's largest, already far greater than the North American market (Canada and the US combined). In 2016, total North American new car sales were 20 million. In China, that number was a mind-blowing 28 million vehicles.[66] By mid-2017, China's EV sales posted a 148 percent year-on-year increase. That's only going to continue as China has strong domestic policy support for EVs. In addition, many Chinese manufacturers are introducing new EV models. In five years' time, the Chinese EV market could be as big as the rest of the world combined.

Musk has already said he doesn't want to just sell EVs in China; he wants to build them there. If future sales will be double those of the United States, he would be foolish not to. It wouldn't surprise me in the least to see an announcement sometime before the end of 2018 that Tesla will be building EVs in the largest market in the world.

Musk is certainly one of the more colorful CEOs. However, he got a little too colorful for the SEC in late 2018. His tweets regarding taking the company private were non-factual. As a result, Tesla's share price soared higher and then dropped back after Musk retracted some of his comments. The SEC sued Tesla and Musk, and eventually a settlement was reached. The company and Musk each had to pay $20 million in fines. Musk agreed to give up his chairman's position but still remains Tesla's CEO.

It can certainly be argued that Tesla has started the twenty-first-century migration to EVs, but they aren't the only car company offering them. In the next chapter I'll look at all of the current and future EV offerings planned by traditional car manufacturers.

NOTES

1. www.boomsbeat.com/articles/323/20140214/50-things-you-probably-didnt-know-about-elon-musk.htm
2. money.cnn.com/2016/11/17/technology/tesla-solarcity-merger/index.html
3. www.boomsbeat.com/articles/323/20140214/50-things-you-probably-didnt-know-about-elon-musk.htm
4. Vance, Ashlee (2015). *Elon Musk: Tesla, SpaceX, and the Quest for a Fantastic Future*. ISBN 978-0062301239.
5. www.cnet.com/news/compaq-buys-zip2/
6. www.boomsbeat.com/articles/323/20140214/50-things-you-probably-didnt-know-about-elon-musk.htm
7. www.shareholder.com/Common/Edgar/1065088/891618-03-1538/03-00.pdf
8. www.vanityfair.com/news/2007/05/tesla200705?currentPage=all&printable=true
9. www.tesla.com/blog/secret-tesla-motors-master-plan-just-between-you-and-me
10. www.tesla.com/blog/secret-tesla-motors-master-plan-just-between-you-and-me
11. www.autoblog.com/2008/02/04/tesla-whitestar-to-be-offered-as-both-an-ev-and-a-rev/
12. web.archive.org/web/20080922222405/greenlight.greentechmedia.com/2008/09/18/tesla-kills-its-gas-electric-hybrid-586/
13. web.archive.org/web/20080809194001/www.cardesignnews.com/site/home/rss_display/item128801/
14. ir.tesla.com/releasedetail.cfm?ReleaseID=477993
15. www.ftc.gov/news-events/blogs/competition-matters/2015/05/direct-consumer-auto-sales-its-not-just-about-tesla
16. https://www.greencarreports.com/news/1107637_tesla-takes-it-to-michigan-opens-gallery-in-state-that-bans-sales-of-its-electric-cars
17. ir.tesla.com/releasedetail.cfm?ReleaseID=477963
18. ir.tesla.com/releasedetail.cfm?ReleaseID=477977
19. ir.tesla.com/releasedetail.cfm?ReleaseID=477977
20. www.tesla.com/blog/tesla-model-s-achieves-best-safety-rating-any-car-ever-tested

21. http://ir.tesla.com/news-releases/news-release-details/tesla-q3-2018-vehicle-production-and-deliveries
22. https://cleantechnica.com/2018/06/12/tesla-opens-10000th-supercharger/
23. Data is from tesla.com quarterly vehicle production and delivery press releases.
24. https://www.theverge.com/2018/1/3/16846860/tesla-2017-deliveries-model-3-production
25. electrek.co/2016/08/23/tesla-100-kwh-battery-pack-quickest-car-ever/
26. electrek.co/2017/06/13/tesla-model-x-5-star-safety-rating-nhtsa/
27. electrek.co/2017/06/13/tesla-model-x-5-star-safety-rating-nhtsa/
28. www.teslarati.com/tesla-settles-lawsuit-hoerbiger-model-x-falcon-wing-doors/
29. electrek.co/2016/09/27/tesla-settles-in-court-with-supplier-over-the-development-of-the-model-xs-falcon-wing-doors/
30. electrek.co/2016/08/23/tesla-100-kwh-battery-pack-quickest-car-ever/
31. www.hybridcars.com/tesla-model-x-reservations-hit-500-24-hours-38538/
32. www.autoblog.com/2014/03/26/does-tesla-really-have-12000-model-x-preorders/
33. gas2.org/2014/09/05/20000-tesla-model-x-reservations-and-counting/
34. www.autoblog.com/2015/09/10/total-tesla-model-x-pre-orders-could-be-over-31-000/
35. Source: tesla.com vehicle production and delivery press releases and https://www.theverge.com/2018/1/3/16846860/tesla-2017-deliveries-model-3-production
36. www.automobilemag.com/news/tesla-in-detroit-our-family-will-grow-197263/
37. electrek.co/2016/03/25/spacex-employees-reserve-tesla-model-3/
38. electrek.co/2016/06/09/tesla-model-3-data-spacex-employees-reservations/
39. blog.caranddriver.com/stand-and-deliver-elon-musk-hands-off-first-tesla-model-3-production-car
40. https://www.bloomberg.com/graphics/2018-tesla-tracker/
41. www.wired.com/story/tesla-model-3-more-than-electric/
42. blog.caranddriver.com/stand-and-deliver-elon-musk-hands-off-first-tesla-model-3-production-cars/
43. blog.caranddriver.com/stand-and-deliver-elon-musk-hands-off-first-tesla-model-3-production-cars/
44. www.tesla.com/blog/master-plan-part-deux
45. electrek.co/2017/09/13/tesla-semi-unveil-unreal-beast-elon-musk-oct-26th/
46. electrek.co/2016/07/21/tesla-model-s-program-director-daimler-cascadia-jerome-guillen-lead-tesla-semi/
47. www.washingtonpost.com/news/innovations/wp/2017/11/17/teslas-latest-creation-an-electric-big-rig-that-can-travel-500-miles-on-a-single-charge/?utm_term=.9d3a124da48c
48. www.bloomberg.com/news/articles/2017-11-24/tesla-s-newest-promises-break-the-laws-of-batteries

49. https://www.fmcsa.dot.gov/safety/data-and-statistics/2016-commercial-motor-vehicle-traffic-safety-facts-sheet
50. www.bloomberg.com/news/articles/2017-11-24/tesla-s-newest-promises-break-the-laws-of-batteries
51. www.cnbc.com/2017/11/17/wal-mart-says-its-planning-to-test-teslas-new-electric-trucks.html
52. https://electrek.co/2018/09/06/tesla-semi-new-order-electric-truck-walmart/
53. business.financialpost.com/news/retail-marketing/loblaw-says-it-ordered-25-tesla-electric-trucks-wants-fully-electric-fleet-by-2030
54. fortune.com/2017/11/17/tesla-semi-truck-meijer-jb-hunt/
55. www.detroitnews.com/story/business/autos/mobility/2017/11/17/meijer-tesla-semi/107777724/
56. www.bizjournals.com/washington/news/2017/11/21/your-next-move-could-be-in-a-tesla-jk-moving-to.html
57. www.wsj.com/articles/dhl-orders-10-tesla-semi-trucks-1511891280
58. www.wsj.com/articles/anheuser-busch-orders-40-tesla-semi-trucks-1512648180
59. electrek.co/2017/12/08/tesla-semi-order-electric-trucks-sysco/
60. www.reuters.com/article/us-pepsico-tesla-orders/pepsico-makes-biggest-public-pre-order-of-tesla-semis-100-trucks-idUSKBN1E61FB?utm_source=Twitter&utm_medium=Social
61. www.theverge.com/2017/12/12/16767422/tesla-semi-truck-pepsi-preorder
62. https://www.reuters.com/article/us-ups-tesla-orders/ups-reserves-125-tesla-semi-trucks-largest-public-pre-order-yet-idUSKBN1ED1QM
63. https://insideevs.com/100000-tesla-semi-sales-spells-18-billion-revenue/
64. www.tesla.com/roadster
65. www.businessinsider.com/teslas-future-depends-on-china-2017-9
66. www.businessinsider.com/teslas-future-depends-on-china-2017-9

CHAPTER NINE

Everybody into the EV Pool

W hile it could be argued that Tesla launched the twenty-first-century transition to EVs, it's certainly not the only one in the game. When all the hoopla over the Model 3 settles, Elon Musk and Tesla have to contend with Big Auto.

WHAT ABOUT BIG AUTO?

Yes, established car companies have been slow to recognize the transition to EVs is real. But when they saw how fast Tesla booked 500,000 orders for its inexpensive Model 3 EV, they quickly revised their future model plans. These are well-established car companies. They have solid sales and existing dealers with repair operations in place. And let's face it: These guys are tough competitors. And some already have competing models to the Model 3.

In this chapter, I'll explore the current EV offerings from each of the major manufacturers. I'll also talk about what might keep some of these companies from being successful in the EV market. In addition, I'll look at some of the secondary effects of transitioning to an all-electric transportation environment. I'll also discuss China. It's a unique environment for EVs. Many of its models will never be sold anywhere outside of the country. I fully expect there will be several new models announced between the time I finish this manuscript and the book is actually published. However, this compendium of models should give you a sense of the size and scope of the global transition to a future in which EVs will quickly become the major mode of personal transportation.

The Impacts of Transitioning to EVs

It seems that every day there are multiple car companies announcing new EV models and plans for more. While EVs still represent about 1 percent of all car sales, those sales are growing 20 times faster than the overall market. If you're in the automobile manufacturing and sales business, those figures certainly get your attention. In general, a transition to EV sales and ownership is extremely positive, even if I only measure it by my own two experiences of purchasing and owning an EV.

But what are all of the impacts of migrating away from internal combustion engine (ICE) vehicles? Are they all positive? I'll try to answer both of those questions in this section. For purposes of this discussion, I'm going to assume that EVs will represent 75 percent of all new vehicles sold by 2050.

The first impact, and it's a positive one, will be wealth generation. EV manufacturers that are successful will generate enormous amounts of wealth for their shareholders. Wealth will also shift, and will generally be aligned with the location of EV manufacturing centers. In the United States, Detroit will no longer be the epicenter of automotive design and manufacturing. California will be the major EV design center, and is the initial EV manufacturing location (Tesla). Given the number of batteries that will be required, new battery gigafactories could be located anywhere in the lower 48 states. Tesla's Gigafactory 1 is outside of Sparks, Nevada. China and India will also be major global manufacturing and design sites for EVs. Most existing legacy car manufacturers will go through major transitions. Some will most certainly cease to exist.

Another very positive effect that EV adoption brings to the table is the massive reduction in the consumption of fossil fuels. I'm primarily talking about crude oil. I used to write about Hubbert's theory on peak oil. Back in 1956, Marion King Hubbert (1903–1989) worked as an American geophysicist and geologist for Shell Research in Houston, Texas. His most important contribution, and the work he is most known for, is the Hubbert peak theory and the Hubbert curve.

Hubbert proposed his peak theory in 1956. He postulated that fossil fuel production in any given area over time follows a bell-shaped curve. He assumed that once a reservoir of oil is discovered and production begins, it increases exponentially. However, at some point peak production is reached. It then begins to decline at an exponential rate. Hubbert further said that the increase and decrease are roughly symmetrical. Once the peak is reached, roughly half of the oil in that given reservoir has been produced.

As you can see in Figure 9.1, US production roughly followed Hubbert's 1956 upper-bound curve prediction for US crude oil production. That is until US producers developed shale oil production. Then US crude production began to rapidly increase.

Ironically, history will show that Hubbert's peak oil theory turned out to be correct. But it won't be because the world ran out of oil. It will simply be because the demand for oil will gradually diminish. The shift to a global electrified transportation system in the near future will kill the demand for crude oil. That drop-off in demand will happen much faster than anyone anticipates. I believe prices will drop so low

FIGURE 9.1   HUBBERT CURVE AND US CRUDE PRODUCTION

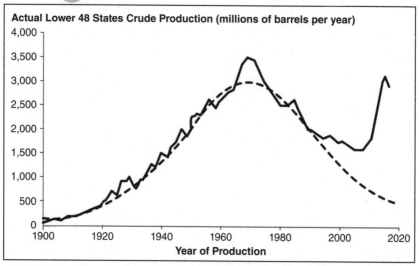

Source: Data from EIA www.eia.gov/dnav/pet/pet_crd_crpdn_adc_mbblpd_a.htm and the following paper: dieoff.org/page191.htm. Accessed October 27, 2017. Sketch provided by author.

that many producers and some refiners will simply go out of business. The Alberta Oil Sands will simply stop producing, as production costs will be far greater than the price of crude.

Another segment of the automotive world that will see an impact from EV adoption will be automotive parts suppliers and manufacturers. Right now, there are roughly 500,000 businesses in the auto care industry. They provide parts and service for the estimated 268.8 million trucks and cars that were on US roads as of the end of 2017. The industry is currently a $368 billion annual enterprise,[1] equal to about 2 percent of the overall 2016 US GDP of $18.46 trillion.[2] The move to EVs will have a significant, negative impact on automotive parts suppliers. EVs have thousands of fewer parts than their ICE counterparts. Most of the parts that wear on an ICE-powered vehicle are absent in an EV. And it won't just be manufacturers. Parts distributors and consumer parts outlets will all be affected.

Many car dealerships will simply disappear. The dealership profitability model is based on maintenance after the sale. Most dealerships make almost nothing on the sale of vehicles. That business model doesn't compute with EVs. They require almost no post-sales maintenance. That's one of the reasons that legacy car manufacturers are having problems selling EVs. Their dealership networks don't make any money selling EVs, and there is little in the way of future maintenance revenue on an EV. Tesla has no dealers, preferring to sell its EVs online. This has worked great for Tesla, but US dealer network associations have sued Tesla and complained to state and federal legislators in an attempt to stop Tesla from selling EVs outside of dealer networks. They've failed in nearly every instance. Tesla continues to pursue several legal actions regarding sales of their vehicles. As a result of the EV sales model, the legacy dealership network will change significantly.

Oil-changing franchises will slowly go out of business. EVs don't use engine oil, since there's no engine. This will have a lesser but still impactful effect on refineries that produce engine oil for automotive use. With little if any gasoline and diesel being purchased, the current gasoline station/eatery will vanish, or be radically transformed as EV charging stations. Without a charging station, it's hard to imagine why an EV driver would stop at a traditional gas station/convenience store. My wife and I don't.

Brake and muffler shops will only be doing brake jobs. EVs have no mufflers, so the demand for muffler repair will disappear. In addition, the demand for platinum and palladium will be drastically reduced, as they are used extensively in the production of automobile catalytic convertors. With no tailpipe emissions, state and local emissions testing facilities will also disappear. This is, after all, the ultimate goal of sustainable transportation: no emissions.

Speaking of brake jobs, those will be few and far between. EVs turn their motors into generators when the operator takes their foot off the accelerator pedal. The drag on the generator slows down the car. Most EV drivers don't need to use the brake, except when coming to a complete stop. Brake fluid will still be necessary and may need to be changed more often, since brakes are used less.

More good news: The more EVs on the roads, the less people dying prematurely every year from air pollution. According to researchers at MIT's Laboratory for Aviation and the Environment, 200,000 Americans die early every year from air pollution. Their research shows that most of that pollution comes from emissions from vehicles.[3] Worldwide, the number is closer to seven million premature deaths from air pollution according to the World Health Organization.[4] The amount of money saved from treating these individuals will save billions annually. The world's population will be far healthier with lower levels of air pollution.

In addition to reduced air pollution, EVs are far quieter than ICE vehicles, so noise pollution is far lower. This is especially true in cities, where vehicles are operating at speeds of 30 miles per hour or less. And traffic noise has been directly correlated with sleep loss in urban centers. Eliminating the noise will greatly improve the sleep of city dwellers. This will have an indirect but nonetheless significant, positive impact on the health of cities.

Finally, transportation is responsible for 26 percent of all greenhouse gases here in the United States. Once EVs replace ICE-powered vehicles, we remove 26 percent of our greenhouse gas (GHG) problem. We help lower the probability of significant, negative climatic events being caused by elevated levels of GHGs. In 2017, we saw record high temperatures in the Pacific Northwest and dry conditions in California leading to historic wildfires. Monsoon flooding in Bangladesh displaced over 40 million people, and threatens to do that annually. I'll go into more detail on the negative effects of GHG emissions later in the book.

Global Sales Growth

Like just about anything else that's manufactured, EVs are starting to reap the benefits of mass production. As sales ramp up, prices are coming down. For 2017, worldwide EV sales reached 1,223,600 units, up 58 percent over 2016.[5] US EV sales increased 27 percent. If this rate of growth continues, and I see no reason why it won't, EVs will account for 10 percent of all new cars sold by 2025. But I believe EV sales growth is going to increase even more rapidly than it currently is. That's because we are going to hit what I refer to as the EV tipping point. That's the point at which EVs are the same cost or less expensive than their ICE counterparts. The battery pack makes up about one-third of the cost of the average EV. Between 2010 and 2017, lithium-ion cell costs have plummeted 73 percent.[6] As battery pack costs continue to drop, the cost of the overall vehicle comes down with it. Right now, EVs represent a little over 1 percent of all vehicles sold. But the rate at which EVs are selling is 10 times faster than that of their dirty ICE equivalents.[7]

In the following pages, I've attempted to provide a snapshot of every EV manufacturer as of this writing. It is by no means intended to act as a buyer's guide. I've included relevant and interesting aspects of each EV manufacturer.

BMW

BMW, one of Germany's legacy automakers, announced an EV strategy that is markedly different from that of Tesla. In August 2017, it announced it would build ICE, plug-in hybrid electric vehicle (PHEV), and EV versions of its various model series on the same production line. It's hedging its EV strategy. "Nobody knows how many electric vehicles you'll sell in 2020, 2021, and 2025," said BMW CEO Harald Krüger. "You don't know how many plug-in hybrids you will sell, and you don't know how many combustion engines you will sell. The only answer is flexibility [to] deliver all three."[8]

BMW is already implementing this unified strategy at its plant in Spartanburg, South Carolina. That's where BMW assembles its X$_5$

crossover. BMW has already integrated both ICE and PHEV versions into the production line. Batteries for the PHEV are produced at the Spartanburg facility. BMW expects the factory will get additional tooling to build and assemble EV versions of all of its vehicle lines manufactured there. These include the X_3 through X_6 crossovers. It will add capability to manufacture its large X_7 crossover towards the end of 2018.

In addition to electrifying its core models, BMW is continuing with its "i" EV sub-brand. The next vehicle coming in this line will be the iNEXT. It will have BMW's advanced autonomous driving capabilities. It is scheduled to be on showroom floors in 2021.[9]

BMW's EV strategy is somewhat confusing. Its integrated manufacturing line concept has most industry analysts scratching their heads, and rightly so. Its plan sounds great in theory, but trying to build three radically different powertrains on one production line means two of them could end up as non-optimized, inferior vehicles. The automotive world is rapidly electrifying and many countries are already requiring it. Why BMW would choose to accommodate engineering and manufacturing space for legacy ICE versions of its vehicles is somewhat baffling. As Tesla has shown, the only way to create a compelling EV is to design, engineer, and manufacture it from the ground up, with no legacy constraints.

Ford

A little more than a century ago, the Ford Motor Company made an initial investment into EV technology. In 1914, Henry Ford confirmed that Ford was working on a low-cost EV. It would use Thomas Edison's newly developed nickel-iron batteries. Most of the parts for Ford's initial EV came right out of the Model T. The front axle, suspension frame, and steering wheel were genuine Model T parts. The car had two battery banks, one where the engine would have been and one under the seats. The car had an electric traction motor located in place of the transmission in a conventional Model T.

Thomas Edison was helping Ford promote the upcoming Edison-Ford EV. Here's what he had to say, as quoted in an interview with the period publication, *Automotive Topics*: "Mr. Henry Ford is making plans for the tools, special machinery, factory buildings and equipment for the production of this new electric. There is so much special work to be done that no date can be fixed now as to when the new electric can be put on the market. But Mr. Ford is working steadily on the details, and he knows his business so it will not be long.

"I believe that ultimately the electric motor will be universally used for trucking in all large cities, and that the electric automobile will be the family carriage of the future. All trucking must come to electricity. I am convinced that it will not be long before all the trucking in New York City will be electric."[10]

The Edison Ford EV would cost between $500 and $700 and would be available for purchase in 1915. Unfortunately, that never happened. A suspicious fire destroyed the storage battery and EV development buildings. After investing $1.5 million and purchasing nearly 100,000 of Edison's batteries, Henry Ford lost interest in EVs and never tried to develop one again.[11]

It's somewhat ironic that a century later, Ford announced a $4.5 billion investment in order to once again bring EVs to the car-buying public. In December 2015, Ford announced it is building 13 new EVs over a four-year timespan. The first is an upgraded electric Focus. The 2018 model has an overall mileage range of 118 city and 96 highway. It has an attractive price of $29,120. Ford expects to have range-competitive vehicles available by 2020.[12] Beyond the Focus, the company expects to ease into EVs with PHEV versions of the Escape, Ford Expedition, and Lincoln Navigator. All three are scheduled for release in 2019. By 2020, Ford plans to introduce the Model E, an all-electric, small SUV with a 300-mile range. Ford is also tackling EVs in China by creating a separate brand. It expects 70 percent of its Chinese models will be all-electric by 2025.[13]

GM

GM entered the EV market with the Chevrolet Volt, a PHEV it introduced in December 2010. By the end of 2017, sales of the Volt totaled 154,849 units.[14] The all-electric range is 53 miles. The overall range is 420 miles.[15] The Chevrolet Bolt is GM's first all-electric subcompact hatchback. It has an all-electric range of 238 miles. The 2017 model entered production in November 2016 and was available for sale in 2017.[16] In 2017, GM sold 23,297 Bolt EVs.[17] The $37,495 price tag (eligible for $7,500 Federal tax credit) is very competitive with Tesla's Model 3.[18]

Beyond the Bolt and the Volt, GM plans 20 all-electric EVs between now and 2023. The first two will hit dealer showrooms in early 2019. GM plans to focus on SUVs and crossovers, currently the heart of its market.[19]

Mercedes

In September 2017, Daimler AG, the parent company of Mercedes-Benz, announced it would offer EV versions of every one of its models by 2022. It's developing a new sub-brand called Generation EQ that will introduce its contemporary EVs. The first one is likely to be a 402 horsepower SUV Coupe. This dual-motor EV is expected to have a range of up to 311 miles and compete with Tesla's Model X.[20]

Of concern to Dieter Zetsche, Daimler's CEO, is the distinct possibility that Mercedes profits will drop significantly as its EV volumes ramp up. That's because EVs aren't as profitable as their ICE counterparts. The main reason is the expense associated with the battery pack. Zetsche announced at Daimler's investment day that the company is working on cutting costs that will ultimately save 4 billion Euros annually by 2025.[21] It's not clear at this point whether Mercedes has decided to manufacture its own battery packs or purchase them from suppliers.

Nissan-Renault Alliance

The Nissan Motors LEAF was one of the first new generation EVs on the market when the Japanese carmaker first introduced it in December 2010. A compact, five-door hatchback EV, it originally came with a 24-kWh battery that gave the car an effective range of 80 to 90 miles. I leased a 2013 LEAF for three years. The car performed flawlessly and the only thing that needed replacement was the windshield wiper blades and the two front tires. Through the end of 2016, Nissan sold over 250,000 LEAFs worldwide. At the time, the LEAF was the world's top selling EV.[22]

Now the Renault-Nissan Alliance has introduced the second-generation, 2018 model year LEAF. The newest LEAF has a 40-kWh battery pack that Nissan expects will deliver an EPA-rated range of 150 miles. It also comes equipped with a larger 110-kW electric power plant, a big jump from the 80-kW motor in the original model. Nissan also indicated an even longer-range battery pack will be available in 2018. This will likely be a 60-kWh battery that should give the LEAF a range of 200 miles or more. This will allow it to compete with Tesla's Model 3 and the Chevy Bolt.[23]

The Alliance unveiled its long-term EV strategy in September 2017. The six-year plan, dubbed Alliance 2022, will launch 12 new all-electric EVs during the plan timeframe. According to the press release, "the vehicles will have new common electric vehicle platforms and components for multiple segments. Seventy percent of EV volumes will be based on shared platforms by 2022. EV range is expected to reach 372 miles (600 km) by 2022 and battery costs should decrease 30 percent from 2016 to 2022."[24] While Nissan delivered the first, widely adopted EV, it is currently playing catch-up to both Tesla and GM. But its third-generation LEAF with the 60-kWh battery will likely be the third low-cost EV to enter the US EV market.

Volvo

In July 2017, Volvo became the first traditional car maker to announce its future direction was headed away from ICE-equipped cars. The Swedish auto manufacturer boasted that its EV strategy was introducing "a new chapter in automotive history," after more than a 100-year domination by ICE vehicles. From 2019 forward, it plans to fit every new car it sells with an electric motor. Not every new car will be all-electric, however. It will offer full-on EVs, but it will also manufacture several variants of PHEVs. Traditional PHEVs will have smaller batteries than EV models. Mild hybrid versions will have a smaller motor and battery that together will be able to capture lost energy. In addition, they will supplement the ICE with short bursts of power. Volvo expects to introduce five all electric models between 2019 and 2021. Three will be Volvo-branded cars and two will be from its new Polestar premium brand. Volvo will produce EVs here in the United States at its new Charleston, South Carolina, factory. Volvo expects to begin producing vehicles from the Charleston plant in 2018. Like BMW, Volvo plans to build its EV variants on the same production lines where it builds ICE-equipped models.[25]

Volvo's announcement was a 180-degree turn for the carmaker. The company stated in its 2016 annual report that EV adoption projections were "extremely uncertain." It further said that "battery costs need to drop significantly." In between March 2017 when the report was issued and a mere four months later, Volvo apparently realized that EV ownership was rapidly increasing and that battery costs were indeed dropping at a rapid pace. Perhaps it saw the UBS study that predicted EV costs would reach parity with similarly equipped ICE vehicles in 2018. When asked about it, Volvo CEO Hakan Samuelsson said, "Things have changed and we can change our mind. Battery costs have come down, and there is some movement on the charging infrastructure." Volvo claims it will be "the second premium carmaker in the world that is becoming all electric."[26]

Volvo's decision to go "all-electric" was based primarily on the extremely tough CO_2 emissions regulations that affect its top three markets: the United States, Europe, and China. Europe is requiring automakers drop CO_2 emissions to an average of 95 grams per kilometer, equivalent to 57 miles per gallon (mpg) by 2021. China has a lower limit of 47 mpg by 2020, and the US mandate is currently 54.4 mpg by 2025.[27] Without electrification, it's practically impossible for any car manufacturer to meet those numbers. Because of the rapid decline of diesel-equipped vehicle sales in European markets, Volvo finds itself particularly exposed. Not too unlike our next manufacturer.

Volkswagen

Volkswagen's CEO, Matthias Müller, when asked about EVs at the Vienna Auto Show in early 2017, said, "the future of driving is electric." And there's no question that VW has plans to be part of it. The company announced that it was making a $10 billion investment to move its EV concept cars forward into production models. The investment would span a five-year timeframe. It represents a big step forward for the German automaker, which only spent about a third of that current investment on EVs in the past five years.[28] Apparently, Müller thought that the response to VW's $10 billion investment announcement was muted because in September 2017 Müller announced that VW would now spend approximately $84 billion to bring 300 EV models to the global market by 2030.[29] That's not a typo.

VW plans to spend part of that money on a new US manufacturing plant that would begin EV production by 2023, according to a plan it unveiled on November 30, 2017. The location will most likely be Chattanooga, Tennessee, where the company has an existing manufacturing location. The vehicles manufactured at the new plant would be destined for North American customers.[30]

Interestingly, the bulk of VW's new investment ($60 billion) would be invested in EV battery production in order to support VW's massive EV ambitions. VW sees the need for as many as 40 Tesla-sized gigafactories worldwide to support the transition to EV production. This announcement is the death blow to ICE vehicles, at least as far as VW is concerned.[31] VW's first EV will have an Audi badge. The Audi e-tron quattro, a high-end SUV, will be offered to the European market first. It will come with a 95 kWh battery pack capable of delivering 310 miles of range per charge. However, real-world range estimates are somewhat lower, at 275 miles.[32] Nonetheless, VW's first EV will provide some serious competition to Tesla's Model X SUV.

EV CHARGING: A CLASSIC CHICKEN-AND-EGG PROBLEM

Electric vehicle (EV) sales are starting to reach significant numbers. In 2017, worldwide EV sales hit 1,227,117 units. The forecast for 2018 is expected to increase 64 percent over 2017. EVs were still only 0.4 percent (one in 250) of all vehicles sold last year.[33] But get this: ***The sales growth rate of EVs is 20 times faster than that of the overall vehicle market.***[34]

One of the obstacles to the rapid adoption of EVs has been the lack of available charging stations. But that's changing much faster than most folks realize. Consumers aren't going to rush out and buy them if they don't have plenty of recharging stations available. The fear of being stuck somewhere is a real issue with lower-capacity batteries like Nissan's original LEAF battery, which was 24-kWh. That limited earlier models to a range of about 75 miles.[35] (Its current offering is a 30-kWh battery capable of a 107-mile range.[36]) On the flipside, who's going to spend lots of money to build EV chargers when few cars are going to use them? It's the classic chicken-and-egg problem.

One of the easiest ways to solve the charging anxiety problem is to make charging stations available at the workplace. Britain's National Grid plc does just that. National Grid is a gas and electric utility company focused on distribution and transmission of both gas and electricity in the UK and the United States. It installed six charging stations at its headquarters in the UK. Since their installation, the number of plug-in hybrid EVs has jumped from 177 to 375. National Grid fully supports EV adoption and it was both amazed and excited by the response.[37] Like many urban dwellers here in the United States, UK city folk may not have off-street parking.

So charging at work is the perfect alternative. If it's free, that's a nice workplace benefit. But even if EV owners have to pay a small fee, it's still a good deal. Unlike their ICE counterparts, EVs are very tech-savvy. Through a tablet or phone app, they report their charging status to their owners. This makes it easy to see when charging is complete. It's especially important to Tesla owners when on the road. When charging is complete at a Tesla Supercharger, car owners have a minute or two to unplug their car. Otherwise, Tesla will bill them $0.40 per minute for every minute their car remains connected to the charger. Another great benefit of a workplace charger is being able to preheat or cool your vehicle right before you leave to drive home. Using charger electricity to heat or cool the car saves on battery life. I'm sure National Grid (or their employees) have put together a charging coordination calendar or app to manage charging schedules. But company parking lots aren't the only places EV charging stations are popping up.

The European Union (EU) recently approved a new regulation regarding EV chargers. All new and renovated homes in EU member countries must have an EV charger installed by 2019. Talk about a tipping point. That is a HUGE deal when it comes to mass adoption of EVs. It's a huge advertisement for EV viability in homes of potential buyers. And it's cheaper to install them during construction or renovation.

EV adoption is like an avalanche. Once a few people start using EVs and talking about them to their neighbors, more and more people will see the advantages of them. Of course, the EU is a little more forward thinking when it comes to EVs and sustainability.

Here in the United States, California is generally at the forefront of sustainability and certainly EV adoption. The Golden State, with half of all EV sales, leads the United States. So it's no surprise that California is spending big bucks on EV charging infrastructure. I'm not talking about a few million dollars. The three largest utilities in California – Southern California Edison, Pacific Gas & Electric, and

San Diego Gas & Electric – have already spent $200 million on EV charging infrastructure. To this point, they've focused on apartment complexes, workplaces, and disadvantaged neighborhoods. But they're just getting started. Through 2022, according to documents they've filed with the California Public Utilities Commission, they want to spend $1 billion more. Moving forward, their focus would be on electric bus and truck chargers, fast-charge stations for EVs, and new incentives and rates for EV owners.[38]

How have carmakers themselves attempted to smooth the way for EV adoption, either by addressing the need for EV charging infrastructure or appealing to consumers' sustainability concerns? GM has the Chevy Bolt EV. The Bolt's range and price are comparable to the Tesla Model 3, and it beat the Model 3 to market by nearly a year. And BMW has its futuristic i3. It even has a small range-extending engine, although that defeats the whole purpose of buying an EV in the first place. And it doesn't matter anyway. Both models have failed to capture the public's imagination. Buyers aren't clamoring for either model. There's an overshadowing reason why. They are traditional carmakers with an EV model.

Tesla on the other hand is a sustainable energy company. All of its vehicles are EVs. Its owners can jump in their EVs and take a long road trip without getting range anxiety. They have access to Tesla's proprietary, global supercharger network. As of the beginning of 2017, Tesla had 830 supercharging sites in 31 countries. It operates 5,400 individual charging connectors at those stations. In June 2018, Tesla opened its 10,000th charging connector.[39] It also expects to expand its Destination Charging network – charging points at restaurants, hotels, and parking garages – from 9,000 to 15,000 connectors over the same timeframe.[40]

The company also has plans to make charging "ubiquitous in urban centers." This would be where Tesla customers who don't have off-street parking would still have access to reliable charging on a daily basis. In a Tesla blog post, the company stated, "To better serve the needs of owners who are traveling or those who don't have access to reliable home charging, we will continue to aggressively expand our public charging networks."[41] This will be particularly important as Tesla rolls out its much-anticipated Model 3 EV. It's a bit of a policy change for Tesla, who in the past has indicated that its Superchargers were for travelers and not for everyday charging.

What other charging options do EV owners have? Right now in the United States it's a hodge-podge network that's mostly at hotel parking garages. That's not exactly convenient for a cross-country jaunt. As of October 2017, US EV drivers had 50,991 public and private charging outlets at their disposal.[42] To put that number in perspective, the annual sales of EV chargers is expected to hit 500,000 annually by 2020. That will certainly be a huge shot in the arm for badly needed charging infrastructure for the rapidly growing EV fleet here in the United States.[43] Around the world, the growth in EV charging infrastructure is expected to hit a compound annual growth rate of 46.8 percent from 2017 through 2025.[44]

Nowhere is the growth in EV charging infrastructure more evident than in California. It is the undisputed leader in EV charging outlets with about 15,930 (not including home chargers).[45] That's not a surprise since California also has the lion's share of EVs sold to date in the United States. Between 2010 and October 2017, Californians have registered over 295,500 EVs.[46]

The EV charging industry is still evolving, especially here in the United States. Six of the top eight leaders in the sector (ABM, ChargePoint, Clean Fuel Connection, Envision Solar, EVgo, EV Connect, SemaConnect, and Volta) are headquartered in California. Just four of them (ChargePoint, EV Connect, EVgo, and SemaConnect) are collectively responsible for the operation of 49 percent of all of the private and public charging points in the United States. In addition, they operate 57 percent of California charging points.[47] There's no question that the Golden State is the gold standard for EV regulatory policies. Other states constantly look to California to model their own EV policies.

The amount of charging infrastructure required to support the rapid growth of EVs is far greater than what is currently available. By 2025, annual sales of EVs are expected to exceed 1.2 million vehicles, hitting over 7 percent of yearly sales by 2025. By that time, the number of EVs on the road is expected to reach 7 million cars and light trucks. In 2025, that will equate to approximately 3 percent of the 258 million vehicles registered in the United States. That number of EVs will require roughly 5 million charging ports.[48] That represents a significant EV charging infrastructure investment.

Charging infrastructure, referred to as a charging station or a charge point, comes in several different configurations. But it is generally differentiated and categorized by power level:

- **Level 1 (L1):** Chargers operating at the L1 level use 120-volt, alternating current (AC) power. Level 1 charging is accomplished by plugging a manufacturer-supplied cord into a standard wall electric outlet. It can take 12 hours or longer to charge a fully drained 50-mile battery. Level 1 chargers are able to charge at the rate of 4 miles of range per hour.
- **Level 2 (L2):** Chargers operating at the L2 level use 240-volt, AC power. Level 2 chargers are typically wall or pedestal mounted. Charging the same 50-mile battery takes approximately three to five hours. Level 2 chargers charge at the rate of 10 to 20 miles of range per hour.
- **DC Fast Charger (DCFC):** These chargers convert either 240-volt or 480-volt AC power to direct current (DC). This voltage is then supplied directly to the vehicle battery pack. DCFC chargers can charge at rates of 50 to 100 kWh or greater. An EV connected to a DCFC charger can generally replenish the entire battery capacity in 30 to 45 minutes. Not every EV can utilize DCFC chargers.[49]

The cost to install EV charging systems varies widely. A Level 1 charger is simply a heavy duty extension cord and can be had for less than $50, depending on length. A Level 2 charging system including installation generally costs about $1,500, depending on the amount of additional wiring, permits, and inspections required. A DCFC installation costs $10,000 or more, depending on the engineering, permits, and costs to get power to the site. Sites with multiple connection points can run $100,000 or more. Outside of the home, much of today's available charging infrastructure has been funded by the EV company (in the case of Tesla), or co-funded with a site host, like a hotel or restaurant or other commercial property owner. More than two million public and workplace charging ports will be required by 2025 in order to meet increasing EV adoption.[50]

In addition to workplace and commercial EV charging sites, electric utilities in a number of states are also involved in EV charging point development. Not surprisingly, California is at the forefront of this activity. The California Public Utilities Commission approved EV charging pilot projects for its regulated electric utilities that will add 12,500 additional EV charging points in the state by 2020. Besides California, electric utilities in Missouri, Georgia, Washington, and Kansas are all involved in providing a total of 1,300 new EV charging points in their respective states.[51]

In the mountainous West, Colorado governor Jared Polis and governors of six surrounding western states are planning a network of DCFC stations. The network is initially slated to cover over 5,000 miles. In Colorado, initial corridors targeted include Interstates 25, 70, and 76. The other states taking part in the initiative, called the Regional Electric Vehicle West plan, are Nevada, Utah, Idaho, Montana, New Mexico, and Wyoming. Over 20,000 EVs and plugin hybrids are already registered in the member states. Colorado has the fourth highest rate of drivers switching from ICE vehicles to EVs. Colorado offers new EV buyers a $5,000 state tax credit. Denver alone has plans to add over 300 DCFC stations in the next two years. That's triple the number currently available in the Mile High City.[52]

Even the federal government sees the need to increase the number of EV charging points. In November 2016, it announced the creation of a network of 55 routes in "alternative fuel corridors" covering 35 states. The network was created based on a request by the US Department of Transportation's Federal Highway Administration (FHWA). It sent requests in July 2016 to all US states asking them to identify important transportation corridors in their respective areas. As a result, the initial network was created, and it contains nearly 85,000 miles of highways (see Figure 9.2).[53] States will be eligible to request (on the fed's dime) new signage alerting drivers to the existence of the new refueling points.

While the FHWA's initial effort is a great first step, it's clear that many areas of the country are underserved. Looking at Figure 9.2, we can see that the West Coast and the Northeast and mid-Atlantic areas of the country have extensive networks. Oklahoma, Texas, and Illinois also have good coverage. But there are no routes passing through Montana, North and South Dakota, Wyoming, Arizona, New Mexico, Louisiana, Arkansas, Alabama, and Mississippi.

F I G U R E   **9.2**   **US ALTERNATIVE FUEL CORRIDOR MAP**

Source: hepgis.fhwa.dot.gov/fhwagis/ViewMap.aspx?map=Highway%2BInformation
%7CElectric%2BVehicle%2B%28EV%29. Accessed November 29, 2017.

In addition to the new refueling corridors, the federal government has an initiative that makes $4.5 billion in loan guarantees available in support of large-scale deployment of EV charging infrastructure. It's a superb opportunity for utilities to earn additional revenue while combating climate change. According to Chris Nelder at the Rocky Mountain Institute, utilities would end up with a more resilient grid, too. "If every light vehicle was an EV, total US electricity demand would increase about 25 percent. But it could be done without increasing peak generation and it could reduce the unit cost of electricity by eliminating the need to invest in peaking capacity."[54]

The US Department of Energy's office of Energy Efficiency and Renewable Energy maintains the Alternative Fuels Data Center. It maintains a running tally of all EV charging stations (excluding private and home stations) and the total number of charging points available in the United States. As of October 2018, there were 19,617 EV charging stations with 55,735 charging points in the United States.[55] For EV owners planning a trip, this interactive website is essential to help find EV charging stations along a proposed route.

The Alternative Fueling Station Locator has every station on a US map and includes an interactive map with detailed information on every charging location for EVs.[56]

The biggest initiative to establish a US EV charging network is coming from the private sector. As part of Volkswagen's court settlement for falsifying its diesel vehicle emissions data, it was directed to spend $2 billion to create a US EV charging infrastructure plan. In order to accomplish this, Volkswagen created a special subsidiary, Electrify America LLC. Over the next 10 years, Electrify America will invest $800 million in California's EV infrastructure and $1.2 billion in EV infrastructure in all other states. This $2 billion investment is by far the largest of its kind for EV infrastructure.

The first phase of investment called the Cycle 1 Investment Plan totals $200 million in California and $300 million throughout the rest of the country. As part of this cycle, Electrify America will construct more than 2,500 EV charging points at more than 450 EV charging stations. The charging stations will be the most powerful designed and deployed to date, capable of delivering 350 kW of charging power to EV batteries. This will add about 20 miles of range per minute to the EV, enabling even 300-mile battery packs to be recharged in 15 to 20 minutes.[57]

Currently, there are no vehicles on the road that can take advantage of a 350-kW fast-charging station. The higher currents require thicker cables that won't overheat. None of the automakers with EVs in the pipeline have indicated when they will be selling cars with battery packs designed to accept such rapid charging. However, both Electrify America and ChargePoint believe that vehicles able to utilize 350-kW chargers will be on America's roads by 2019.[58] Tesla, which has its own proprietary charging network, is modifying some of its Superchargers to be able to supply 145 kW to its battery packs. However, those have not yet been deployed.

Sites are expected to be located between 70 and 120 miles apart. Each station will have between 4 and 10 charging points, each with a DCFC. In addition, Electrify America will install more than 300 community-based charging stations outside of California. These will be in retail, workplaces, municipal lots and garages, and multifamily residential locations. These stations will be a mix of Level 2 and DCFC units. The metropolitan areas include Boston, Chicago, Denver,

Houston, Miami, New York City, Philadelphia, Portland (Oregon), Raleigh, Seattle, and Washington, DC.[59]

What does it cost to charge an EV? That depends on what EV you buy. Just like gasoline and diesel-powered cars, some EVs carry a higher efficiency rating than others. The typical gasoline-powered engine vehicle is able to convert 17 to 21 percent of the energy stored in the gasoline to power at the vehicle's wheels. EVs, on the other hand, are able to convert 59 to 62 percent of the electrical energy obtained from the grid to power at the EV's wheels.[60]

The average EV uses about 30 kWh of electricity to power the vehicle for 100 miles. The Nisan LEAF carries an EPA rating of exactly that: 30 kWh per 100 miles.[61] The Tesla Model S, however, carries an EPA rating anywhere from 32 to 35 kWh per 100 miles.[62] Not surprising, since the Model S is a much larger and heavier car. The most efficient EV for sale in the United States is the Chevrolet Bolt. It has an EPA rating of 28 kWh per 100 miles.

In 2016, the sales-weighted average fuel economy of all new cars and light trucks sold in the United States was 25.3 miles per gallon.[63] The average cost of a gallon of regular gasoline in the two-year period of 2016 and 2017 is $2.28 per gallon.[64] Let's assume the average person drives 15,000 miles per year. Their yearly cost for gasoline amounts to $1,351 per year.

Now let's look at what it costs to operate at a typical EV for a year. Since most of the electricity used in the United States is produced domestically, the cost remains relatively stable. The average cost of a kilowatt-hour of electricity is $0.12.[65] So that same person driving an average EV 15,000 miles annually pays $540 a year to charge it (15,000 miles/(100 miles/30kWh) × $0.12/kWh). While electric rates vary widely across the United States, they are far more stable than the price of gasoline over time. Gasoline and diesel are tied to the price of crude, and crude is subject to geopolitical events that regularly occur in the large oil producing countries in the Middle East.

So in order for an EV to cost as much to drive as an ICE-equipped vehicle, the price of electricity would have to rise to 2.5 times the current national average, or $0.31 per kWh. The average EV driver, therefore, saves about $810 per year in fuel costs alone. And that's assuming crude prices stay at current levels. I believe they're headed much higher. That makes the cost savings even more dramatic. With far fewer moving parts, EVs cost much less to maintain. Combine maintenance cost savings with fuel savings, and it's clear that EVs are a far less costly alternative to ICE vehicles. Most EV owners will find (like my wife and I did) that making one's home more energy efficient can completely eliminate transportation fuel costs. By replacing every single light bulb with an LED equivalent version, my wife and I save $840 annually in electricity. The bulbs pay for themselves in two to three years, and they last 20 years or more. It's a great way to save on electricity and drive as much as you did before. Other energy saving measures like programmable thermostats and newer energy efficient appliances can save even more on annual electric bills.

The amount of time saved by charging an EV at home and/or at work saves my wife a day and a half's worth of time annually by not having to stop at a gas station every week to pump gas. That's time you'll never get back if you have an ICE vehicle.

In the remainder of this chapter, I'll briefly discuss the major clean transport initiatives that governments around the world have announced. Let's start with China. It's the country with the largest auto market. Many are closely watching the Red Dragon.

THE CHINA FACTOR

There's no question that EV sales are really starting to take off. For instance, it took 17 months to go from one million EVs sold to two million. But it took just six months to go from the third million to the fourth million. And we should hit five million sold in March 2019.[66] The first time annual global EV sales eclipsed the one million mark[67] (see Figure 9.3) makes 2017 a notable year. Perhaps not too surprisingly, China registered more than half of those sales, and the European Union, another 24 percent. Moving forward, 42 percent of all EVs sold will go to China, 26 percent will head to Europe, and 25 percent will be in the United States.[68] The Chinese government is intently focused on increasing EV sales. Why? Most of the citizens in its large cities are choking on gasoline and diesel fumes from ICE-equipped vehicles. The Chinese are keen to crack down on all sources of pollution, and the transportation sector is a big one. Besides playing a role in curbing pollution, China wants to be the world's leading producer of EVs (just like it is for many other consumer-purchased items).

FIGURE 9.3   QUARTERLY GLOBAL EV SALES, 2015–2017

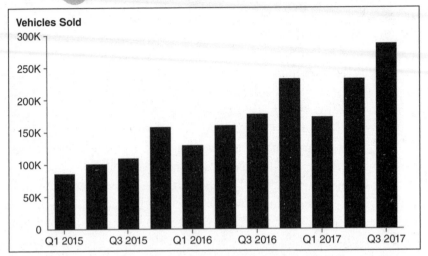

Data source: www.bloomberg.com/news/articles/2017–11–21/global-electric-car-sales-jump-63-percent-as-china-demand-surges and author. Accessed November 30, 2017.

Make no mistake, the EV market, while a small portion of overall sales today, is poised to become the dominant subsector of all light vehicle sales. Some industry forecasts predict that the EV market could surpass 60 million vehicles annually by 2040.[69] And Chinese automakers are the ones positioning themselves to meet that demand.

The sales of EVs in China are fueled by government incentives. Right now, central government subsidies can make an EV purchase there close to 40 percent less expensive than a comparable ICE-equipped vehicle.

In September 2017, China announced that all foreign automakers producing cars there must produce EVs by 2019. The government is expected to gradually raise quotas for EVs, PHEVs, and fuel-cell vehicles as it seeks to curb pollution and nudge carmakers toward the production of greener models. In the first year (2019) most Chinese domestic and foreign carmakers must make at least 10 percent EVs. That rises to 12 percent in 2020. The rule applies to car manufacturers that make or import more than 30,000 cars annually.[70] Both Ford and GM have already formed alliances with Chinese carmakers that will focus on the design and production of EVs.

Volvo is owned by Geely Auto, an automaker based in Hangzhou, China. Volvo announced it is ceasing production of ICE-equipped vehicles at the end of 2019.[71] It's already producing all-electric versions of London's black cabs.[72] In addition, it's rumored that Uber may be purchasing up to 24,000 all-electric Volvos.[73]

In October 2017, Great Wall Motors said it planned to form a joint venture with BMW, Germany's iconic brand. The joint venture plans to begin production on a brand new fleet of EVs for sale to Chinese buyers.[74]

It's clear that China is serious about transitioning away from fossil fuels and electrifying its transportation sector. It's the opportunity of the coming decade for the world's largest automakers. There's plenty of room for all of them in the nascent Chinese EV market.

When you talk about electric vehicles in China, the name BYD will quickly become part of the conversation. The BYD Company has a market cap of $7.7 billion. It's the world's largest manufacturer of EVs and electric buses. Electric buses? Yes, in 2016 China's cities bought 115,700 of them, followed by another 89,546 in 2017.[75] Shenzhen's bus fleet is 100 percent electric, with 16,359 on the road.[76] That's more buses than the total bus fleets of the top five North American cities.[77]

As of May 2018, China had 99% of the 385,000 electric buses operating in the world.[78] Right now, 20 percent of China's buses are electric. It wouldn't surprise me if they were all electric five years from now.

Globally, BYD is quickly expanding. On December 10, 2017, BYD announced it was setting up a factory in Morocco on a 125-acre site. The factory will build all-electric passenger cars, trucks, and buses. It will employ 2,500 people. The project is Africa's first EV manufacturing facility. Vehicles made there will be sold in Morocco and exported to other countries.[79]

In September 2008, legendary investor Warren Buffett bought a 10% stake in BYD.[80] Back then BYD was a little known cell phone battery maker. But BYD had a plan, and Buffett is a patient man. Well his patience is starting to pay off. His original $230 million stake is now worth about $756 million. But it's soon going to be worth a lot more. BYD is already China's largest manufacturer of passenger EVs and electric buses. But the company has even bigger plans. Here in the United States, BYD is manufacturing electric buses electric trucks at its Lancaster, California plant. The plant has the capacity to produce

1,500 buses per year. The factory has been expanded to meet increased demand and is now three times the size it was in 2015.[81]

In September 2017, the Chinese government said it wants to end the sale of ICE-powered vehicles.[82] It hasn't set a date yet. However, there's no question that China will want to be perceived as being behind European countries, so I wouldn't be surprised to see a date of 2030 or before.

EV INITIATIVES IN OTHER COUNTRIES

We've looked at China's EV plans. But other countries have even more aggressive goals to rid their skies from fossil fuel fumes. Let's take a look at some of them.

Norway has banned the sale of ICE-powered cars by 2025.[83] In addition, all heavy-duty vans, 50 percent of all new trucks, and 75 percent of new long-distance buses must be zero emission vehicles by 2030.[84] It's a surprising goal because one of Norway's main exports is crude oil. Even though it wants to rid its own skies of fossil fuel emissions, it seems to have no problem exporting carbon elsewhere. Why are EVs so popular in Norway? They have big government support. If you purchase an EV there, you don't have to pay the high sales taxes ICE-equipped vehicle purchasers do. EV owners can use bus lanes and they don't have to pay any tolls on the nation's toll-highways. Most parking lots and highways have EV chargers that are free to use. It's the equivalent of free gasoline. Some of the country's critics argue that its EV adoption policy is somewhat paradoxical. They suggest it should trim the supply of fossil fuels, not just the demand coming from its countrymen.

In what is already the second largest vehicle market, India has gone on record saying it plans to ban the sale of ICE vehicles by 2030. India's central government will finance the effort. Some outsiders doubt that India can accomplish such an aggressive goal in the next 11 years. But at least it *has* a goal.

France is also aiming to ditch ICE-equipped cars and light trucks by 2040, a little less ambitious than Norway's target. France made its announcement a day after Volvo announced it plans to phase out the internal combustion engine. Like Norway, France is serious about limiting climate change. In addition to the ICE ban, France stopped issuing new crude and natural gas exploration permits at the end of 2017. By 2022 it will cease using coal to produce electricity.[85] As an interim step, France expects to have 2.4 million EVs and PHEVs by 2023.[86]

Roughly 131 years after Karl Benz applied to patent a "vehicle powered by a gas engine" in Germany, the country plans to ban those very engines. It looks like Germany could ban the sale of new ICE vehicles by 2030. Even then, it may be difficult for the country to meet its 2050 climate targets.[87] Germany wasn't the first to consider banishing ICE vehicle sales, but it was the first country to make it a law. It's not a decision that the German government took lightly. After all, it's the world's fourth largest car manufacturer.

Shortly after France announced its ICE vehicle sales ban last year, Britain announced it would do the same and is also spending $4.06 billion to improve its air quality. Struggling with growing air pollution, the island nation announced the sale of new gas and diesel cars would end by 2040.[88] Like France, Britain is committed to the Paris Climate Agreement and the reduced levels of pollutants associated with it.

You can bet by the time this book is published, other countries will have enacted ICE-powered vehicle bans. It's one of the easiest ways to meet the Paris Climate Agreement targets.

NOTES

1. www.autocare.org/who-we-are/
2. en.wikipedia.org/wiki/Economy_of_the_United_States
3. lae.mit.edu/air-pollution-causes-200000-early-deaths-each-year-in-the-u-s/
4. www.who.int/mediacentre/news/releases/2014/air-pollution/en/
5. http://www.ev-volumes.com/news/global-plug-in-vehicle-sales-for-2017-final-results/
6. evannex.com/blogs/news/bloomberg-tesla-projected-to-win-the-us-electric-car-race
7. thinkprogress.org/electric-vehicle-sales-are-soaring-worldwide-5718b58441c7/#.7birvvmxb
8. www.autonews.com/article/20170807/OEM01/170809780/bmw-future-proof-ev-strategy
9. www.autonews.com/article/20170807/OEM01/170809780/bmw-future-proof-ev-strategy
10. www.thetruthaboutcars.com/2015/12/ford-motor-co-invests-4-5b-evs-century-henry-ford-gave-electric-cars/
11. www.thetruthaboutcars.com/2015/12/ford-motor-co-invests-4-5b-evs-century-henry-ford-gave-electric-cars/

12. www.wsj.com/articles/ford-to-spend-4-5-billion-in-electric-vehicle-development-1449785859
13. www.autonews.com/article/20170828/OEM04/170829799/ford-evs
14. https://insideevs.com/december-2017-plugin-electric-vehicle-sales-report-card/ and www.hybridcars.com/nissans-quarter-millionth-leaf-means-its-the-best-selling-plug-in-car-in-history/
15. www.hybridcars.com/2016-chevrolet-volt-rated-for-53-miles-electric-range/
16. www.hybridcars.com/first-chevy-bolt-evs-delivered-today/
17. https://insideevs.com/december-2017-plugin-electric-vehicle-sales-report-card/
18. www.hybridcars.com/first-chevy-bolt-evs-delivered-today/
19. www.forbes.com/sites/joannmuller/2017/10/02/gm-plots-all-electric-future-with-20-new-evs-and-fuel-cell-vehicles-coming-by-2023/#66d2b6f176ec
20. www.engadget.com/2016/09/29/mercedes-eq-electric-cars/ and www.engadget.com/2017/09/11/mercedes-benz-electric-versions-2022/
21. www.engadget.com/2017/09/11/mercedes-benz-electric-versions-2022/
22. nissannews.com/en-US/nissan/usa/channels/us-nissan-2017-ces/releases/press-kit-nissan-intelligent-mobility-at-ces
23. electrek.co/2017/09/05/nissan-leaf-2018-next-gen-3/
24. newsroom.nissan-europe.com/eu/en-gb/media/pressreleases/426204678/alliance-2022-new-plan-targets-annual-synergies-of-10-billion-and-forecasts-unit-sales-of-14-million?utm_campaign=NewsAlert_151190&utm_medium=Email&utm_source=newsroom.nissan-europe.com
25. www.autonews.com/article/20170710/OEM05/170719961/volvo-electric-gasoline-combusion
26. www.autonews.com/article/20170710/OEM05/170719961/volvo-electric-gasoline-combusion
27. www.autonews.com/article/20170710/OEM05/170719961/volvo-electric-gasoline-combusion
28. electrek.co/2017/04/28/vw-invesment-electric-vehicles/
29. electrek.co/2017/09/11/vw-massive-billion-investment-in-electric-cars-and-batteries/
30. fortune.com/2017/12/01/volkswagen-vw-manufacturing-electric-cars-united-states/
31. electrek.co/2017/09/11/vw-massive-billion-investment-in-electric-cars-and-batteries/
32. electrek.co/2017/04/24/audi-opens-reservations-all-electric-vehicle-e-tron-quattro/
33. http://www.ev-volumes.com/country/total-world-plug-in-vehicle-volumes/
34. www.ev-volumes.com/news/global-plug-in-sales-for-2016/
35. www.autoblog.com/green/
36. www.fueleconomy.gov/feg/Find.do?action=sbs&id=37066&id=37067&id=34918&id=34699
37. www.fleetnews.co.uk/news/fleet-industry-news/2017/03/23/national-grid-hq-chargepoint-usage-grows-by-334

38. www.greentechmedia.com/articles/read/california-utilities-seek-1b-to-build-out-electric-vehicle-infrastructure#gs.5puHjfY

39. https://cleantechnica.com/2018/06/12/tesla-opens-10000th-supercharger/

40. www.theverge.com/2017/4/24/15408040/tesla-supercharger-expansion-details-electric-car-charging-cities

41. www.tesla.com/blog/charging-our-priority

42. Calculations do not include residential outlets. Charger types included are AC Level 1, AC Level 2, and DC fast charging. U.S. Department of Energy, citing figures dated October 23, 2017 (www.afdc.energy.gov/fuels/stations_counts .html).

43. ENERGY STAR, "Market and Industry Scoping Report: Electric Vehicle Supply Equipment (EVSE)."

44. Grand View Research, Inc., "Electric Vehicle (EV) Charging Infrastructure Mark Analysis By Charger Type (Slow Charger, Fast Charger), By Connector (CHAdeMo, Combined Charging System), By Application, By Region, And Segment Forecasts, 2014–2025."

45. Calculations do not include residential outlets. Charger types included are AC Level 1, AC Level 2, and DC fast charging. U.S. Department of Energy, citing figures dated October 23, 2017 (www.afdc.energy.gov/fuels/stations_counts .html).

46. EV Hub, citing figures dated October 23, 2017 (app.powerbi.com/view?r= eyJrIjoiYWMwOGNiMmItMjBmYi00NmQ0LWFiYjYtMmU4YzA3ODBi Y2Q0IiwidCI6IjFiYjQ4ZGE0LTMxNDMtNDAzMS1iZGFlLWNjYzA0 MDc1MDhmZSIsImMiOjF9&pageName=ReportSection)

47. www.evassociation.org/uploads/5/8/0/5/58052251/evca_2017_state_of_the_ charge.pdf

48. www.edisonfoundation.net/iei/publications/Documents/IEI_EEI%20PEV %20Sales%20and%20Infrastructure%20thru%202025_FINAL%20%282 %29.pdf

49. www.edisonfoundation.net/iei/publications/Documents/IEI_EEI%20PEV %20Sales%20and%20Infrastructure%20thru%202025_FINAL%20%282 %29.pdf

50. www.edisonfoundation.net/iei/publications/Documents/IEI_EEI%20PEV %20Sales%20and%20Infrastructure%20thru%202025_FINAL%20%282 %29.pdf

51. www.edisonfoundation.net/iei/publications/Documents/IEI_EEI%20PEV %20Sales%20and%20Infrastructure%20thru%202025_FINAL%20%282 %29.pdf

52. www.denverpost.com/2017/10/04/western-governors-electric-vehicle-charging-network-spanning-seven-states/

53. www.utilitydive.com/news/dept-of-transportation-unveils-national-electric-vehicle-charging-network/429775/

54. www.utilitydive.com/news/white-house-plan-to-boost-ev-adoption-includes-45b-in-loan-guarantees/423174/

55. https://www.afdc.energy.gov/fuels/stations_counts.html
56. www.afdc.energy.gov/locator/stations/
57. www.electrifyamerica.com/our-plan
58. www.electrifyamerica.com/our-plan
59. www.electrifyamerica.com/our-plan
60. www.fueleconomy.gov/feg/evtech.shtml
61. pluginamerica.org/how-much-does-it-cost-charge-electric-car/
62. www.fueleconomy.gov/feg/bymodel/2017_Tesla_Model_S.shtml
63. pluginamerica.org/how-much-does-it-cost-charge-electric-car/
64. Data from www.eia.gov/dnav/pet/pet_pri_gnd_dcus_nus_a.htm with calculations by author.
65. pluginamerica.org/how-much-does-it-cost-charge-electric-car/
66. https://www.greentechmedia.com/articles/read/total-global-passenger-ev-sales-to-hit-4-million-this-week#gs.1xpSnT4
67. www.bloomberg.com/news/articles/2017-11-21/global-electric-car-sales-jump-63-percent-as-china-demand-surges
68. https://www.greentechmedia.com/articles/read/total-global-passenger-ev-sales-to-hit-4-million-this-week#gs.1xpSnT4
69. data.bloomberglp.com/bnef/sites/14/2017/07/BNEF_EVO_2017_ExecutiveSummary.pdf
70. www.wsj.com/articles/china-sets-new-deadline-for-electric-car-production-1506608295
71. www.autonews.com/article/20170828/OEM05/170829828/volvo-thinking-evs
72. europe.autonews.com/article/20170424/ANE/170429944/how-volvo-helped-to-electrify-the-london-black-cab
73. electrek.co/2017/11/20/uber-volvo-xc90/
74. www.barrons.com/articles/is-possible-bmw-great-wall-motor-jv-over-hyped-1508144245
75. https://www.google.com/url?sa=t&rct=j&q=&esrc=s&source=web&cd=2&ved=2ahUKEwilnoHmuITeAhVLneAKHePnDswQFjABegQIBhAE&url=https%3A%2F%2Fevobsession.com%2Fchina-100-electric-bus-sales-drop-to-89546-in-2017%2F&usg=AOvVaw0ygYngfN5mwbAyK-VTnbNG
76. https://www.citylab.com/transportation/2018/05/how-china-charged-into-the-electric-bus-revolution/559571/
77. www.bloomberg.com/view/articles/2017-12-08/china-goes-all-in-on-the-transit-revolution
78. https://www.citylab.com/transportation/2018/05/how-china-charged-into-the-electric-bus-revolution/559571/
79. northafricapost.com/21176-another-chinese-giant-sets-electric-transportation-eco-system-morocco.html
80. https://www.bloomberg.com/news/articles/2018-05-02/bulls-flee-buffett-s-china-investment-as-shares-lose-9-billn
81. cleantechnica.com/2017/10/07/byd-triples-the-size-of-lancaster-bus-factory/

82. https://www.bloomberg.com/news/articles/2017-09-10/china-s-fossil-fuel-deadline-shifts-focus-to-electric-car-race-j7fktx9z81
83. www.nytimes.com/2017/06/17/world/europe/norway-climate-oil.html
84. https://futurism.com/these-7-countries-want-to-say-goodbye-to-fossil-fuel-based-cars/
85. www.nytimes.com/2017/07/06/business/energy-environment/france-cars-ban-gas-diesel.html
86. https://futurism.com/these-7-countries-want-to-say-goodbye-to-fossil-fuel-based-cars/
87. https://money.cnn.com/2017/08/21/news/economy/germany-diesel-gas-cars-ban-angela-merkel/index.html
88. https://futurism.com/these-7-countries-want-to-say-goodbye-to-fossil-fuel-based-cars/

CHAPTER TEN

EVs and Stranded Oil (Peak Demand Is Here)

In the latter part of the nineteenth century, US crude oil production was just getting started. Initially, kerosene was considered the most useful product of crude refining. Gasoline was deemed useless, and was dumped in rivers or burned. At the start of the twentieth century, wood and coal were still the top energy fuels. Incredibly, they were responsible for over 90 percent of global energy consumed. But all that changed in 1910[1] when Henry Ford and others began mass-producing cars and light trucks with internal combustion engines (ICE) fueled by gasoline. Fast-forward to the early part of the twenty-first century, and we see that the interdependent relationship between ICE vehicles and crude oil, which transformed society, is starting to fray. It used to be that the growth of Western countries would move in parallel with their energy consumption. Not anymore. For the first time, we are seeing a decoupling of that phenomenon in some advanced countries.

In fact, there's going to be a lot of crude oil demand destruction coming in the next several years. That's going to completely disrupt the oil industry. We could see hundreds of companies filing for bankruptcy. And the Saudi Aramco initial public offering just might not happen . . . not now, not ever.

Think I'm kidding? Just look at what happened from 2015 to 2017 in the deep water drilling industry.

- **Atwood Oceanics, Inc.** (NYSE: ATW)   −81.98%
- **Seadrill Ltd** (NYSE: SDRL)   −98.85%
- **Transocean LTD** (NYSE: RIG)   −79.31%
- **Diamond Offshore Drilling Inc.** (NYSE: DO)   −75.89%

And the list goes on and on. Why are shares of these companies down so far? Simple. The demand for expensive oil has come and gone. I used to write about $100 (a barrel) oil returning as supply and demand rebalances. But I don't believe $100 oil is in the cards. Now or ever. Producers are becoming much more discriminatory when deciding which of their oil fields to develop. With electrification looming large, only the very productive and lowest-cost fields will make the grade. Producers just won't be competitive otherwise. Why are they worrying about this now? Because oil field development can cost billions of dollars on the front end. And that money must be invested 5 or even 10 years ahead of production, especially for a large field that needs pipeline infrastructure to connect to refineries and terminals. But the story gets even worse. Starting in the early part of the next decade, the world will gradually start using *less oil, not more.* And by 2040, we could see 20 million barrels per day of demand permanently disappear.[2] Figure 10.1 tells the story.[3]

The solid line up until now represents existing global demand for crude. The widely dispersed projections into the future assume a number of improvements. Let's start at the top and work our way down. The oil industry, including OPEC, believes the demand for oil will rise for decades to come with no letup in sight. The second prediction is from the International Energy Agency (IEA). It believes oil demand will slow, but still increase. The third line, "Efficiency," simply expects existing internal combustion engine (ICE) vehicles will get much more efficient. Not an unreasonable assumption. The fourth line, "Electric Vehicles," represents a seismic downward shift in the demand for oil. EV adoption is going to happen much faster than anyone realizes. The bottom line, "Fuel Switching," includes the effects of adding biofuels into our current fuel mix.

These changes are coming like a freight train. Think Fessler's Second Law of Technology: "When it comes to technology, changes happen

FIGURE **10.1**   **GLOBAL OIL DEMAND**

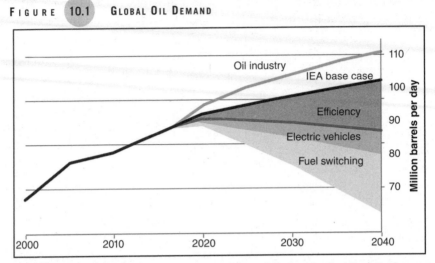

Data source: www.eia.gov/dnav/pet/pet_crd_crpdn_adc_mbblpd_a.htm (and the following paper) dieoff.org/page191.htm. Accessed October 27, 2017. Sketch provided by author.

much faster than anyone expects they will." That's because, as with any new and "better" technology, the time always comes when purchasing the old no longer makes any sense, economically or otherwise. Some examples include gasoline cars in the early twentieth century. They replaced horse and buggies as well as steam cars. In the 1970s, everyone had a color TV. Manufacturers soon stopped making black-and-white versions. Starting with the introduction of the iPhone in 2007, smartphones began to replace traditional cellphones. A decade later, nearly every new phone made and sold is a smartphone.

No one can predict these technological shifts. But think of Fessler's Third Law of Technology: "New technology is almost always disruptive and transformative." When these shifts do happen, they have the power to change the world. And now, EVs are poised to do that again. I believe the period from 2020 to 2030 will be the EV decade. Mass adoption happens when prices are no different than ICE-equipped vehicles. And even though I'll be in my late 80s, I might live long enough to see it.

In 2015, EV battery prices dropped more than 50 percent. They dropped another 16 percent in 2016 and will drop at least another 16 percent by the end of the decade.[4] At Tesla's shareholder meeting in June 2018, an interested shareholder asked if Tesla had broken the $100 per kWh price barrier. Here's what Elon Musk said in response: "We think at the cell level probably we can do better than $100/kWh maybe later this year [2018]...depending upon [stable] commodity prices...[W]ith further improvements to the cell chemistry, the production process, and more vertical integration on the cell side, for example, integrating the production of cathode and anode materials at the Gigafactory, and improved design of the module and pack, we think long-term we can get below $100/kWh at the pack level. Which is really the key figure of merit for a car. But long-term meaning definitely less than two years."[5]

That puts unsubsidized EVs on track to cost less than their ICE counterparts by 2020. By 2040, long-range EVs could easily cost less than $22,000 (in 2019 dollars) according to industry projections, and 35 percent of all cars sold globally will plug in.[6] Non-EV drivers have some common misconceptions about charging time, vehicle cost, speed, and range. Once they realize these are unfounded, they will quickly become adopters.

Amin Nasser is the CEO of Saudi Aramco. In July 2017, Nasser voiced his contrarian view regarding the peaking of crude demand: "Even when legacy fuels begin to lose market share, history tells us that absolute demand for them continues to rise."[7] As an example, he cited coal's absolute growth throughout the twentieth century even as its relative share of the global energy supply continued to decline. But most analysts take issue with Nasser's view. China and India constitute the major part of the developing world in the twenty-first century. Both have high ambitions regarding EV battery technology development, high-volume EV battery production, and the deployment of EVs. If they follow through on their plans, they won't be holding back EVs at all. In fact, they will be the driving force accelerating EV adoption ahead of the United States and Europe. China is already the largest EV market. Chinese authorities have plans to mandate that all taxis in major cities be either electric or natural gas-fueled. And the thought that the Chinese government is taking affirmative action to move its transportation system to alternative fuels is already sending chills down the back of the world's major oil producers. In China, companies like the BYD Company are already dominating EV production and lithium-ion EV battery manufacturing. There's no question Chinese companies will drive EV battery costs down in a similar fashion to the decreased cost of PV solar panels.

Let's get back to oil's coming demise. What a difference a decade makes. In 2008 I was writing about "peak oil." Back then the concern was that demand would outstrip supply. But the American shale oil revolution took care of those worries. Now, it looks like the opposite is slowly happening. And some Big Oil shareholders could be stuck with big losses. Once again, the relentless march of technology is to blame (happily).

Remember the old adage "the stone age didn't end because we ran out of stones." It describes in broad terms how technological advances can displace one technology (cars with internal combustion engines) or resource (gasoline and diesel) with another (EVs and renewable energy). I'll bet most car dealers would laugh if you tell them this is what's coming. In 2013, all of the top oil company CEOs would have scoffed at the idea as well. They aren't scoffing now.

"THE TIMES THEY ARE A-CHANGIN"

Every country in the world has embraced the Paris Climate Accord. Only the Trump administration doesn't think climate change is real. So Trump thumbed his nose (and the United States's) at the rest of the world. Fortunately, there are people out there with money, vision, and the drive to initiate change. People like Elon Musk. Someone had to go first when it comes to sustainable energy. And the climate change problem gets solved quite handily as well with EVs and renewable energy.

Big oil companies are faced with a gut-wrenching dilemma. Do they focus on maximizing shareholder returns from their existing legacy businesses? Or do they go all-in, making billion-dollar bets on renewables? All of them are wrestling with those questions.

The biggest energy companies in the world are quietly prepping for change. What is it? It's the biggest energy consumption shift since the Industrial Revolution. The demand for oil has relentlessly moved higher ever since Edwin Drake pounded a pipe into the ground in Titusville, Pennsylvania, back in 1859 and hit oil. But that's all coming to a screeching halt. What's changing?

Incredibly, Big Oil economists are now telling upper management that there's a paradigm shift coming in oil consumption. And we're starting to see the first signs that they are listening *and* changing their business models. It's not just EVs. New technology is vastly increasing fuel efficiency of vehicles with internal combustion engines (ICEs). That's gradually reducing the overall demand for oil. When new global carbon rules from the Paris Accord go into effect, engineers will continue to improve vehicles with ICEs to eke out additional increases in fuel efficiency. However, EVs will begin to rapidly see big gains in market share.

The growth of Western economies used to be directly coupled to their energy consumption. But that's not the case anymore. The disruption in several technologies is changing how much energy is used, and more importantly where it's coming from. Take battery technology. In the early twentieth century, EVs were commonplace. However, the battery technology of the time left them range-bound. Henry Ford's newly designed Model T with its ICE spelled the end of those early EVs. Now, we are seeing the reverse. Modern EVs have ranges of 200 to 300 miles. And that will most likely double in the next three to five years as battery energy densities improve.

The range argument is no longer an issue for an EV buyer. When EVs are no different in range or price from ICE vehicles, buyers will be compelled to buy EVs. The more EVs on the road, the less gasoline and diesel used. A decline in oil demand will send shockwaves through the industry. The big question isn't if, but *when*. For investors and oil companies alike, getting the timing correct will sort out winners and losers. Declining oil demand is quickly becoming an industry flashpoint and a focus for energy economists.

Bob Dudley, the CEO of British oil giant BP plc was asked during the 2017 St. Petersburg International Economic Forum when the peak demand in oil would occur. He answered, "June 2, 2042."[8] Everyone laughed. They knew it wasn't possible to know the answer down to the precise day. But he wasn't kidding. The 2017 edition of the BP Energy Outlook calls for the peak of global crude demand in two and a half decades, plus or minus a year.[9] Do the math.

While Dudley predicts the peak of demand will occur in 2042, he doesn't seem to be repositioning BP to deal with that inevitability. Quite the opposite. It's currently the fastest growing member of Big Oil. In 2017, it launched seven new oil and gas fields. That's more than in any other year in the company's history. It expects to launch an additional nine before 2020. In total, they will add about 800,000 barrels per day of oil and gas to BP's annual production. By the end of the decade, it will be pumping out four million barrels per day, the amount it was producing right before the *Deepwater Horizon* explosion in 2010.[10]

At turn of the twenty-first century, BP was on a path toward renewables. It even adopted a new sunburst logo, and laid out plans to invest $8 billion in renewables over a 10-year period. It was manufacturing solar panels in the United States, Spain, and Australia. And it erected wind farms in the Netherlands and the United States. What a difference twenty years makes. The company has since exited or scaled back its investments in renewable energy. It sold its solar panel business in 2011. Today, with its renewed focus on petroleum, BP just doesn't seem to be buying the idea that the demand for petroleum is at its peak.

BP isn't alone in its thought process. Chevron's CEO, John Watson, apparently also thinks there's no end in sight for oil. "There is no sign of peak demand right now. For the next 10 or 20 years, we expect to see oil demand growth." Watson retired in early 2018, so his successor, Michel K. Wirth, will be left holding the bag if he's wrong.

ExxonMobil Corporation is another one of the majors that believes the demand for oil will continue at least through 2040.[11] But it has invested in liquid natural gas assets as well as other natural gas properties. It believes demand for both is going to continue to increase and is using its investments as a hedge against any drop in the demand for crude. But in spite of Exxon's crude forecast, it boosted the number of EVs it expects in 2040 from 65 million to 100 million.[12]

Remember, Norway plans to ban all new ICE-powered vehicles in 2025. Statoil ASA is the Norwegian state oil company. So it's not too surprising that the country is rapidly refocusing on natural gas, solar, and wind. It believes EVs will account for 30 percent of all new car sales by 2030.[13]

The French oil giant, Total SA, isn't waiting around for a decline in the demand for oil. It's proactively moving to become a major electricity supplier. It even created a new "gas, renewables, and power" business segment. Total's CEO, Patrick Pouyanné, believes demand won't peak until sometime in the 2040s. It's one of the reasons Total has been investing heavily in solar power.[14]

Ben van Beurden, CEO of Royal Dutch Shell, believes the peak demand for oil could hit in the next 15 years. At the St. Petersburg forum, he said, "The energy transition is unstoppable."[15] Shell is rapidly diversifying into EVs and renewables. The company expects to spend $1 billion annually by 2020 on renewable energy initiatives to help tackle climate change issues. In October 2017, Shell purchased the biggest EV charging network in Europe. Dutch-based NewMotion manages more than 30,000 charging point for EVs in Western Europe. There are currently less than 100,000 public charging points in Western Europe, but Morgan Stanley believes one to three million will be needed by 2030.[16]

Other energy organizations and industry research think tanks have their own forecasts regarding the peak in demand for crude. The World Energy Council (WEC) published a report it created in collaboration with Accenture Strategy. If peak oil demand takes place in the 2030 timeframe, it believes the peak would be somewhere between 94 and 103 million barrels of oil per day. The WEC expects per capita energy demand to peak before 2030 because of "unprecedented efficiencies created by new technologies and more stringent energy policies."[17]

The IEA believes that the demand for crude is actually growing. It doesn't see global consumption peaking before 2040.[18] It says oil markets are tighter than they have been in some time. The IEA believes any drop in demand from the introduction of EVs will be offset by growth in the petrochemicals, road freight, and aviation sectors. It says, "The growth in those sectors together is greater than the growth in global oil demand."[19]

Some researchers believe the biggest blow to oil demand will be the increased fuel economy of new ICE-powered vehicles. Research firm FGE believes fuel economy gains will be responsible for slashing 11.3 million barrels per day from global demand by 2040. It says that will be more than double the 5.3 million barrel per day cut that will come from PHEVs and EVs.[20]

So I think we could see peak oil demand in the 2025 to 2030 timeframe. And based on Fessler's Third Law of Technology, "New technology is almost always disruptive and transformative," some Big Oil companies are going to be in a world of hurt. The Carbon Tracker Institute recently performed an analysis of the biggest publicly traded oil and gas companies. It provides a method of determining if their collective

crude supply is aligned with demand levels in a 2°C carbon budget scenario. It determined which of the top 69 oil and gas producers are at
risk – and by how much – through 2025. The results are stunning:

- About one-third of the potential capital expenditures (capex)
  through 2025 – $2.3 trillion – should *not* be spent in a 2°C carbon
  budget scenario.
- The level of individual company exposure varies from less than
  10 percent to more than 60 percent.
- About two-thirds of the surplus oil and gas production is under the
  control of private sector companies.[21]
- While state-owned oil companies also face an increased risk of
  stranded assets, it's the private sector, publicly listed companies
  that have the bulk of the exposure.

It's their responsibility to shareholders to provide them with regular
communications regarding new project development. Otherwise, it's
difficult for shareholders to test and understand how aligned the company is with a 2°C carbon budget scenario. As far as the oil majors go,
ExxonMobil Corporation is the most vulnerable to a 2°C carbon budget scenario. Half of its capital spending through 2025 is unnecessary
in the peak demand scenario. Royal Dutch Shell, Eni SpA (in Italy),
and Chevron could see 30 to 40 percent of their capital expenditure
dollars wasted. Apache Corporation and Southwestern Energy were at
the top of the list in the study with as much as 60 to 70 percent of their
exploration capex wasted in the peak demand scenario.[22] In fact, the
study concludes that there should be no capex spending growth beyond
2016 levels. Companies that plan to increase capex spending with rising
oil prices are throwing money away, according to the Carbon Tracker
Initiative study.

Remember, it was a 10 percent loss of market share (due to the
shutdown of old coal-fired power plants) that caused the collapse of the
coal mining industry in the United States. A similar retraction of market
share is coming in crude oil over the next five years. It's good news
for EVs, consumers who buy them, the health of inner-city residents,
and our planet. Not so good news for oil companies in denial of the
electrification of transportation.

That concludes the second section of the book. In the next section, I'll look at how energy storage is completely transforming our energy systems, from cars to home energy storage to utility-scale energy storage.

NOTES

1. cleantechnica.com/2016/03/30/electric-vehicles-will-deflate-demand-for-oil/
2. Data came from chart using math.
3. moneyweek.com/chart-of-the-week-a-seismic-shift-in-energy-markets/
4. electrek.co/2017/01/30/electric-vehicle-battery-cost-dropped-80-6-years-227kwh-tesla-190kwh/. Percentage drop calculated by author.
5. https://cleantechnica.com/2018/06/09/100-kwh-tesla-battery-cells-this-year-100-kwh-tesla-battery-packs-in-2020/
6. www.bloomberg.com/features/2016-ev-oil-crisis/
7. www.ft.com/content/37e6ad06-6576-11e7-8526-7b38dcaef614
8. www.bloomberg.com/news/articles/2017-07-11/remember-peak-oil-demand-may-top-out-before-supply-does
9. www.google.com/url?sa=t&rct=j&q=&esrc=s&source=web&cd=2&ved=0ahUKEwjUmr7t4O7XAhWoRt8KHfFgAG8QFggvMAE&url=https%3A%2F%2Fwww.bp.com%2Fcontent%2Fdam%2Fbp%2Fpdf%2Fenergy-economics%2Fenergy-outlook-2017%2Fbp-energy-outlook-2017.pdf&usg=AOvVaw21DbGtozGFH3PPlKqRNNvH
10. www.reuters.com/article/us-bp-ceo/bps-dudley-seen-reigning-for-years-to-restore-majors-might-idUSKBN19614U
11. https://oilprice.com/Energy/Oil-Prices/Are-Supermajors-Spooked-By-Peak-Oil-Demand.html
12. www.bloomberg.com/news/articles/2017-07-14/big-oil-just-woke-up-to-the-threat-of-rising-electric-car-demand
13. www.bloomberg.com/news/articles/2017-07-14/big-oil-just-woke-up-to-the-threat-of-rising-electric-car-demand
14. www.bloomberg.com/news/articles/2017-07-11/remember-peak-oil-demand-may-top-out-before-supply-does
15. www.bloomberg.com/news/articles/2017-07-11/remember-peak-oil-demand-may-top-out-before-supply-does
16. www.reuters.com/article/us-newmotion-m-a-shell/shell-buys-newmotion-charging-network-in-first-electric-vehicle-deal-idUSKBN1CH1QV
17. www.worldenergy.org/news-and-media/press-releases/world-energy-scenarios-2016-report-global-energy-demand-growth-set-to-fall/
18. www.reuters.com/article/us-oil-outlook-iea/oil-demand-wont-peak-before-2040-despite-paris-deal-iea-idUSKBN13B0OP

19. www.reuters.com/article/us-oil-outlook-iea/oil-demand-wont-peak-before-2040-despite-paris-deal-iea-idUSKBN13B0OP
20. www.reuters.com/article/us-oil-demand/fuel-economy-bigger-threat-to-gasoline-demand-than-electric-cars-fge-idUSKCN1BW2AI
21. 2degreeseparation.com/reports/2D-of-separation_PRI-CTI_Summary-report.pdf
22. https://oilprice.com/Energy/Energy-General/Oil-Industry-To-Waste-Trillions-As-Peak-Demand-Looms.html

Cheap Battery Storage: The Biggest Energy Disruptor

CHAPTER ELEVEN

The Rise of Energy Storage

The US electric grid is an engineering marvel. It starts with large, utility-owned generation facilities. Engineers designed these for one-way energy flows: from the generator to the end user. For over 100 years, this is how we've made and used electricity. It's fundamental to our lives. It's the power behind 40 percent of everything we do. It powers the $74 trillion global economy. The grid has largely operated without the ability to store the product it delivers. But that's all about to change. The current system is technologically inflexible. What's more, big utilities control most of it. And most of the time, their interests aren't aligned with their customers in mind, but rather their shareholders. Simple buy-sell transactions and electric market structures govern electricity sales between utilities and between a utility and the customer. It's all highly regulated by state public utility commissions (PUCs).

Today's energy supplies are rapidly changing. Wind and solar power are on the rise. In Chapter 4, I discussed how solar energy is making up an increasingly larger share of our energy supply. Now, energy users with solar panels can send their excess power to the grid, which means the number of energy suppliers overall to today's grid is rapidly increasing. This combination results in complex, two-way energy flows.

The grid is gradually becoming smarter. We're starting to see digital control of the electromechanical infrastructure. Behind-the-meter energy management systems are becoming more commonplace.

But the grid isn't just smarter. It's more resilient, more flexible, and more dynamic. Remember Fessler's First Law of Technology: "Technology marches on." Of course, all this added complexity comes at a price. Transactions and market structures are no longer simple. They are becoming complex, too. State PUCs are rewriting regulations around renewables. Net metering and distributed generation sources (microgrids, solar, and wind) are under review.

WHAT'S DRIVING THE TRANSFORMATION?

If I asked this question of the average electricity user, they would likely reply solar or wind energy. But that's not the case. It's energy storage. You see, we've never been able to store energy cheaply before. But now, changes in consumer behavior, technological advances, and market dynamics have enabled the installation of cost-effective energy storage systems throughout the electric grid. And energy storage is at the heart of the energy disruption triangle. As I acknowledge in this book's subtitle, energy storage is going to dramatically change how we generate, deliver, and use energy.

Being able to store electricity reduces its dependence on time. Remember, we use electricity as soon as utilities generate it. The ability to store it means we can "time-shift" it to a period of higher demand. We can then meet peak demand with batteries. Natural gas-fired peaker plants will quickly become a thing of the past.

Imagine a cloud drifting over a 100-megawatt (MW) solar field. A peaker plant wouldn't be able to respond fast enough to keep the supply from dropping. A drop in voltage (known as a brownout) occurs. Lights dim, and some equipment or appliances stop working. The solution is simple. A utility puts batteries near vulnerable installations like solar or wind farms. When sensors detect even a small drop in voltage, the batteries make up the difference. It's a great way to balance grid intermittency.

But it gets even better. A natural gas–fired peaker plant takes 12 to 18 months to build. A utility can order, build, and bring a battery storage facility online in less than 6 months. And utilities don't have any choice about storage. Distributed sources of generation – solar, wind, and others – are here to stay. Utilities must integrate storage into their grid to accommodate them. Estimates are that between 2017 and 2025, US customers will install 71.8 GW of distributed solar.[1] Smart inverters give utilities some control over distributed solar or wind. But for the ultimate flexibility, storage assets are the best choice. As long as it's on the grid, its placement can be anywhere.

For the energy cloud, storage isn't an option. It's a requirement.

THE ENERGY-STORAGE INFLECTION POINT

During the past decade, advances in energy storage technology have happened nearly on a daily basis. Battery costs have rapidly dropped, and manufacturing capacity has rapidly increased. But here's the most important thing: The value of stored energy – on the grid – is finally being recognized.

How fast is storage growing? In 2017, US installations grew by a blistering 284 percent. At the end of 2017, 922.8 MW of grid-connected storage existed in the United States.[2] In 2018, an additional 393 MW of energy storage is projected to be installed. By 2023, that number could balloon to 3,890 MW.[3] By 2022, continued advances in energy storage and utility grid planning could drive the installation of more than 40 GW of energy storage.[4] That will create billions of dollars of grid efficiencies and improve its overall performance.

TODAY'S DISRUPTED GRID

As I mentioned, our current grid is an engineering marvel. It was largely developed and expanded by the nation's electric utilities. The majority of electric consumers – homeowners and large and small businesses – depend on large, central generating stations and the one-way flow of electricity they produce. Every area of the country essentially gets the same services.

The huge power plants that are central to the operation of the twentieth-century grid took several years to plan and several more to build. They were constructed to last for 40 to 50 years or more. But once constructed, these plants have almost no ability to acclimate to changes in energy requirements. Remember, electricity is instantaneous, traveling at close to the speed of light to its destination. It's perishable, and must be used immediately after it's produced. That means the grid must have enough capacity to meet the highest expected (and mostly infrequent) peaks in customer demand. As virtually all customers are painfully aware, the existing grid is vulnerable to many types of disruptions, from storm-related damages to transformer failures, and everything in between.

Compare that to nearly every other critical network. Natural gas, transportation, data, and our food supply all have abundant sources and plenty of storage capacity. It's estimated that most of our critical networks have storage equal to or greater than 10 percent of our daily usage. Compare that to the US power grid, which has excess capacity equal to 20 minutes of our daily usage. Applying the 10 percent model means we should have nearly 2.5 hours' worth of storage. Clearly, our electric network is terribly underdeveloped when it comes to providing for today's increasing reliability requirements, changing generation mix, increased need for grid resilience, and the overall increasing electrification of our economy.

Increasing electrification is coming from data center build-out, communications, electrification of transportation, manufacturing and industry, and heating, ventilating, and air conditioning our buildings. Many of these networks are interconnected and interoperable. But they all are extremely reliant on a high-functioning electric grid. The demands of the twenty-first century have brought our electric grid into everyone's focus. Today's antiquated, centralized grid is responsible for expensive, and sometimes lengthy, disruptions to our lives and our economy.

All of the applications mentioned previously require consistency in electric supply. A very common type of grid issue is caused by variations in weather. Major heat waves can require a utility to ramp up a slow-moving thermal generating plant or a faster peaker plant. Peaking plants are used so infrequently that they generally have overall utilization rates as low as 5 to 7 percent[5] of their nameplate capacity. But utility customers pay for those assets nonetheless. They represent billions of dollars of excess, stranded generating capacity.

The grid must also be capable of handling near-instantaneous changes in demand. Even a minor variation in frequency can cause motors to slow or stop working. That can have disastrous effects on manufacturing production lines and the like. System-wide blackouts, like those sustained in Puerto Rico in 2017 after Hurricane Maria, can have devastating effects on the economy and its citizenry. Clearly, our electric grids have an unsustainable model with regards to the twenty-first-century electrified economy.

Once a utility brings a large, centralized, fossil fuel-powered generating plant online, it is reluctant to turn it off, even though it's easier to ramp it down than to ramp it up. Every time a thermal plant is cycled, it costs more and shortens its life. As a result, most of the North American grid is producing more power than is required on average. Utilities do this in order to be able to make sure they can meet *peak* demand, whenever it occurs. As additional solar resources are deployed on utility grids, midday power prices drop. This decreases baseload power plant value. In the evening, grids with a large component of wind generation can experience power generation that is over and above customer demands. This can create negative wholesale energy prices.

Unfortunately, untold thousands of megawatt-hours (MWh) of renewable energy never get used every year. This sustainable, emissions-free energy is simply wasted. The reason? Today's grid can't store and time-shift it to periods during the day when it can be used. Aligning our electricity supplies with demand can't be achieved on today's grid without the addition of energy storage. Today's grid is constantly straining to meet peak power demands. Those peaks are the biggest inefficiency when it comes to overall system planning. That's because every portion of the grid, including transmission lines, distribution lines, and substations, must be sized to meet *peak* demand, not the long-term average demand. Producing those 10 percent of additional peak demand hours is responsible for over 40 percent of overall energy costs.[6]

Adding energy storage to the grid is key in order to be able to address grid vulnerabilities. Those can come from cyber threats, physical disruptions, a supply/demand imbalance, or an extreme weather event. Every one of those increases the cost of electricity to the customer. Most small network disruptions can be fixed quickly, even without network storage. But every disruption costs money. In 2016 (the latest data available), the financial impact resulting from all grid disruptions was estimated to be a $150 billion hit to the US economy.[7] And that number just continues to go up every year.

GRID DISRUPTIONS: GETTING MORE EXPENSIVE EVERY DAY

The biggest driver increasing the cost of grid disruptions has to do with our increasing dependence on new technology that needs electricity. While electronics continue to shrink in size, they are growing in power. Our cellphones are now more powerful from a computing standpoint than a room-size computer was in the twentieth century. Cloud-based web servers are an increasingly large user of electricity. These server farms and data centers are part of today's communications, banking, and transportation networks. Because of their inextricable link to today's businesses, their uptime requirements are 100 percent. And that translates into a grid reliability of 100 percent. While a grid outage may have minimal effect on the average homeowner, the impact to the quality of life is very high. Food refrigeration, heating, cooling, and water pumps are key functions that need electricity. For businesses, grid outages are estimated to be as high as $20,000 per MWh.[8] For data centers and server farms, power loss costs can run as high as $9,000 per minute.[9] As individuals and businesses continue to transition applications and storage to the cloud, downtime costs are only going to get more expensive.

Credit card verification systems are particularly vulnerable to power outages. Without power, these massive computer networks are unable to verify consumer transactions at thousands of business point-of-sale terminals around the world. Buildings with highly automated lighting, intelligent HVAC systems, and high-speed video and data networks are also vulnerable in the event of a power outage. Highly automated warehouse distribution centers and highly automated industrial manufacturing plants depend on clean, reliable electricity to run robotic inventory and robot-heavy manufacturing lines. Diesel-belching buses, waste removal trucks, and other urban vehicles are rapidly becoming electrified. As a result, widespread outages will have increasingly deleterious effects on our transportation network.

There's no question that the intrinsic value of our grid and every kilowatt-hour it produces and delivers are becoming more valuable. As more and more technology-rich networks are added to our lives, the impact, frequency, and cost of grid disruptions continue to rise and gain notoriety. Our electric supply is more distributed, non-dispatchable, and bidirectional than ever before.

By 2050, over 3,500 terawatt-hours (TWh) of new grid capacity will be required to handle the electrification of building systems and the transportation network.[10] The United States currently uses about 4,200 TWh of electricity annually.[11] EVs are likely to be the biggest share of new grid load. And they will add a big dynamic component that will affect grid performance. As EVs move from the workplace to the home garage, so will the dynamic electric power component due to EV charging. By 2050, the EV landscape will be a lot different than it is today. Autonomous EVs will constitute an increasingly large portion of global transportation networks. Similar to Uber, but without drivers, this century's emerging electrified transportation network will create new disruptions and dynamic power demands. A reliable grid will be absolutely necessary in order for it to function.

The biggest challenge facing today's grid is variable power demand, system congestion, and fuel security (natural gas, coal, and processed uranium fuel rods). The fuel security risk associated with our current transportation network (gasoline and diesel supplies) will be gradually mitigated as the network is electrified. Adoption of electrified mass transit systems will further mitigate fuel security risks. Computer-controlled dispatch of autonomous vehicles will mitigate transportation delays and should have a leveling effect on overall grid load. The more predictable grid disruptions are, the easier the grid can be configured to react. The more flexible the grid is, the easier that unpredictable disruptions can be handled. There's no question that energy storage is the key grid element needed to handle disruptions, especially unpredictable ones. Otherwise, billions would need to be spent on costly additional generating capacity. And all it would do is sit idle most of the time. And unlike energy storage systems, adding inflexible legacy generating capacity makes no sense. It costs too much, and adding it to today's grid would make it far less reliable and reactive.

Without the flexibility that grid storage provides, today's grid will become increasingly less able to provide power to many of today's dynamic sectors. Today's grid must be able to instantly smooth out load curves, adapt to constantly changing grid power demands, reduce overall peak demands, and provide additional instantaneous capacity where and when it's needed. Energy storage is the key grid element that is essential to the electrification of transportation, manufacturing, data, buildings, and communications.

New electric grid disruptors are coming along at a furious rate. As our transportation network is electrified, the concentration of value is greater than ever before. And it means that even a small grid disruption may have a wide-ranging impact and affect millions. It's clear that the foundation of today's disruption-proof grid isn't a generating station, a transmission or distribution line, or a substation. It's energy storage. Modern energy storage systems can respond to real time fluctuations. No legacy coal-fired plant idling on standby is needed. Today's energy storage systems are truly utility-scale. They can sit on a transmission or distribution network and provide backup power for entire neighborhoods, towns, or even a small city. Utility-scale storage can easily mesh the needs of dynamic demands and intermittent generating resources like solar and wind. The entire resiliency of a grid is vastly improved by adding distributed energy storage. No more blackouts, brownouts, or voltage surges. The customer gets clean, smooth electric power, exactly what he's paying for. Time-shifting large quantities of electricity to ensure that both supply and demand are always matched is the beauty of distributed storage. Having storage distributed around the grid means it will be able to rapidly self-heal after a major, widespread outage.

Imagine for a moment we are traveling down the New York Thruway in the not-too-distant future. Most of the cars traveling along with us are EVs. A traffic jam occurs, delaying the 100,000 commuters that use the thruway every day. As a result, they arrive home an hour later than normal. The EV battery in each of their cars requires three times the electricity to charge as a typical home uses in one day. When all 100,000 EV owners plug in to charge, they are using as much power as 300,000 homes. The power company needs to provide enough generating capacity to meet the needs of those EV owners, whenever they decide to charge. The average coal-fired plant generates 500 MW of power and serves about 400,000 homes. So that means the power company has to have a 500-MW coal-fired plant at the ready to be able to handle a time-shift in power all because of a traffic jam. Distributed energy storage eliminates the need for the power plant altogether, by time-shifting the power necessary to charge the EVs to a later point in the day.

One of the great things about energy storage is that it scales easily. So far, the largest lithium-ion battery energy storage system is in South Australia. The 129-MWh system was installed by Tesla, Inc. The installation was needed to help South Australia avoid intermittent power supply issues that were commonplace in the region. South Australia had suffered a string of blackouts during 2016 and 2017. Tesla's battery storage system is part of a $390 million plan to increase South Australia's grid reliability.[12]

In the next chapter, I'll take a look at different battery storage technologies. Battery storage is growing rapidly, especially at the utility-scale level.

NOTES

1. naatbatt.org/energy-storage-enables-transformation/
2. https://www.energy-storage.news/news/us-has-gone-past-1gwh-of-installed-battery-capacity-with-help-from-utilitie
3. https://pv-magazine-usa.com/2018/09/05/us-triples-energy-storage-installations-residential-grows-10x-to-become-largest-sector/
4. http://energystorage.org/energy-storage/facts-figures
5. www.google.com/url?sa=t&rct=j&q=&esrc=s&source=web&cd=1&cad=rja&uact=8&ved=0ahUKEwiut4_sgbXYAhUHct8KHQ20ACgQFggpMAA&url=https%3A%2F%2Fwww.eia.gov%2Ftodayinenergy%2Fdetail.php%3Fid%3D14611&usg=AOvVaw19-NqFuWtIzPEe-Ws80Agt
6. www.mass.gov/service-details/peak-demand-reduction-grant-program
7. powerquality.eaton.com/blackouttracker/default.asp?act=smtc&id=&key=&Quest_user_id=&leadg_Q_QRequired=&site=&menu=&cx=3&x=18&y=12
8. Ibid.
9. technology.ihs.com/551385/the-cost-of-server-application-network-downtime-survey-calculator-2016
10. files.brattle.com/system/news/pdfs/000/001/174/original/electrification_whitepaper_final_single_pages.pdf?1485532518
11. www.eia.gov/electricity/monthly/epm_table_grapher.php?t=epmt_1_1
12. cleantechnica.com/2017/11/23/tesla-completes-worlds-largest-li-ion-battery-129-mwh-energy-storage-facility-south-australia-notfree/

CHAPTER TWELVE

Energy Storage Technologies

In this chapter, I'm going to cover the current technologies used for energy storage. There are plenty of ways to store electrical energy besides lithium-ion batteries. I'll cover the most common ones before we delve into battery storage. Energy storage is defined as capturing energy produced in the present and storing it for use at a later time. When we think of storing electricity, we generally think of a battery. But stored energy comes in other forms, too.

The most common form and vast majority of energy storage in use today is pumped hydroelectricity. It comes from hydroelectric dams and the reservoirs behind them. The water represents gravitational potential energy. When it is released and allowed to flow through turbines connected to generators, that kinetic energy is transformed into electrical energy. In a pumped hydroelectric facility, there are generally two reservoirs involved. During periods of low electric use, giant pumps move water from the lower reservoir to the upper one. Then during periods of high electric demand, water is released from the upper reservoir and it passes through turbines and generators to generate power during peak demand times. Pumped hydro storage is an example of a system that provides relatively short-term energy storage, usually several hours to a few days. Most pumped hydro systems range in efficiency from 70 to

85 percent.[1] But most hydroelectric generators can be dispatched in as little as 16 seconds.[2]

A conventional hydroelectric dam and lake like the Hoover Dam and Lake Meade can be considered a long-term energy storage system. Lake Meade is the largest reservoir in the United States when full. It has a total capacity of 28.5 million acre-feet of water. It sits on the border between Nevada and Arizona. After numerous upgrades, the power-house at the bottom of the dam is 2.08 gigawatts (GW). The problem with hydroelectric energy storage is simple. It's entirely dependent upon the weather. During wet years, the level of Lake Meade rises. But due to a prolonged drought from 2010 through July 2016, the power produced was significantly reduced and limited to periods of peak demand. If the water gets below 1,050 feet, Hoover Dam's generators will no longer be able to generate power.

Compressed air energy storage (CAES) also stores energy produced at one time for use at another. Compression is accomplished with electrically powered turbo compressors. When needed to produce power, the compressed air is used to drive an air engine connected to an electrical generator. The storage vessel for a CAES system can be very large. Above-ground tanks and below-ground aquifers and mined-out caverns are used.

Another method of storing energy, using air, is also being evaluated by a number of companies. Referred to as **liquid air** (really liquid nitrogen), the technique involves using electricity produced by wind farms in the middle of the night when demand is low to compress and cool nitrogen in the air down close to –200°C. When generation is needed, the liquid nitrogen is allowed to expand and warm up to drive a turbine and generator pair. It can then be recaptured to allow the cooling and liquefaction process to begin again. The system is only about 25 percent efficient by itself. But when the system is co-located with a conventional fossil fuel–fired or nuclear power station, ambient waste heat used by the system can boost the efficiency to about 70 percent. The nitrogen is liquefied using off-peak, low-cost power. Highview Power Storage, based in London, is evaluating the technology with a pilot plant it's built in the UK. If the technology proves viable, the UK. government could possibly fund a commercial-sized plant.[3]

A flywheel energy storage power system uses mechanical inertia to store energy. During off-peak hours, when excess electricity is available, an electric motor accelerates a very heavy rotating disc to a very high speed. When electric power is needed, the motor can quickly be reconfigured as a generator. Now the energy stored in the rotating disc as kinetic energy powers the generator as the disc slows down. The amount of power produced is based on the size and mass of the disc, the speed at which it rotates, and the friction in the system. Flywheels are placed in a vacuum and supported on magnetic bearings. These requirements mean flywheel energy storage systems are expensive. Typical applications that use flywheel storage need high bursts of power for very short durations. Electrical load leveling on railway power systems, as well as high-power laser systems, use flywheel energy storage systems. Another more critical application is in data centers. Here, the uninterruptable power supply (UPS) may use a flywheel energy storage system to provide bridging or ride-through power. That is the time it takes the UPS to switch from grid power to the alternate source power (usually a diesel-powered generator).

Power-to-gas energy storage is a less common, but potentially very viable energy storage technology. There are currently two methods being studied. The first uses electricity to split water molecules into hydrogen and oxygen. The resulting hydrogen can then be injected into the natural gas grid. A second method, while less efficient, may be even more attractive than the first. It converts carbon dioxide and water to methane using electrolysis and what's known as the Sabatier reaction, discovered by French chemist Paul Sabatier in the early part of the twentieth century. First, water is separated using electrolysis into hydrogen and oxygen, as in method one. Then, the hydrogen is combined with carbon dioxide at elevated temperatures (300–400°C) and pressures, and in the presence of nickel, which is used as a catalyst.

The result is water and methane. The methane can then be injected into the natural gas stream. Gaseous hydrogen can be stored in a conventional natural gas network. A good example is the German natural gas network, which can store 23,800 million cubic meters, the fourth-largest storage system in the world. That is enough to power the German electrical grid for about 80 days.[4] Another advantage of converting excess electricity to hydrogen or methane is that the transport of either substance through a natural gas network is done with far less loss (1.4 percent, plus or minus 0.5 percent[5]) than electricity through a power network (8–15 percent[6]).

Power-to-ammonia is another interesting energy storage technology that has the potential to be used for non-carbon, large-scale energy storage. During hours when there is a surplus, electricity can be converted into ammonia for use later as a fuel. Ammonia is produced using electrolysis to first split water molecules into hydrogen and oxygen. The hydrogen is then combined with nitrogen from the air under high pressure and temperature. This creates ammonia. It can be cryogenically cooled and stored in tanks, like with liquid propane. Ammonia is a great hydrogen storage and delivery vehicle. When ammonia is burned, as it would be in a fuel cell, it does not release CO_2, since it contains no carbon. The byproducts are water and nitrogen. Ammonia is also the basis for many chemicals, including fertilizer. The other big advantage of power-to-ammonia energy storage is that the infrastructure for the safe distribution, transport, and use of ammonia already exists in the United States and elsewhere.

Another interesting and relatively new method of storing electrical energy is in a superconducting coil. It is known as superconducting magnetic energy storage, or SMES for short. An SMES system is broken down into three parts:

1. A coil, made of superconducting wire
2. A cryogenic cooling system, or super refrigerator to cool the coil
3. A power conditioning system that includes inverters, rectifiers, and other control electronics

Because of the high cost of the superconducting wire and the energy to refrigerate the coil, most SMES systems are used for short-term energy storage requirements. The aim and end result is an improvement in power quality. An electrical coil can only store energy if the voltage flowing through it is DC, or direct current. In order for the coil's magnetic field to store energy, it must be cooled below its superconducting critical temperature. Today, there are practical limitations that keep SMES systems from being deployed on a wide scale. For instance, the coil loop size would need to be 100 miles in length, requiring a significant amount of land. In addition, superconducting wire only occurs at cryogenic temperatures. When and until room temperature superconducting materials are developed, the 100 miles of coil would need to be held in a vacuum container of liquid nitrogen. That's not at all practical or cost effective.

Thermal energy storage systems use molten salts to store thermal energy from the sun or energy that is produced from excess electricity generated from renewable sources. Giant concentrated solar power (CSP) systems use thousands of mirrors to focus the sun's rays on a tank of molten salt mounted on a solar tower. The heat stored in the molten salt in the tank can be run through a heat exchanger to create superheated steam. The steam is used to power a conventional steam turbine/generator. In this way, power can be generated during inclement weather or at night. With proper insulation the energy in the molten salt can be stored for a week.

One of the simplest ways to store energy uses something we're all very familiar with: gravity. Imagine a group of shuttle trains that are able to transport heavy masses between an upper and lower storage yard. When the grid has excess energy available, shuttle trains draw excess energy and use it to transport themselves to a higher altitude storage yard. When the grid energy demand reaches peak levels, the shuttle trains move to a lower storage yard. Along the way, shuttle motors are reconfigured as generators and pump power generated by regenerative braking back into the grid. A company in Nevada is attempting to raise funds to build a 50-MW grid-scale energy storage facility. Advanced Rail Energy Storage (ARES) envisions 12.5 MWh worth of storage to help balance intermittent renewable sources like wind and solar.[7]

Most of the energy storage systems discussed previously have cost or size limitations or both. This restricts their use to a few specialized applications and locations. But battery storage is compact, scalable, and increasingly less expensive. The current rechargeable battery technology of choice is lithium-ion. These batteries are in use wherever rechargeable power is needed. Laptop computers, e-readers, tablets, mobile phones, and now EVs and power storage applications are all using some variation of lithium-ion chemistry in their batteries. I expect that will remain the case for the foreseeable future. High-speed, automated manufacturing continues to drive lithium-ion battery costs down. That will only speed up adoption and deployment of battery storage applications.

Prior to its use in battery applications, lithium was relatively unknown. Lithium is the lightest of any metal. Back in 1800, Brazilian naturalist José Bonifácio de Andrada e Silva was exploring Utö Island off the coast of Sweden. He discovered a whitish, gray mineral now called petalite. A couple of decades later in 1817, a Swedish chemist by the name of Johan August Arfwedson (1792–1841) noticed that petalite contained an element that wasn't known by the scientific community.[8] While he couldn't completely isolate the element, Arfwedson named it lithium, which means "stone" in Greek. He later demonstrated that lithium was also present in two other minerals, lepidolite and spodumene.

Lithium wasn't completely isolated until William Thomas Brande and Sir Humphrey Davy did so in 1821. They started with lithium oxide and used electrolysis. Lithium production in commercial quantities began by Metallgesellschaft AG in 1923 in Germany. Its chemists also used electrolysis, but they started with a molten mixture of potassium chloride and lithium chloride.[9] Lithium's first major application was in high-temperature grease for aircraft engines during World War II. Lithium grease has a much higher melting point than normal grease. Nuclear fusion weapons produced during the Cold War dramatically increased the demand for lithium. It was used as a form of fuel inside of hydrogen bombs.

Between the 1950s and the mid-1980s, the United States became the largest producer of lithium. Another use for lithium includes decreasing the melting temperature of glass. This was the dominant use of lithium until the mid-1990s. Once lithium-ion batteries became popular for portable devices, the demand for lithium began to increase. By 2007, lithium-ion batteries became the largest user of lithium.[10] As you can see from Figure 12.1, the demand for lithium is starting to skyrocket. This is primarily due to the demand from lithium-ion EV batteries and energy storage applications.

Lithium hydroxide is one form of lithium used to produce the part of the battery called the cathode. Lithium carbonate is another. Here's how lithium use breaks down, according to the USGS: batteries, 7 percent; ceramics and glass, 38 percent; lubricants, 11 percent; synthetic rubber and pharmaceuticals, 13 percent; chemical manufacturing, 13 percent; miscellaneous chemicals, 12 percent; air treatment, 4 percent; and all other uses, 2 percent.[11] But lithium isn't the only element that is heavily used in lithium-ion cells. Let's take a little deeper look at the battery chemistry that is in use in today's EVs and storage applications.

Prior to the current ramp-up in EVs and battery storage, lithium and the other main battery component, cobalt, were relatively obscure

FIGURE   12.1   LITHIUM PRICES

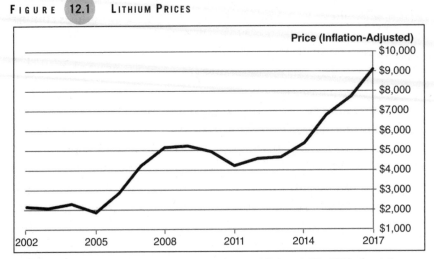

Data source: www.metalary.com/lithium-price/. Accessed February 27, 2018. Graph by author.

elements used in small quantities. With the advent of the lithium-ion cell, both have been thrust into the limelight.

Around the world, there are currently 26 battery gigafactories under construction, in use, or set to be ready by 2021. These are not unlike the one Elon Musk continues to build in Nevada for his Tesla cars and energy storage units. Most of these gigafactories have a cell manufacturing capacity of 1 GWh or more per year. Perhaps not too surprisingly, China is shaping up to be the dominant lithium-ion EV battery maker. Right now, it looks like China will have 49 percent (169 GWh) of worldwide cell manufacturing. The European Union will have 23 percent (78.5 GWh) and the United States should have 15 percent (53 GWh) of worldwide capacity. Tesla believes it will eventually be able to produce 150 GWh worth of cells from its Nevada plant. The plant is nowhere near its final size, and Tesla had planned to expand it between now and 2021.[12] I expect to see numerous announcements for building new gigafactories in 2018.

It's clear that the market is underestimating the rate of EV adoption, and the coming lithium commodity supercycle. Each kWh of storage in an EV battery uses about 1 kilogram (2.2 pounds) of **lithium carbonate equivalent (LCE)**. That means the average 75 kWh EV battery pack uses 165 pounds of LCE. Prices for LCE continue to increase, and are currently about $12,000 per ton. With additional supplies coming online in 2019, we could see prices of $9,000 per ton. I don't see that as a problem for producers, most of whom can make LCE for $3,000 per ton.[13] With 2018 being the assumed EV tipping point, I think we'll see demand for LCE remaining strong.

In 2017, lithium production totaled 43,000 metric tons. That was a 13.1 percent jump from 2016's production of 38,000 tons. If EV production hits 10 million by 2025, as the International Energy Agency predicts, then lithium production alone would have to hit 80,000 tons a year just to meet EV battery demand. Consumer electronic demand would need another 7,200 tons annually. Energy storage, another 6,400 tons.[14] By 2020, lithium-ion EV batteries will consume 75 percent of worldwide lithium demand. That's not surprising when you consider the huge growth ahead for EV batteries. Based on the above numbers, we're looking at a compound annual growth rate of 29.6 percent for overall lithium demand through 2020. That's a lot of future lithium demand. Musk says he believes 200 gigafactories will be needed to totally transition away from gasoline and diesel-powered vehicles to all-electric ones.[15] Musk also believes that mass production will reduce the cost of EV batteries by more than 30 percent.

So what's inside the current EV lithium-ion battery? If we're talking about Tesla, it's the 18650 cell, named after its dimensions in millimeters. Tesla's P85D (85 kWh) battery pack consists of 16 battery modules each with 444 of the 18650 cells. That's 7,104 cells. Why does Tesla use such small cells? The answer is: These cells have an extremely high energy density. They have been in use for years and their charge/discharge characteristics are well known. In addition, they have no memory. That means they don't have to be periodically completely discharged.

So what's inside an 18650 cell? Each cell is a two ampere-hour battery. It contains lithium, graphite, and one other element. This element is even scarcer and costs far more than lithium. I'm talking about cobalt. Its prices have soared over the past several years. Since hitting a low on February 1, 2016, cobalt prices have increased 263 percent.[16] Let's look into cobalt a little further.

Because of its name, the average person thinks that lithium-ion batteries contain mostly lithium. That's not true. Lithium-ion batteries contain about 5 percent lithium. Most lithium-ion cells contain anywhere from 15 to 33 percent cobalt. The batteries really should be called cobalt-nickel batteries. Cobalt could be in short supply as well, and as early as 2018. Tesla has forecast that it will produce 35 GWh worth of batteries in 2018. That's equal to the entire global production in 2013. That means one factory (one of Tesla's gigafactories) will produce 100 percent more than all the battery factories *combined* did in 2013.

Each 18650 cell in a Tesla battery pack has three major parts. The anode is made from graphite. The second part of the battery is an electrolytic solution containing lithium salts. The third part of the battery is the cathode. It contains a number of different chemicals, but most designs contain some cobalt. Tesla battery cells contain anywhere from 15 to 33.3 percent cobalt. (Apple iPhone batteries contain 100 percent cobalt in their cathodes.) Both lithium and cobalt are critical for EV battery production. The problem is, EVs are about to take off like wildfire. Much faster than any of the industry analysts are predicting.

The cost of lithium and cobalt will be the two main drivers of EV battery costs. Most of the world's lithium is produced from brines that come from two of the countries that make up the lithium triangle: Argentina and Chile. Bolivia has huge deposits of lithium, but it is just starting to allow the Chinese to develop them.

The world's supply of cobalt is a completely different story. The main supplier has been the Democratic Republic of the Congo (DRC). It's by far the largest source of cobalt, producing 65 percent of the world's supply.[17] The problem is the DRC has been accused of using child labor in its cobalt mines. As a result, most EV companies are shunning cobalt coming from DRC mines. Besides the DRC, there is no other large cobalt producer. China, Canada, Russia, Australia, and Zambia each produce less than 10 percent of the world's cobalt. Each is trying to challenge the DRC's dominance as a cobalt supplier.[18]

Goldman Sachs believes the cobalt market could mushroom to $244 billion by 2025.[19] They may be on to something. Based on the coming demand from EVs, lithium and cobalt demand is expected to rise exponentially. See Figure 12.2.

FIGURE **12.2**   COBALT DEMAND FROM LITHIUM-ION BATTERIES

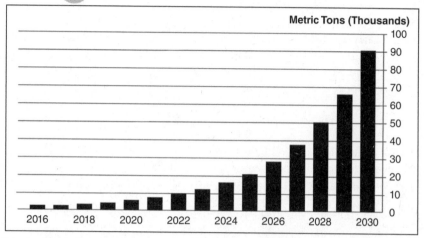

Data source: www.bloomberg.com/news/articles/2017-06-08/cobalt-upstarts-eye-glencore-s-turf-for-244-billion-ev-spoils. Graph by author.

In 2016, cobalt supply was about 100,000 metric tons. However, demand was rising and it opened a 1,500-ton deficit. According to the CRU Group, that deficit could triple this year. By 2020, the cobalt supply deficit could reach 5,340 tons.[20]

It is clear that by 2030 or so, most of the new vehicles produced will either be full electric or some form of electric hybrid. That means just about every model will have a battery pack on board. We've looked at the current state of lithium-ion batteries. Lithium-ion chemistry will be the dominant EV battery chemistry for at least the next decade. There are dozens of new battery chemistries under investigation by various university laboratories around the world. Listing them all here is beyond the scope of this book.

In the next chapter, I'm going to take a look at why cheap energy storage matters, since it's relatively new. What does it mean to be able to store energy? I've explored the advantages for the transportation sector. EVs are now more than just a flash in the pan. They are quickly replacing internal combustion engine-powered vehicles. But what are the advantages and implications for energy storage when we're talking about homes, businesses, and utilities? Let's take a look.

NOTES

1. www.electricitystorage.org/technology/storage_technologies/pumped_hydro
2. www.fhc.co.uk/dinorwig.htm
3. www.technologyreview.com/s/514936/liquefied-air-could-power-cars-and-store-energy-from-sun-and-wind/
4. www.germanenergyblog.de/?p=16962
5. www.sourcewatch.org/index.php/Natural_gas_transmission_leakage_rates
6. schneider-electric.com/energy-management-energy-efficiency/2013/03/25/how-big-are-power-line-losses/
7. www.aresnorthamerica.com/about-ares-north-america
8. www.webelements.com/lithium/history.html
9. www.webelements.com/lithium/history.html
10. minerals.usgs.gov/minerals/pubs/commodity/lithium/450494.pdf
11. Ibid.
12. benchmarkminerals.com/where-is-new-lithium-ion-battery-capacity-located/
13. oilandgas-investments.com/2017/top-stories/lithium-prices-to-stay-high-to-2024-ubs/
14. closeloop.fi/wp-content/uploads/2017/05/Li-raw-materials-20170517.pdf
15. www.just-auto.com/electric-drive-technology/US-Musk-sees-hundreds-of-gigafactories-to-meet-demand_n146111.aspx
16. www.infomine.com/ChartsAndData/ChartBuilder.aspx?z=f&gf=110572.USD.lb&dr=5y&cd=1
17. www.bloomberg.com/news/articles/2017-06-08/cobalt-upstarts-eye-glencores-turf-for-244-billion-ev-spoils
18. www.bloomberg.com/news/articles/2017-06-08/cobalt-upstarts-eye-glencores-turf-for-244-billion-ev-spoils
19. www.bloomberg.com/news/articles/2017-06-08/cobalt-upstarts-eye-glencores-turf-for-244-billion-ev-spo
20. www.bloomberg.com/news/articles/2017-06-08/cobalt-upstarts-eye-glencores-turf-for-244-billion-ev-spoils

CHAPTER THIRTEEN

Why Cheap Energy Storage Matters

Energy storage, cheap or otherwise, is not something we've ever had before. Electricity is used as soon as it is produced. Being able to store it cheaply for use at a later time has profound implications for homes, businesses, utilities, and the transportation sector. In this chapter, we'll look at how energy storage will effect each of the above.

My second law of technology states, "When it comes to technology, changes happen much faster than anyone expects they will." That's certainly been the case with the introduction of energy storage. The reason it's happening so fast is the plummeting price of lithium-ion batteries. That's not a recent phenomenon, either. The price of lithium-ion batteries has been dropping since the early 1990s and energy density has been on the rise. Take a look at Figure 13.1.

The data for Figure 13.1 comes from three different sources. It depicts lithium-ion pricing and battery-energy density. Notice that lithium-ion prices fell from $3.20 per watt-hour to $0.136 per watt-hour over 27 years. It's clear that battery cost improvements haven't stood still. On the contrary: They have continued to drop. The improvements in lithium-ion batteries are not unlike what occurred with solar photovoltaic.

FIGURE 13.1 LITHIUM-ION PRICING AND ENERGY DENSITY

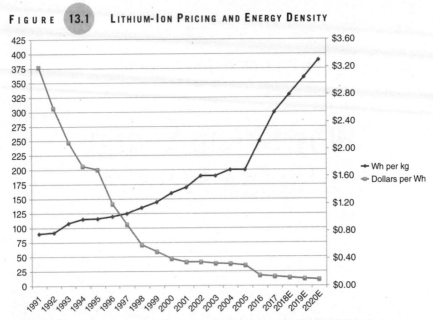

Data sources: dukespace.lib.duke.edu/dspace/bitstream/handle/10161/1007/Li-Ion
%20Battery%20Costs%20-%20Anderson%20-%20MP%20Final.pdf?sequence=1 and
rael.berkeley.edu/wp-content/uploads/2017/07/Kittner-Lill-Kammen-EnergyStorage
DeploymentandInnovation-NatureEnergy-2017.pdf and www.teslarati.com/tesla-partner-
panasonic-20–30-percent-energy-density-increase/. Accessed April 28, 2017. Graph by
author.

We can think of it as an experience curve. It's similar to Moore's law in the semiconductor world. In a general sense, an experience curve means that as any industry ramps up production of its goods or services, prices inevitably drop. With lithium-ion batteries, that's certainly been the case. The energy density of lithium-ion batteries has gone from 90 watt-hours per kilogram to 300 watt-hours per kilogram today. And even more improvements are expected over the next few years. Panasonic believes that lithium-ion energy density can increase by another 20 to 30 percent using existing battery technology.[1]

GRID STORAGE IS GROWING LIKE WEEDS

The point of revisiting lithium-ion battery cost and energy density is this: cheap lithium-ion batteries, while needed for the electrification of our transportation networks, are also crucial for making the small- and large-format battery storage systems necessary for home, commercial, and utility grid storage applications. That's why energy storage is starting to be deployed at the grid scale level today. Continued deployment drives demand and that drives prices down even further. And that will create even more applications for energy storage.

In 2017, the additional cumulative global energy storage deployed was 1.4 GW. Australia added 246 MW and that represented a tripling of its residential storage. The United States added just over 200 MW. When it went into service in November 2017, Australia's big South Australia storage project was the largest in the world. The 100 MW, 129 MWh energy storage system supports a wind farm run by Neoen of France. The storage project was designed and built by Tesla. It worked so well that it generated nearly AUD $1 million in revenues in the first few days of operation.[2] The battery is used to trade power on the wholesale market and also to stabilize the grid. Tesla's massive battery has performed so well that the company has received an order for another one from Neoen. The second battery is a less powerful system (20 MW) than the first one, but will be used in a similar fashion. It will be a part of a 204 MW wind farm located in Western Victoria.[3]

Tesla believes that these projects are just the tip of the energy storage iceberg. It believes that energy storage could experience "significant growth." In 2018, Tesla has a goal of tripling energy storage revenues. Even though Tesla is rapidly increasing production at its Nevada battery Gigafactory, it can't keep up with demand for its energy storage products. It deployed more residential Powerwall systems in Q1 2018 than in any previous quarter. Even so, a backlog of orders for the units continues to increase. Its energy storage revenues increased by 92 percent to $196 million in Q1 2018 over Q1 2017.[4]

Tesla's big battery in South Australia is officially known as the Hornsdale Power Reserve (HPR). That's because it's located close to the Hornsdale Wind Farm, also owned by Neoen. It has been garnering lots of industry and media attention, and for good reason. The HPR is having a huge effect on the electricity market in Australia. On Thursday, December 14, 2017, at 1:59 a.m., one of the largest coal-fired power plants in Australia, the Loy Yang A 3, tripped offline without warning. The trip created a sudden loss of 560 MW of power and caused the frequency, which is nominally 50 Hertz (Hz) to drop below 49.8 Hz. What happened next was astounding.

The HPR, located over 600 miles from the Loy Yang A power plant, sensed the drop and injected 7.3 MW into the electric grid. It responded four seconds ahead of another generator that was contracted by the Australian Energy Market Operator (AEMO) to provide frequency control to the grid. The Tesla energy storage system actually responded in a few milliseconds, far faster than AEMO equipment can measure. The contracted backup plant eventually responded, and added enough power to take the frequency back to its nominal level of 50 Hz. But by that time, the Tesla backup system was just resting.[5] It's clear from the HPR performance that even natural gas peaker plants are going to be replaced by battery storage systems. Today, nothing can respond faster to a grid demand for more power or a drop in frequency than a battery backup energy storage system.

The HPR may be just a fraction of the size of some new energy projects Tesla is working on. Here's what Musk had to say when asked about the performance of the South Australia system and regarding new projects: "I think it had quite a profound effect. South Australia took a chance on doing the world's biggest battery, and it's worked out really well. If you read the articles, it worked out far beyond their expectations because the battery is able to respond at the millisecond level – far faster than any hydrocarbon plant. So, its grid stabilization was much greater actually than even a gas turbine plant, which normally responds quite fast. The utilities that we've worked with thus far have really loved the battery pack and I feel confident that we'll be able to announce a deal at the gigawatt-hour (GWh) scale within a matter of months."[6]

A battery storage system of GWh magnitude would be several times larger than even the largest announced to date. Only two utilities have requested bids on a storage project that is even close to the size Musk is hinting about. One is Xcel Energy's plan for an energy storage system in Colorado. Xcel confirmed that Tesla responded to its request for proposal.[7] If Tesla's design wins, the storage system would likely be three times the size of the one in South Australia. The second large system is for Pacific Gas & Electric. The initial size would be a 730 MWh battery capable of discharging over four hours. The utility has the option to increase the discharge time to six hours and the size to 1.1 GWh.[8]

It's becoming clear that energy storage, when it's paired with solar or wind power or just standalone, is not just cost-competitive with natural gas, coal, or nuclear. It's cheaper . . . much cheaper. Some of the most recent industry forecasts show that there won't be a need for natural gas peaker plants after 2020. When a peaker reaches the end of its useful life, utilities can either replace it or build more transmission lines to bring in more electricity. Both are costly. But renewable energy combined with energy storage is turning out to be the new solution to meet peak energy demands. It's already starting to happen in California.

Near Jack London Square in Oakland, California, Pacific Gas and Electric Company (PG&E) operates a 40-year-old power plant that runs on jet fuel. Because it's a peaker plant, it only runs about 35 days each year, when peak electricity demands dictate. Even on those days, it's only used a few hours each day. The 165-MW plant can't just be closed. That would jeopardize the reliability of Oakland's electric service. To solve the problem, PG&E, working with several environmental groups and Oakland city leaders, came up with an alternative. The Oakland Clean Energy Initiative will replace the plant with a combination of about 35 to 40 MW of solar arrays and 10 MW of battery storage installations in Oakland. In addition to being operationally silent, it will reduce air pollution in the area around the existing plant. PG&E will likely sign power purchase agreements with the system developers.[9]

Three other California natural gas–fired plants are also targeted for replacement with batteries. PG&E is currently looking at replacing three other natural gas peaker plants. They are the Metcalf Energy Center, Feather River Energy Center, and Yuba City Energy Center. The Metcalf Energy Center is a 605-MW power plant located in South San Jose. It's no longer economical to operate today's electricity prices. However, it can't just be shut down. It's necessary to run in order to maintain reliability of the grid. The other two plants are both located in Yuba City, California. Both are 47.6-MW natural gas peaker plants used during periods of high electricity demand. Specifically, PG&E will be replacing the plants with solar- or wind-generating resources combined with energy storage. The plants are to be online and operational before the end of 2018.[10]

NextEra Energy is the world's largest utility company. It generates more electricity from solar and wind than any other company in the world. Fully 22 percent of its 47 GW of generating capacity comes from wind. Another 3 percent comes from solar.[11] Back in 2015, NextEra Energy CEO Jim Robo was thinking way out of the box, and far ahead of his peers. He made a comment while attending an analyst conference at Wolfe Research in New York City, and that statement today makes him sound like a very wise man: "Post-2020, there may never be another peaker built in the United States – very likely you'll be just building energy storage instead." He wasn't just whistling Dixie. He further stated: "We're going to deploy probably $100 million in [energy storage] projects in the next 12 months in places like PJM, California, and Arizona."[12] He was true to his word. By the end of 2016, NextEra Energy already had 90 MW of storage deployed across its grid.[13]

Robo and his energy team are obviously forward thinkers. They surmised correctly that energy storage prices would go through a similar drop in costs to that of solar. They further predicted that solar plus storage would be the death-blow for natural gas peaker plants. And that's exactly what's happening. The cost of energy storage dropped about 70 percent from 2010 through 2016. And by 2020, it could drop another 36 percent to reach a range between $12 and $22 per MWh.[14] These prices will enable the rapid expansion of utility-scale storage. It will also become clear to most utilities that solar plus storage is the way to handle peak energy demands. This will have a disruptive effect on the demand for natural gas peaker plants, gas turbines, and natural gas itself.

GE is the world's largest gas turbine manufacturer. In December 2017, it announced it planned to cut 12,000 jobs in its power business. The company said customers are turning away from fossil fuel–based energy and continuing to embrace renewables. Division Chief Russell Stokes had this to say: "This decision was painful but necessary for GE Power to respond to the disruption in the power market."[15] When I read that the world's largest turbine manufacturer calls what's happening in the energy world a disruption, I knew the title of this book was spot-on.

It's clear that energy storage is going to supplant natural gas peaker plants. But replacing them and backing up solar and wind during periods of dark and no wind aren't the only applications for energy storage. It can also be used to avoid the design and deployment of costly new transmission lines. These can take years to permit, as every local jurisdiction has to weigh in.

According to the International Energy Agency (IEA), renewable energy, primarily wind and solar, continue to grab larger shares of the power generation market. By 2040, the IEA expects solar and wind will be generating more electricity than coal. It estimates that of the $11.3 trillion of new power plant investment expected to occur over the next two decades, renewables will garner about two-thirds of that amount.[16] The trend is clear in the utility space: New fossil fuel and nuclear power generation is out, and solar and/or wind, combined with energy storage, is in.

ENERGY STORAGE TAKES ON COMMERCIAL AND RESIDENTIAL BUILDINGS

Utility-scale, renewable power plants combined with energy storage are expected to grow rapidly over the next decade. By 2026, the annual energy storage revenue tied to systems of 1 MW or greater (considered to be utility-scale) is expected to reach $9.6 billion. But utilities aren't the only entities embracing energy storage. The residential and commercial and industrial (C&I) "behind-the-meter" energy storage applications are expected to exceed $13 billion over the same time period. In fact, C&I and residential storage paired with renewables could account for nearly 70 percent of all storage capacity installed as part of a renewable system over the next 10 years.[17]

There are a number of factors accelerating the deployment of storage for residential and C&I sectors. The main one is the same for both: reduced energy costs. Up until energy storage became practical and affordable, solar PV incentives (like net metering and feed-in tariffs) essentially rewarded customers for sending excess power back into the local grid. But some utilities (like the one I have here in eastern Pennsylvania) only credit solar energy producers with the wholesale power generation rate. That's the rate the utility pays to buy electricity from another utility, and that rate is far less than what the utility charges me. For instance, my electricity costs me slightly more than $0.14 per KWh. That includes generation, transmission, and delivery. But the utility only pays me $0.015 per KWh. In my case, and in the case of many other residential and commercial solar customers, storage makes economic sense. There's no point in sending electricity worth $0.14 per kWh back onto the grid when I can use it later. By the time you read this, I hope to have energy storage installed here at my farm in Pennsylvania.

Solar installation incentives are set to disappear in the early 2020s. The elimination of these could actually help the economic argument for installing solar PV plus storage versus just solar PV by itself. Based on my own experience with buying electricity from and selling it to the grid, it makes sense to believe that customers who are able to store the excess energy they produce will maximize their onsite use. The storage system enables users to time-shift their energy to periods of total darkness if necessary. In addition, energy storage systems can provide many hours of backup power during lengthy power outages.

In addition to lower electricity costs, energy storage can reduce demand charges, something all businesses and some large residential customers have to pay. Demand charges help utilities pay for peaker plants. Peaking plants are those that operate only during periods of high electricity demand. The charges are based on the 15-minute interval with the highest average electric usage within a given month. Customers who use a lot of power in a short period of time likely have high demand charges. In this instance, those charges could actually be the largest part of the bill. Customers who are able to keep their electric usage relatively constant throughout the month will have demand charges that are less than the energy charges.

I mentioned earlier that the reduction and eventual elimination of state and federal solar PV incentives could actually benefit the economic argument for storage. And frankly, solar PV incentives won't be needed anyway. Between 2010 and 2017, solar PV prices plummeted 60 percent.[18] Solar PV systems *alone* are at or below grid parity in many major solar markets. These include Spain, Germany, and California, New York, and Hawaii here in the United States. And while it's true that low solar PV prices increase the economic case for solar PV, it also increases the case for solar plus storage. A system with solar PV plus energy storage can now be installed for the price of a standalone solar system of just a few years ago.

Energy storage system costs continue to drop. We could see prices drop another 50 percent for some applications. As the volume of energy storage systems produced continues to increase, higher manufacturing volumes will reduce system prices. Customers in the C&I sector are generally interested in power resilience in the event of the local utility's grid failure. Battery storage combined with solar PV can provide resilience even if the outage occurs at night. In addition, most solar PV systems have a safety interlock that shuts them down when the grid goes down. The addition of storage batteries and a smart controller will allow solar PV generation to continue even if there is a grid outage. I believe we'll see many markets (in addition to California) implement programs that incentivize solar PV systems combined with energy storage.

HOW ENERGY STORAGE CAN BOOST THE ADOPTION OF EVs

When it comes to the transportation sector, energy storage can solve the biggest problem EVs have right now. I'm talking about the "chicken and egg" problem regarding EV adoption that I discussed in Chapter 9. EVs are starting to turn heads here in the United States and, more importantly, their adoption rate is starting to increase. Through the end of September 2018, over one million battery EVs (BEVs) were sold here in the states.[19] That equates to about 1 percent of all cars sold. But the EV tipping point is at hand and once it happens we could see 10 to 11 million BEVs on US highways by 2030, according to McKinsey.[20]

There's just one problem: lack of available access to charging infrastructure. Potential customers without garages or long commutes need access to public charging stations. Publicly accessible charging points need to dramatically increase in number. As of the end of March 2018, there were more than 48,000 publicly available charging stations in the United States. These include Level 1, Level 2, and three different DC Fast Charging configurations (including Tesla).[21] The roadblock to wider deployment of DC Fast Charging stations is cost. They are expensive to install and have too few visitors to break even or make a profit for their owners. But without them, EV adoption rates just won't increase. And unless BEV sales increase, no one wants to build out more charging infrastructure. Hence the chicken-and-egg problem.

The biggest problem today with EVs is waiting to get a full battery charge. Potential and current EV customers don't want to idle away their time at a recharging station. Today, most of the charging stations are "Level 2." Their charging capacity, measured in kilowatt-hours (kWh), is 7 to 19. That means, using my Tesla Model X (with its 90 kWh battery) as an example, would take 5 to 13 hours to fully charge at a Level 2 station. Fortunately for Tesla owners, the company has deployed a network of 1,229 Supercharger stations with 9,623 individual charging bays.[22] Each Supercharger is capable of charging a

Tesla battery at up to 120 kW per hour, which means that even to fully recharge, the average stay at a Tesla Supercharger is 30 minutes or less. A longer stay at a charging station would be an immediate turn-off to a would-be EV buyer.

The other big problem is the outright cost of a DC Fast Charging station. Costs run upwards of $150,000 per 150 kW station. But the biggest cost of a DC Fast Charging station is its operating costs. As discussed previously, commercial customers pay for the energy they use as well as demand charges. These charges can be as cheap as $2.00 per kW to $90 per kW. In the case of charging stations, demand charges make up the lion's share of the monthly bill. For the power-hungry EV owner who pulls in to charge up, demand charges could cost as much as $25 to $50 per visit.[23] Folks simply won't pay that. But if there were more EVs, overall demand charges for the charge station would be lower and that cost would be spread among many more EV visitors to the site. Because of the high costs and long payback times, few investors are interested in building new charging stations. And without more of them, consumers are reluctant to make the jump to an EV.

But there is a solution to the EV charging station deployment problem: simply add battery storage to the site. The batteries are connected to the grid alongside the charging bays. The system is programmed to charge only when electricity costs are at their lowest. Conversely, they source power during periods of high demand. This is an industry practice called peak shaving. Shaving the peaks off of demand spikes dramatically cuts down on demand charges. With a properly sized system, arriving cars can be charged from the battery and the grid. The battery pack lowers overall power demand and peak demand, increasing the economics of the station.

As EVs increase in number, even battery storage won't be enough to help with lower demand charges. But the sheer number of EVs that will split a station's demand charges will ensure that the charges are a small portion of the cost of a customer's visit. In addition to creating economics that work for charging station investors, battery storage can generate additional income streams. These can come from other grid services such as demand response and frequency regulation.

In this chapter we covered the effects cheap battery storage will have on the utility, C&I, and residential sectors of the energy storage market. In the next chapter, I want to review the effects cheap battery storage will have on the US energy supply and address the implications for utilities and other forms of power generation.

NOTES

1. www.teslarati.com/tesla-partner-panasonic-20-30-percent-energy-density-increase/
2. electrek.co/2018/01/23/tesla-giant-battery-australia-1-million/
3. electrek.co/2018/01/04/tesla-powerpack-battery-australia/
4. www.utilitydive.com/news/teslas-musk-talks-gigawatt-hour-scale-storage-project/522988/
5. reneweconomy.com.au/tesla-big-battery-outsmarts-lumbering-coal-units-after-loy-yang-trips-70003/
6. electrek.co/2018/05/05/tesla-record-1-gwh-energy-storage-announced-soon/
7. electrek.co/2018/03/14/tesla-bids-new-world-largest-powerpack-battery-system-colorado/
8. https://electrek.co/2018/06/29/tesla-pge-giant-1-gwh-powerpack-battery-system/
9. www.sfchronicle.com/business/article/Proposal-to-go-solar-at-old-Oakland-power-plant-12408069.php
10. www.sfchronicle.com/business/article/Batteries-could-replace-three-California-power-12428238.php
11. www.investor.nexteraenergy.com/~/media/Files/N/NEE-IR/may-2018-investor-presentation.pdf
12. www.greentechmedia.com/articles/read/nextera-on-storage-post-2020-there-may-never-be-another-peaker-built-in-t#gs.ZwdHSqs
13. www.nexteraenergy.com/company/work/battery-storage.html?cid=esnee2018wphcs1
14. www.investor.nexteraenergy.com/~/media/Files/N/NEE-IR/may-2018-investor-presentation.pdf
15. www.bloomberg.com/news/articles/2017-12-07/ge-is-said-to-plan-12-000-job-cuts-as-new-ceo-revamps-power-unit
16. www.bloomberg.com/news/articles/2017-12-07/ge-is-said-to-plan-12-000-job-cuts-as-new-ceo-revamps-power-unit
17. www.greenbiz.com/article/expect-strong-growth-year-commercial-energy-storage
18. www.greenbiz.com/article/expect-strong-growth-year-commercial-energy-storage
19. https://insideevs.com/1-million-electric-cars-sold-us/
20. www.mckinsey.com/business-functions/sustainability-and-resource-productivity/our-insights/how-battery-storage-can-help-charge-the-electric-vehicle-market#0
21. https://insideevs.com/number-of-charging-stations-in-u-s-increased-to-48000-15000-in-california/

22. www.tesla.com/findus#/bounds/49.73070615469516,-86.39947673359376,
    46.994318026897425,-92.09588786640626,d?search=supercharger&name=
    North%20America&place=bellefontepasupercharger
23. www.mckinsey.com/business-functions/sustainability-and-resource-
    productivity/our-insights/how-battery-storage-can-help-charge-the-electric-
    vehicle-market#0

CHAPTER FOURTEEN

Disrupting the US Energy Supply

I n this chapter, we'll look at the future effects cheap battery storage is going to have on the US energy supply. I'll address the implications for utilities, the coal-mining sector, and other forms of power generation.

President Trump may still be digging coal but America's electric utilities don't seem to be. From 2008 to 2017, almost all of the utility-scale power plants that retired were of the fossil fuel variety. Not surprisingly, 47 percent of them were coal plants. By the end of 2017, 17 percent of all US coal-fired generating capacity had completely retired. Utilities converted another 4 percent to natural gas.[1] That's what caused coal's drop from 51 percent to 31 percent of all US electrical generation in 2017.[2] And more shutdowns are coming. An August 2018 study indicated that half of the remaining coal-fired plants are likely to shut down by 2030 or before. Or they may be converted to natural gas–fired plants. It turns out that 18 percent of the remaining ones already have a target retirement date.[3]

Solar or wind (plus storage) generation systems are now at or below grid parity in the United States. More than 72.5 gigawatts (GW) of wind and 43.5 GW of solar are coming online over the next several years. And the reason is simple: market economics. Coal simply can't cut it economically. It's that simple. Building a new coal-fired power plant is only economical when compared to a similar-sized nuclear plant. Otherwise, it's more expensive than wind and solar. Trump may dig coal but – presidential rhetoric aside – utilities dig market economics. Here are a few examples of recent utility decisions to abandon their coal plants and why they chose to do so.

THE LAND OF ENCHANTMENT

New Mexico's largest electricity provider is the Public Service Company of New Mexico, owned by PNM Resources, Inc. (NYSE: PNM). As of 2015, 56 percent of its electricity generation came from coal-fired plants. In April 2017, it released its five-year integrated resource plan (IRP), which PNM developed to see what mix of generating sources made the most sense for its 510,000 customers.[4]

The results surprised everybody. The IRP suggested that PNM's best and low-cost option for reliable power was to move entirely to solar and natural gas plus energy storage. PNM is adding capacity to its transmission lines that access eastern New Mexico. It's there that constant winds provide cheap wind power. It expects to start retiring coal plants by 2022. A little more than a decade from now, in 2031, New Mexico plans to shut off its last coal-fired plant. By 2035, its generation mix is going to be almost 36 percent renewables and 33 percent natural gas. That's a smart increase from 2017's levels of 11 percent and 6 percent, respectively.[5] In addition to eliminating coal use PNM expects to significantly improve its grid reliability.

AMERICA'S DAIRYLAND

Wisconsin has coastlines on both Lake Michigan and Lake Superior. Wisconsin's largest utility is We Energies, serving over 2.2 million customers. As of 2015, coal made up 50.6 percent of its total generating capacity.[6] And for motorists on Interstate 94, the water vapor billowing from We's Pleasant Prairie coal-fired generating station was a familiar sight.

But soon, those billowing clouds will cease. And so will the plant's pollution. In November 2017, We Energies elected to shutter the 1.2 GW Pleasant Prairie units in early 2018. This is notable since Pleasant Prairie only started operating in 1985. It recently had

$325 million in additional pollution controls installed.[7] But none of that mattered. Economics took center stage in the decision to close the plant.

In recent years, the plant ran intermittently. And last spring, it was completely shut down for three months. Pollution aside, that's the problem with large legacy coal-fired plants. If they're not running at full capacity, they are apt to lose money ... lots of money. And now, with cheap natural gas, solar, and wind, more and more of them like Pleasant Prairie can't compete. We Energies plans to replace part of Pleasant Prairie's capacity with a 350-MW solar array. Slated to be the largest in Wisconsin, it's expected to be complete and operational by 2020.[8]

DEEP IN THE HEART OF TEXAS

In Texas, Luminant has almost 18 GW-worth of generation. By the end of January 2018, it permanently closed its 1.8 GW Monticello coal-fired power plant. The reason? It can generate or buy power much cheaper than Monticello can produce it. It also expects to close two other coal plants that together have a 2.3 GW capacity. They are also economically challenged. The three plants represent about 12 percent of Texas's entire coal-fired fleet. The good news is that Texas energy consumers have saved billions as utilities shift to clean energy from renewables.

More good news: there has been no impact on grid reliability in Texas due to the closures. And the wind keeps on blowing. Texas's wind capacity surpassed the 21-GW mark at the end of 2017. The Lone Star State is rapidly adding solar, too. It expects an additional 14 to 27 GW of solar will be sourcing power by 2030.[9]

MISSOURI'S BIG SWITCH

The most significant utility in Missouri is Ameren Missouri. In September 2017 it announced that it's retiring half of its coal fleet (about 2.65 GW). To replace some of the lost capacity, Ameren is spending $1 billion on 100 MW of new solar and 700 MW of new wind capacity. It's all expected to be operational by 2020.[10] Once again the reason for the switch is simple economics. The utility will spend far less to operate the new wind and solar plants. And Ameren customers will save money on energy. The story is the same nearly everywhere.

MONTANA'S BIG POLLUTER

Montana is one of the last places you would expect to find one of America's biggest greenhouse gas emitters. But the 2.2-GW Colstrip power plant has that dubious title. Its owners are planning to close it by 2027 or sooner. That's 20 years faster than the owners estimated in 2012.[11]

The story is the same. Cheap renewables will replace the lost capacity. The bottom line is this: Everywhere across America, utilities are choosing renewables plus storage. They are cleaner and less expensive than many existing coal-fired plants. As of this writing in fall 2018, I expect we'll see even more coal plant closures announced before year's end. Even the president can't change the economics of renewables.

COAL'S VANISHING CUSTOMERS

The coal industry has a big problem: disappearing customers. The US coal industry's last hope is exporting coal to Asia. Unfortunately, that's turning out to be another dead end for US coal producers. Why are US utilities shunning coal? It's a combination of three factors.

The first is increasing state mandates for renewable energy. Utilities are being forced by states to obtain anywhere from 10 percent to as much as 50 percent (in California) of their electricity from renewable sources. A few of the western mountain states are using existing hydropower plants to help meet state renewable objectives. Most of them are turning to wind and solar plus storage.

The second factor is that coal is just plain dirty. It's the dirtiest fossil fuel. It's responsible for most of the pollutants produced by fossil fuels. According to the Clean Air Task Force, retiring one coal-fired generating plant prevents:

- More than 29 premature deaths
- 47 heart attacks
- 491 asthma attacks
- 22 asthma emergency room visits

For the Environmental Protection Agency (EPA), dirty coal plants are low-hanging fruit. Over the past 10 years, the EPA has been continually reducing acceptable levels of the worst pollutants (mercury, sulfur dioxide, carbon dioxide, and others) that utilities can emit. To meet

EPA objectives, utilities have been adding pollution abatement equipment to their newest and largest coal-fired plants. That brings me to the third factor: cost. It's expensive to build new coal-fired plants and it's not cost-effective to add pollution-control equipment to older and smaller coal-fired plants.

Instead, utilities are simply retiring those plants and replacing them with renewables. One statistic tells it all. Clean energy (including hydro-powered generation) and natural gas are responsible for *93 percent of all new power plants over the past 25 years.*[12] Coal and nuclear are the obvious laggards. And policy issues have nothing to do with it.

The reason solar and wind are the "new normal" in power generation is purely economic. Utilities have responsibilities to the public utility commissions that govern them, their boards of directors, their customers, and to shareholders. Since 2006, renewables have been the biggest source of annual generating capacity build-out.

President Trump should have more than a little egg on his face. "Digging [more] beautiful, clean coal" was a top focus of his campaign, and continues to be one during his presidency. But here are the sobering facts. More coal-fired capacity has closed in 2018 than in President Obama's first three years in the White House.[13]

Since 2010, 270 coal plants have closed. There are 260 left.[14] Closures are going to continue. In 2018, utilities are set to shutter another 11.4 gigawatts of coal capacity.[15] They won't replace some of it. The rest will be with solar, wind, or natural gas–fired plants. There's no way coal is coming back, here or anywhere else. It's just too dirty. It's a secular decline with no end in sight. Even those utilities with plenty of coal-fired generation are moving away from it.

Coal's Last-Ditch Effort

US customers burn up roughly 90 percent of American coal production. That's a problem for coal because it's no longer competitive with renewable generation here in the United States. As a result, the coal mining industry is rapidly dying. In a last-ditch effort to save America's coal mining industry, coal company executives are shifting their focus toward exports. But that market peaked at around 125 million tons in 2012[16] and it's been volatile ever since. In 2016, exports dropped to about 60 million tons. They surged to 97 million tons in 2017. Demand could fall by 30 million tons in 2018. A business plan based on a market with that kind of volatility is a recipe for disaster. Building one with disappearing customers is even worse.

No New Capital, No New Plants, No New Demand

No wonder coal's biggest problem is its shrinking customer base. Since 2010, US utilities have retired more than 50,000 megawatts of coal-fired generating capacity. Utilities are spending their capital on renewables for new capacity. Wind is now responsible for 6 percent of America's power generation. In windy states like South Dakota, Oklahoma, Iowa, and Kansas, wind power is at least 30 percent of overall generation capacity.[17]

Solar is also cutting into coal's market share. That's because solar generates most of its power during peak daytime periods. Historically, that's been a traditional stronghold for coal-fired plants. It's when they earn most of their revenue. For instance, Texas utilities are bringing 3.5 gigawatts of new solar capacity online in the next few years. That will compete head-to-head with what remains of Texas coal-fired plants.

The public relations website pages of coal companies wax poetic about future possibilities with exports. An investor could get hoodwinked into believing these companies have a bright future. But they don't. The Securities and Exchange Commission rules require companies to disclose real market expectations. That's where you'll find accurate future market projections. They are anything but rosy.

For instance, Cloud Peak Energy Inc. (NYSE: CLD) saw its shares slide from a high of $21.87 in April 2014 to $2.49 in October, 2018. That's a decrease of 88.6 percent. And Cloud Peak Energy isn't the only coal producer with those kinds of negative returns. They all look like that.

Pollution problems aside, coal isn't an economical source of energy anymore. The bad news is I expect most American coal-mining companies will eventually go out of business. The good news is the clean energy sector is responsible for over a million jobs. And that's far more than the number of jobs lost in the coal sector.

AMERICAN BUSINESS AT ODDS WITH TRUMP

One thing has become clear during Donald Trump's presidency: He's not afraid of ruffling anyone's feathers. His proposed steel and aluminum import tariffs in spring 2018 were just the latest in what was a year of upsetting apple carts.

On the one hand, Trump professes to want to help American businesses. But sometimes, it seems as if he could care less about the opinions of corporate America. For instance, his views on coal and climate change directly fly in the face of world opinion. Trump has signed legislation to make it easier to burn coal and he's rejected the Paris Climate Accord, something every other country has embraced (even Syria has signed) – the United States now stands alone in its rejection of climate science.[18]

So how does corporate America feel? Are companies just rolling over and requesting coal-fired power for their energy needs? Quite the contrary. American businesses have broken ranks from Washington on energy policy and have done so in significant numbers.

As of October 10, 2018, and even with America's non-participation in the Paris agreements, 2,142 businesses and investors, 280 cities and counties, 345 colleges and universities, and 10 states are all aligning their emission reduction plans with the Paris goals. The companies alone have a business worth of $9.46 trillion. These businesses represent 169 million people, across all 50 states.[19] Ironically, but maybe not too surprisingly, they have made the most significant commitment to reducing emissions of any in the group.

WE ARE STILL IN

And then there are the groups who have signed the "We Are Still In" declaration. In short, it's a list of folks who believe in climate change and are committed to honoring and abiding by the terms of the Paris Climate Accord. It includes leaders from over 2,500 of America's businesses, city halls, college campuses, and state houses. They represent over 130 million Americans and are responsible for $6.2 trillion of US economic interests. And here's one other interesting bit of information: They all vote.[20]

Unfortunately, progress in renewable energy and energy storage seems to be falling on deaf ears in the White House. Trump's had coal industry advocates like Murray Energy CEO, Robert Murray, continually blowing in his ear. Murray is about as biased toward coal as one can get. Not too surprising. He's the CEO of a coal mining company with one of the worst track records in the business.

Murray is the one behind the rule that Energy Secretary Rick Perry proposed. It would have paid coal-fired generating plants to maintain massive, 90-day coal piles to keep plants running "in times of crisis." The Federal Energy Regulatory Commission (FERC) thought the idea was silly. They voted it down.

In June 2018, Trump told Perry he needed to take "immediate steps" to keep coal- and nuclear-fired power plants open, especially those that were in immediate danger of closing. The White House Press Secretary, Sarah Sanders, said in a statement that the President believes that "keeping America's energy grid and infrastructure strong and secure protects our national security, public safety and economy from intentional attacks and natural disasters." She further went on to say that the President felt that retiring "fuel-secure" power plants, in particular coal and nuclear-powered ones, "harms America's power grids and reduces their resilience." Incredibly, Trump is considering ordering utility grid operators to buy electricity from these struggling plants for a period of at least two years in order to keep them running.[21]

This action by the Department of Energy, if it comes to pass, would be an unprecedented intervention into America's energy markets. This is absolute nonsense. I'm not the only one saying that. The PJM Interconnection, one of the largest power grid operators in the United States, said that retiring four nuclear plants from its grid would not affect system reliability. PJM further said that forcing coal and nuclear plants to sell electricity at prices higher than other sources will just end up costing electricity consumers money.[22] There's no reason for the government to intervene in America's energy markets. They've been working just fine for decades and all Trump is doing is trying to solve a problem that doesn't exist. If Trump tries to invoke this order, it will likely be challenged in the courts by a number of states as well as various utility interconnect organizations.

BUSINESS AS USUAL

After Trump withdrew from the Paris Accord, and climate change believers in the business world launched the "We Are Still In" group, the statement from these US organizations to the world was clear: that they affirm the United States move toward a greener direction in energy. And it's not like the United States is the only country getting rid of coal plants. Coal and its economics are as out of favor in Europe as they are here. Half of European coal plants are money losers. And by 2030, almost every one will be.

In the UK, coal-fired generation provided 40 percent of electricity in 2013. As of 2018, coal's share has dwindled to 2 percent. In fact, during the period from Monday, April 16, 2018, to Thursday, April 19, 2018, the UK reported a stretch of nearly 55 hours of coal-free electricity generation. That's the first time the UK powered itself without coal since the first coal-fired generating station opened in London back in 1882.[23]

Australia's largest power producer, AGL Energy is closing one of its largest coal-fired power plants and replacing it with renewables and natural gas-fired units.[24, 25] Even China is starting to ditch coal. In October 2017, China unveiled a list of 151 coal plants that must close or stop construction. The capacity is equal to 95,000 megawatts. That's equal to the total power requirements of Germany and Japan.[26]

Why are businesses and entire countries abandoning coal? Besides coal's obvious pollution issues, coal plants are just too expensive. Since 2010, the cost of a solar energy system has dropped by 70 percent. Wind system prices fell 25 percent in the same timeframe.[27]

And of all places, China is fueling the dropping cost of renewables. Instead of funding new coal plants, the Red Dragon plans to drop more than $360 billion on wind and solar power by 2020. Volume purchases like that will continue to drive costs down. China expects it will create 13 million renewable energy sector jobs by 2020 as well.[28] In 2008 China took over the dubious title of the world's biggest GHG emitter but 10 years later it produces twice as much as the United States Now China has a clear mission to do its part to reduce GHG production. In the absence of any federal plan to do that here, we're fortunate to have 1,700 business leaders who want to do their part.

In short, coal-fired power production is rapidly losing ground here in the United States and around the world. The "culprit" is economical solar and wind paired with energy storage. Cheap energy storage overcomes the intermittent nature of wind and the lack of solar during nighttime hours by allowing the time shifting of those energy sources. As a result, we are going to see more and more coal become stranded in the ground. Many existing mines will close, and the few remaining will drastically have to downsize. The export market for coal isn't going to save America's coal industry.

Some US states are "behind the eight ball" when it comes to forward thinking regarding energy. For instance, the Pennsylvania Chamber of Business and Industry claims it's not against renewables, but "they don't see it as a reliable source that can fully meet Pennsylvanians' energy needs barring some significant technological breakthrough."[29] I'm not sure what "breakthrough" they are waiting for, but cheap energy storage is a breakthrough, and it will eventually dethrone all fossil fuels, including natural gas. Pennsylvania produces roughly one-quarter of all of the natural gas in the United States.

But even Pennsylvania, with its massive natural gas deposits and its numerous coal-burning power plants, is moving away from coal. The reason is simple economics. Coal plants are just too expensive to run and maintain. In Pennsylvania, during the period from 2010 through 2015, total greenhouse gas emissions from coal-fired generating plants dropped by 25 percent.[30]

It's a transformative time in American energy. We've had other energy transformations in the past, as the country moved from wood to coal, and then coal to oil. Now, the world is moving away from fossil fuels at a fairly rapid pace. When utilities plan future generation, energy storage is part of the solution. Utilities are signing power purchase agreements (PPAs) for solar plus storage. As costs continue to drop, solar plus storage is becoming even more attractive than any other form of power generation.

NOTES

1. https://www.eia.gov/todayinenergy/detail.php?id=34452
2. https://www.eia.gov/tools/faqs/faq.php?id=427&t=3
3. https://www.greentechmedia.com/articles/read/report-nearly-half-of-u-s-coal-plants-could-close-by-2030
4. www.forbes.com/sites/energyinnovation/2017/12/18/utilities-closed-dozens-of-coal-plants-in-2017-here-are-the-6-most-important/2/#4067fe667059
5. www.forbes.com/sites/energyinnovation/2017/12/18/utilities-closed-dozens-of-coal-plants-in-2017-here-are-the-6-most-important/2/#4067fe667059
6. www.jsonline.com/story/news/2017/11/28/we-energies-coal-fired-power-plant-pleasant-prairie-shut-down-2018/901891001/
7. www.jsonline.com/story/news/2017/11/28/we-energies-coal-fired-power-plant-pleasant-prairie-shut-down-2018/901891001/
8. www.jsonline.com/story/news/2017/11/28/we-energies-coal-fired-power-plant-pleasant-prairie-shut-down-2018/901891001/

9. www.forbes.com/sites/energyinnovation/2017/12/18/utilities-closed-dozens-of-coal-plants-in-2017-here-are-the-6-most-important/2/#4067fe667059

10. www.forbes.com/sites/energyinnovation/2017/12/18/utilities-closed-dozens-of-coal-plants-in-2017-here-are-the-6-most-important/2/#4067fe667059

11. www.forbes.com/sites/energyinnovation/2017/12/18/utilities-closed-dozens-of-coal-plants-in-2017-here-are-the-6-most-important/2/#4067fe667059

12. www.greentechmedia.com/articles/read/renewable-energy-generation-nuclear-bnef#gs.vz7FzTI

13. www.greentechmedia.com/articles/read/trump-cant-save-coal#gs.mdkZGpA

14. https://content.sierraclub.org/coal/victories

15. https://energytransition.org/2018/06/americas-coal-plants-closing-despite-trump/

16. ieefa.org/ieefa-update-americas-coal-industry-trouble/

17. Ibid.

18. https://www.theatlantic.com/science/archive/2017/11/syria-is-joining-the-paris-agreement-now-what/545261/

19. https://www.wearestillin.com/

20. www.wearestillin.com/we-are-still-declaration

21. www.power-eng.com/articles/2018/06/trump-orders-immediate-steps-to-boost-coal-nuclear-plants.html

22. www.power-eng.com/articles/2018/06/perry-pjm-interconnection-react-to-trump-directive-on-coal-nuclear.html?cmpid=enl_pe_power_engineering_e-newsletter_2018-06-08&pwhid=2bb71543f97d6dc6da41d4b5652a6a6a735c8dabc6f15061235368f662666b5ebd83032edcfe697279767714bcfc1f90ae0bf66ea4b40c1b4aadb176d3a9caa1&eid=288141552&bid=2131707

23. www.independent.co.uk/environment/uk-no-coal-power-renewable-energy-record-electricity-climate-change-wind-solar-a8312116.html

24. https://www.reuters.com/article/australia-power-agl-energy/australias-agl-energyditches-coal-plant-for-gas-renewables-idUSL3N1O904D

25. https://insideclimatenews.org/news/03012018/clean-power-renewable-energy-jobs-technology-grids-policy-2017

26. reneweconomy.com.au/china-halts-150-coal-fired-power-plants-84937/

27. insideclimatenews.org/news/03012018/clean-power-renewable-energy-jobs-technology-grids-policy-2017

28. www.nytimes.com/2017/01/05/world/asia/china-renewable-energy-investment.html?_r=0

29. www.pennlive.com/politics/index.ssf/2018/04/bills_that_sets_100_percent_re.html

30. www.philly.com/philly/health/Trump-environmental-rollback-likely-too-late-for-not-Pennsylvania-coal-plants.html

CHAPTER FIFTEEN

Say Goodbye to Conventional Power Plants

In Chapter 14, we looked at some of the parties interested in adopting energy storage systems, and the reasons they are replacing legacy-generating facilities with solar, wind, and supplemental battery storage. In this chapter, we'll look at the specific effects that battery storage systems will have on future power plant construction. The effect of cheap storage combined with local generation (solar and wind) will keep a lot of power plants from ever being built. Let's look at some of the specific reasons energy storage is becoming such a game-changer in the energy space. Some of this material can get very technical, but I have done my best to clarify and simplify the concepts for you.

BLINK AND YOU'LL MISS IT

Remember that the electricity in non-storage, electrical-grid networks is used as soon as it is generated. All power generated worldwide is alternating current (AC) power. Here in the United States, the **nominal frequency** is 60 **hertz** (Hz). Most of Europe, Asia, and Africa generate 50 Hz power. Most networks have excess generating capacity that is available to add to the grid as demand increases. When an electric generating plant trips offline suddenly and unexpectedly, there is an immediate dearth of energy on the grid. This causes a drop in frequency on the grid. If the frequency falls too far, other generators may not be able to supply enough energy to the system fast enough to keep the grid stable. If that happens, those other stations could also trip off the grid. Eventually, a blackout would ensue as the electrical load becomes too big for remaining generators to handle. And all of that would occur within the first half-second after the original generator trips off. That's about the time it takes us to blink.

This problem has only gotten bigger as higher levels of renewables continue to be deployed on global electrical grids. As their levels increase, grid stability becomes progressively more at risk. The **inertial response** that a turbine-driven spinning generator provides to the network is what keeps networks stable. But as they are replaced by renewables, new ways of maintaining grid stability (in that blink-of-an-eye example above) are crucial.

THE CHALLENGE: MATCHING SUPPLY AND DEMAND

In order to keep the grid stable, the amount of power being supplied and the demand being drawn from customers must be closely matched all the time. When a power grid is in balance, the frequency is stable (60 Hz here and 50 Hz across most of the rest of the world, as noted above). But when an unexpected fault occurs and a generating plant trips off the grid, the frequency starts to drop. In order to avoid a catastrophic networks failure, the drop must be quickly stopped and reversed.

As depicted in the waveform shown in Figure 15.1, there are two areas of concern after a fault occurs.

The first area is the ROCOF, the Rate of Change of Frequency. That's simply how quickly the frequency changes. If the ROCOF is greater than 1 Hz per second, other power stations on the grid could trip offline or, even worse, sustain damage.

The second area is the Nadir. That's the minimum frequency to which the grid drops after a fault occurs. Below 59 Hz (in a grid with a nominal frequency of 60 Hz), the potential for additional power stations to trip off the grid goes up rapidly.

FIGURE **15.1**   POWER FAULT WAVEFORM

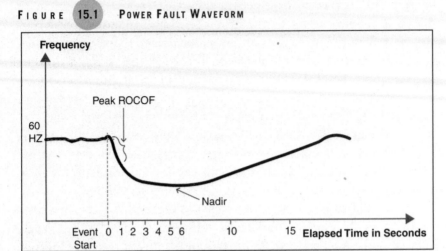

Data source: s2.q4cdn.com/601666628/files/doc_presentations/2017/Everoze-Batteries-Beyond-the-Spin.pdf. Accessed May 21, 2018. Graph redrawn and modified by author.

Actively managing ROCOF is the easiest way to reduce the Nadir to a level that keeps other power stations online. However, it's becoming a growing challenge to manage ROCOF as the system nonsynchronous penetration (SNSP) has increased. There are three ways to manage ROCOF at high SNSP levels.

1. The first way is to increase the tolerance of existing generators to higher levels of ROCOF. This is something implemented in grid control software that will improve overall grid resilience to **frequency faults.**

2. The second is to reduce the level at which the **thermal synchronous generator** operates, or add additional types of synchronous inertia. If combined-cycle gas turbine generators can run at lower load levels, operation will accommodate higher levels of SNSP. Potential sources of synchronous inertia include pumped hydro storage, synchronous compensators, compressed air energy storage, and rotational stabilizers.

3. The third way, and the most relative to our discussion of energy storage, is to increase the **synthetic or emulated inertia** on the grid. The level of SNSP on grids with significant wind and/or solar penetration is often 75 percent or higher. Synthetic inertia can keep

ROCOF within manageable and reasonable levels, even with a 75 percent SNSP level. Battery storage systems with sophisticated control software are capable of achieving low ROCOF, even at high SNSP levels.

SYNCHRONOUS GENERATORS VERSUS BATTERY STORAGE

Let's compare the frequency fault response of **synchronous generators** and batteries on a typical grid. When the frequency drops suddenly on a grid with nothing but additional backup synchronous generators, those generators automatically respond immediately by slowing down. This adds additional energy that is stored in these massive rotating masses (the generator armature assembly); it is called the **synchronous inertial response (SIR)**. The average generator can provide an increase in grid power of 7 to 14 percent of its total rated capacity. The average SIR response time for a large fault is 0.05 seconds.[1] But here's the catch: In order to respond, a synchronous generator *must already be running* to create analog inertia. And each additional unit can only provide a small amount of the total required power, as noted above. In order to protect a grid, a large amount of reserve synchronous generators have to be running. This defeats the whole purpose of creating an efficient grid. It also eliminates the need for additional renewables, slowing the transition to a sustainable energy grid.

A battery energy storage system, on the other hand, has no moving parts. With sophisticated control software, this system begins to respond as soon as the frequency fault can be measured. Reaction times of current systems are in the range of 0.1 seconds. Note that the response of battery systems is slightly slower than standby synchronous generators. But once a grid fault is detected by grid control software, a battery system can ramp to full power in less than 0.2 seconds. And unlike synchronous generators, which require a lot of fuel (coal, natural gas, oil) to keep running in standby mode, a battery energy storage system just sits there, fully charged, waiting to respond.

In a real world example, the island country of Ireland installed a 10-MW **energy storage array**. It began operations on January 5, 2016. The Kilroot Advancion Energy Storage Array is owned by AES Corporation and is the first grid-scale battery storage system in the United Kingdom. It helps keep the island's energy supply and demand in balance. The array assists system operators in efficiently managing existing generation assets. More importantly, it greatly facilitates the integration of renewable power sources into Ireland's power grid.

The initial 10-MW storage array works so well AES is planning to install a 100-MW energy storage array on the grounds of the Kilroot Power Station. That would be the largest energy storage array in all of Europe, and would be the equivalent of 200 MW of flexible generating resources. That array, once installed, is expected to provide $11.3 million in savings annually. In addition, it will avoid 123,000 tons of CO_2 emissions annually.[2]

Batteries have much higher ramp rates when compared to standby synchronous generators. Once batteries reach full power, the battery system can maintain that level for minutes or hours, as dictated by the size of the battery system. Installing battery storage systems allows grid operators to automatically respond to grid faults much faster than conventional standby generators. It therefore allows renewable generation to replace more conventional synchronous generation and reduce or eliminate standby synchronous generators. More importantly, all those dirty, polluting, and greenhouse gas-emitting fossil fuels that power those generators are no longer necessary.

SOLAR AND WIND, PAIRED WITH STORAGE, ARE DISRUPTING ELECTRIC POWER GENERATION

The year 2017 saw a dramatic drop in both wind and solar energy prices. This reverberation was felt around the world across the global electricity generation sector. In 2017, wind and solar installations nearly reached 155 GW. That's more than all of the power capacity currently installed in the United Kingdom. Renewables are far outpacing coal and nuclear plant development. It's good news for electric customers as well. Prices for solar energy generation dropped 50 percent from levels reached in 2014 and 2015.[3]

The rapid drop in solar is creating a rapid shift away from fossil fuels. Examples of large utilities shedding fossil fuel generators are NTPC of India, NextEra in the United States, and ENGIE in France. In Italy, ENEL has only had its green power division in existence since 2008. Remarkably, half of its generating capacity now comes from its 39.4 GW of renewable generating assets around the world.[4]

As the amount of renewables deployed goes up, economies of manufacturing scale kick in, and prices go down, a situation compounded by advances in technology, government renewable targets, and inexpensive financing. It's Fessler's first and second laws of technology in action. As a result, solar power purchase agreement (PPA) price records were broken not one but *four* times in 2017. This technology-driven change is happening all over the world. During 2017, 75 GW of solar PV capacity was turned on by the top three thermal power generating countries: China (53 GW), the United States (12 GW), and India (10 GW). In total, that's more power capacity than all of Indonesia or Australia.[5]

NextEra Energy is one of the world's leading clean energy providers. Based in Juno Beach, Florida, NextEra has 46.79 GW of net generating capacity online; it is the largest producer of wind energy in North America, with 16 percent of all US wind energy capacity. It has almost tripled the amount of wind energy it's deployed over the past decade. It currently has 14 GW of wind energy online, with plans to add an additional 2.4 to 4.1 GW by the end of 2018. Its wind energy projects are located in 20 states and four Canadian provinces.

NextEra is also the world's largest producer of solar energy, having pioneered utility-scale solar nearly 30 years ago. In 2016 alone, NextEra tripled its solar energy plants and now has 2.262 GW of solar energy online. It expects to nearly double that number over the next seven years, including one plant in 2018 that will contain 2.5 million solar panels when complete. Its solar deployments are in 10 US states and Canada. NextEra believes that by 2025, renewable power in the United States will be less expensive than either coal or natural gas–fired power plants. In addition to solar plants that it owns, NextEra Energy designs, builds, finances, and operates solar energy plants for third-party owners. These are located on commercial building rooftops, vacant land, and parking structures. In 2018, it had 20 solar plants in development or under construction in eight states, representing an investment of over $300 million.[6]

NextEra Energy has continued to lead its peers with additional planned deployments of both solar and wind. But it's also the leader in energy storage here in the United States, with over 100 MW of battery energy storage in operation on its grids. Its Babcock Ranch Solar Energy Center is a 74.5-MW solar power plant combined with a 10-MW battery storage system. It's currently the biggest combined solar-plus-storage system in the United States.[7]

In Arizona, the company has a 20-MW, solar PV generating system with 258,000 solar panels. Located on 257 acres of land in Casa Grande, the Pinal Central Solar Energy Center has 10 MW of lithium-ion battery energy storage. The batteries can provide 10 MW of power for a four-hour period. The system cost $60 million to design and install. The owner is the Salt River Project, one of Arizona's largest utilities. The battery system is one of three that the Salt River Project expects to install on its power grid.[8]

A decade ago, the cost of renewables was still in the pre-commercial stage. The only countries that were spending large amounts of capital on them were the United Kingdom, Germany, and Denmark. Now, we've reached the renewable energy tipping point. Today, renewables aren't just commercially viable. They are the cheapest game in town when it comes to energy generation, especially when paired with battery storage. As a result, we see South Korea, France, Japan, the United States, India, and Taiwan all with plans for a rapid ramp-up of renewable energy generation. India could reach fossil-fuel parity by 2020.

Renewables are no longer classified as "other" when compared to coal, natural gas, and nuclear. Their rapid deployment has given rise to a rampant deflationary trend in new power generation costs. This has not gone unnoticed by many governments that are making the shift from fossil fuels to sustainable energy sources. Renewables aren't plagued with the kind of stranded asset issues thermal power plants wrestle with. In addition to countries mentioned above, the UAE, Mexico, Australia, Chile, Canada, and Argentina are all favoring renewable-energy generation. I believe that by the end of this decade, renewables – when paired with storage – will be the least cost generating option everywhere.

RENEWABLES REPLACING NEED FOR MORE NATURAL GAS CAPACITY

In January 2018, much of the United States, including New England was subject to an extended period of cold weather. Unfortunately, New England is underserved in available natural gas transmission line capacity. As a result, spot prices for natural gas hit $35.35 per thousand cubic feet (Mcf) at the Algonquin Citygate, New England's main trading hub for natural gas. But just 250 miles away, in the vast Marcellus shale region of Pennsylvania where the gas comes from, that same gas was priced at between $1 and $2 per Mcf. During that weather pattern, New Englanders paid the highest recorded price for natural gas anywhere in the world. It was 13 times higher than the main US natural gas pricing location, the Henry Hub in Louisiana.

While New England homeowners paid hundreds of dollars more than their counterparts in Ohio and Pennsylvania, they aren't New England's biggest customers for natural gas. Those are the utilities that own natural gas–fired power plants in the region. Natural gas turbines turn generators that produce 50 to 60 percent of New England's daily power requirements.[9]

Looking at New England's problem based simply on natural gas demand, one might conclude that it's absolutely essential that New England have more natural gas pipeline capacity. Without it, especially during winter cold snaps, the reliability of New England's entire power grid could be at risk. And that was exactly the conclusion that ISO-New England, the region's power grid operator, stated in a report it published in January 2018. The report, titled "Operational Fuel Security Analysis," claimed that if nothing was done to alleviate the natural gas pipeline bottleneck to the region, by the mid-2020s, New England could be subject to rolling blackouts during periods of severe winter cold.[10]

The New England Power Pool is the region's group of electricity stakeholders. When this type of analysis is done, they are usually included in the process. But ISO-New England neglected to include them. It didn't include the owners of New England's two LNG import facilities. ISO also made a few assumptions that were way off the mark. It assumed that natural gas demand for use by utility customers would see huge increases. It was an overestimation that resulted in an erroneous conclusion that New England would see complete depletion of natural gas during cold snaps. ISO's other misstep in its report was to completely underestimate the positive effects energy efficiency would bring to the table over the next decade.

It was clear that ISO-New England's study was sending a message to readers that only more natural gas can solve New England's future energy supply issues. But in reality, more natural gas capacity into New England just prolongs that region's move toward a sustainable energy model and creates even more dependence on natural gas. One of the other factors that ISO-New England failed to take into account was the Energy and Diversity Act of 2016 passed by the Massachusetts state legislature. It requires Massachusetts to import clean hydro energy from Canada and contract for 1.6 GW of offshore wind by 2027. Roughly one-third of that wind capacity should be online by 2023. Had ISO-New England taken this information into account when it did its study, its determination would not have been as dire.

In fact, it would have shown that a diversified energy mix, including renewables and storage, improves the reliability of any energy grid. And ISO-New England's conclusions fly in the face of another study commissioned by the attorney general of Massachusetts back in November 2015. It concluded that, "there's no reliability problem though 2030 so long as we continue to pursue our national leading energy efficiency and renewable programs."[11]

The bottom line is New England doesn't need more natural gas capacity and the pipelines it would need to get it. What it really needs is a focused program to increase the amount of renewables and battery storage on its grid. Adding more natural gas makes it even more difficult to meet climate change goals. And it would create even more stranded assets that ISO-New England's customers would eventually end up paying for. Its grid reliability goes up as the amount of renewables goes up and reliance on natural gas goes down. Renewables plus storage just seems like a no-brainer when you take the pair at face value. They provide grid resilience and stability, which completely flies in the face of what some legacy-loving individuals are advocating. But we are at a renewable tipping point, and their inclusion into twenty-first-century grid planning and development is unstoppable. In fact, having them as part of any modern electrical grid architecture is a basic requirement.

HUGE EXPENDITURES ON TRANSMISSION AND DISTRIBUTION INFRASTRUCTURE ARE OVER

For the last hundred years or so, utilities expanded **generation, transmission,** and **distribution infrastructures** in anticipation of future load expansion. And it was a plan that worked. The annual 2 to 3 percent load growth that the average US electric grid saw was directly correlated to the growth in US **gross domestic product (GDP).**

That's no longer the case. And it's almost entirely due to the rapid growth in rooftop solar as well as energy efficiency measures like LED bulbs and more efficient appliances, all of which are driving the demand for electricity down. But at the same time, electric vehicle charging is starting to drive it up.

This is a real problem for grid planning engineers. They have to make investment decisions on assets that are designed to last 50 years. And the information they have to base their decisions on is extremely fluid. For the first time since electric grids were first designed and built, engineers must deal with the very real possibility that new thermal generation, transmission, and distribution infrastructure added to keep the grid "stable" might not be needed.

COAL-FIRED ELECTRIC GENERATION IS HISTORY ... IS NUCLEAR NEXT?

The collapse of coal-fired power generation has had devastating effects on America's coalmines. But cheap renewable and natural gas–fired generation is also weighing heavily on America's remaining nuclear power plants. Nuclear power was once hailed as the world's "cleanest" source of energy. But now, there is a nuclear renaissance in reverse in the United States. And it's being fueled by renewables and natural gas. It's another no-brainer. And once again, it's pure economics.

Back in the heyday of nuclear power, it was hailed as "too cheap to meter." Fast-forward to 2018 and nuclear is anything but too cheap to meter. In an electricity market dominated by cheap energy from solar, wind, and natural gas, nuclear power is rapidly failing. Let's look at the newest nuclear power generators under construction in the United States. They are Vogtle Units 3 and 4.

This massive boondoggle is being sold to Southern Company's Georgia Power customers. They will be paying for this project for generations to come. The original construction estimate for Vogtle was $14 billion. Units 3 and 4 were scheduled to be online in April 2016. After cost overruns totaling billions, the new price tag has soared to $29 billion. But don't expect these units to be producing power anytime soon.[12]

Southern Company estimates Vogtle will cost an additional $3.9 billion to complete by 2022. But existing current and future debt service is straining Southern Company's balance sheet. Not too surprising, Moody's has a negative outlook on the company's stock, which is rated Baa2. That's only a level or two above junk status.

At the end of 2017, Southern Company had long-term debt of $44.46 billion.[13] Just imagine if Southern Company had bet on solar and natural gas instead of Vogtle. It would already be producing plenty of clean energy. What's more, its customers wouldn't be on the hook for tens of billions of dollars. It's an expensive lesson for Southern Company. It's too soon to tell if Vogtle will ever be completed. Let's look at why other nuclear plants are closing here in the United States.

NUCLEAR PLANTS ARE DROPPING LIKE DOMINOS

At last count, there are 99 nuclear power plants licensed to operate here in the United States.[14] Sixteen have scheduled closing dates of 2025 or sooner.[15] That means over the next seven years, 25 percent of America's nuclear power fleet will be gone. It's just too expensive to keep these giant maintenance nightmares running. In January 2018, California officials voted to close the last operating nuclear plant in the state. By 2025, the Diablo Canyon Power Plant will be closed.[16]

In April 2018, FirstEnergy Corporation (NYSE: FE) announced it is closing three nuclear power plants in Ohio and Pennsylvania.[17] The reason? They cost too much money to run. So much for "too cheap to meter." Utility executives at FirstEnergy and at other utilities are appealing to lawmakers for money. Their nuclear plants just can't operate profitably.

The latest announcement came in August 2018. NextEra, the owner of the Duane Arnold nuclear plant in Iowa, says it's closing the plant early. NextEra claims that closing the plant now will save Iowans $42 annually in electricity costs starting in 2021. If all of the planned nuclear plant closings move forward, the U.S. nuclear plant fleet will drop from its current level of 99 plants to 89 by 2025.[18]

And state public utility commissions aren't willing to have customers shoulder the costs. But nearly all state and federal lawmakers are turning a blind eye toward the utilities' nuclear woes. In January 2018, the Federal Energy Regulatory Commission (FERC) sidelined a Trump administration plan to prop up coal and nuclear power plants. Energy Secretary Rick Perry suggested coal and nuclear plants should have a 90-day fuel supply on hand. He also suggested US taxpayers should pay for it. FERC disagreed, and voted the measure down.

In October 2018, a Trump nominated Bernard McNamee to FERC. He replaces outgoing commissioner Ron Powelson. McNamee is a big champion of Trump's coal and nuclear bailout. Trump is still hopeful FERC will pass his plan, which has been regularly denounced by former FERC commissioners, various consumer groups, and the solar, wind, natural gas, and energy efficiency sectors.[19]

The oldest operating nuclear plant belongs to Exelon Corporation (NYSE: EXC). It's the Oyster Creek plant located in Lacey Township, New Jersey. The plant originally went online on December 1, 1969. The plant's biggest problem is lack of storage for cooling water. The company is closing the plant in October 2018,[20] over a year ahead of schedule. Exelon cites excessive maintenance costs and cheap power from natural gas and renewables as the reason.

Another very real example of unnecessary generation expansion occurred in South Carolina. As I mentioned earlier, in 2008, nuclear industry executives predicted a "nuclear renaissance."[21] Never mind that no utility had started a new reactor project since the 1970s. Fast-forward a decade. In August 2017, two South Carolina utilities announced they were abandoning the V.C. Summer nuclear project. The project was to have two reactors when completed sometime in 2018. Today, the reactors are each about 40 percent complete. Cost to date? About $9 billion. The original cost estimate was $11.5 billion. The estimate to complete them now is $25 billion.

The SCANA Corporation and Santee Cooper, South Carolina's state-owned electric and water utility, jointly own the V.C. Summer project. The two new reactors were under construction next to an existing nuclear reactor. In order to keep the project afloat, the two utilities appealed to "high White House officials," according to SCANA's CEO Kevin Marsh. This included Energy Secretary Rick Perry. His answer? No response. It appears even Washington isn't interested in reviving American nuclear power.[22]

What's wrong with America's nuclear industry? The engineering expertise and the robust supply chains needed to build these plants no longer exist. They've been atrophying for the past 30 years. That's one issue facing today's nuclear projects. Another is the reactor supplier. The Westinghouse Electric Company had been building nuclear reactors for decades. But on March 29, 2017, Westinghouse filed for bankruptcy protection. That was a big nail in the coffin of the V.C. Summer project.

But the biggest nail of all is the overall cost of nuclear power generating plants. They take one or two decades to permit and construct. Even the most ambitious solar and wind projects are permitted and constructed in a year or two. And for tens of billions of dollars less. But the bottom line is the final cost of the energy they produce. Nuclear power, when the costs of the plant, storing the toxic waste it produces, and the operating costs are all taken into account, is the most expensive power source on the planet. There's no question nuclear power served America well for more than half a century.

The disruption of nuclear power is one that utilities didn't see coming. In the case of nuclear (and coal) the disruption is an economic one. Many existing plants are eligible for 20-year extensions from the Nuclear Regulatory Commission. But economics trump license extensions. I wouldn't be a bit surprised if most of our nuclear power plants closed over the next several decades. Expensive nuclear has no place in today's world of cheap, renewable energy. The twenty-first century is going to be one of energy disruption: The "nuclear sunset" and the "rise of renewables" are all part of it.

PJM Interconnection is one of the **regional transmission organizations (RTOs)**. It overlooks the transmission grid that covers most of Delaware, Illinois, Indiana, Kentucky, Maryland, Michigan, New Jersey, North Carolina, Ohio, Pennsylvania, Tennessee, Virginia, West Virginia, and the District of Columbia. PJM is responsible for coordinating the movement of electricity (at the wholesale level) between major markets and the generators tied to the grid serving those markets, and it acts as a referee in a price-competitive market. Ultimately, it's responsible for grid reliability for over 65 million Americans.

As part of its duties, PJM has to estimate the growth of electrical loads within the aforementioned areas. That has never been an easy task. And for the last decade, PJM has consistently overestimated its summer peak load. Its projections specified that in 2017 load growth was going to increase. But it never materialized. That's a real problem for customers. They're the ones footing the bill me personally, because I live in PJM's coverage area.

Today we see progressive organizations taking a much more cautious view toward any transmission and distribution upgrades. In 2017, Arizona Public Service (APS) had a big little problem. The small village of Punkin Center, 90 miles northeast of Phoenix, needed more power.

Only 600 people live in this tiny hamlet. APS could upgrade 20 miles of a 21-KV transmission line that serviced the village. The line would have to traverse very mountainous terrain. Constructing it would be very expensive.

So APS looked into a battery storage system. It found the cost to be far less than the transmission line. It installed two MW-worth of storage on land it owned in Punkin Center. Now, on the 20 to 30 days during the year when Punkin Center's load would have overloaded the existing transmission line, APS can source additional power from the battery system. The overall cost ended up being less than half of the transmission line upgrade.[23] It's a great example of not having to install a thumbtack with a sledgehammer. The project is one of several APS has installed in its territory, and the utility now considers storage as part of any new transmission and distribution upgrade discussion.

Another advantage of battery storage, often overlooked by its detractors, is its flexibility. An upgraded transmission or distribution system can only provide relief to one place. And transmission and distribution lines can take years to permit and install. A battery storage system can be permitted and installed in six months, whereas a battery storage system can source power onto a grid that can then be directed anywhere. What's more, if storage is no longer needed in one place, it can be dismantled and moved to another. Storage can solve headaches for utilities and soothe the wallets of utility ratepayers. Everybody wins.

A NATURAL GAS CRISIS WITH AN ENERGY STORAGE SOLUTION

The Aliso Canyon Oil Field and Natural Gas Storage Facility is an underground oil reservoir containing both oil and natural gas. It's located in the Santa Susana Mountains, north of Los Angeles. It was initially discovered in 1938 and underwent rapid development. Oil production from Aliso Canyon peaked in the 1950s. After the depletion of its oil and gas resources, the Southern California Gas Company (SoCalGas), a subsidiary of Sempra Energy, converted it to an underground natural gas storage reservoir in 1973. The reservoir has a capacity of more than 86 billion cubic feet of natural gas.[24] That makes it the second-largest underground natural gas storage facility in the United States.

SoCalGas used Aliso Canyon to store natural gas for future use during winter peak heating periods. It also withdrew natural gas during peak summer months as air conditioners created more demand for electricity. Gas is accessed via one of 115 injection wells on the property. There are 38 miles of interconnecting pipelines from the wells to distribution and transmission pipelines. The average thickness of the reservoir is 160 feet, and it's located roughly 9,000 feet below the surface.[25]

On October 23, 2015, SoCalGas employees found a huge natural gas leak at Aliso Canyon. Natural gas was leaking from a well on the property. It was not until February 11, 2016, that SoCalGas brought the leak under control. A week later on February 18, California state officials announced that a permanent plug had successfully been installed in the leaking well.[26] The duration of the leak resulted in a massive natural gas release. At its peak, the well was leaking 4.5 metric tons of ethane. But its 60 metric tons of methane leaking every hour was twice the methane emissions rate of the entire greater Los Angeles area. Altogether, 97,100 metric tons of methane were released as a result of the leak, making the Aliso Canyon leak the largest natural gas atmospheric spill in US history.[27]

As a result, San Diego Gas & Electric (SDG&E), the electric utility for Southern California, now had a big problem. It relied on natural gas from the Aliso Canyon Storage Facility to power its peak natural gas–fired turbine generators during peak summer periods of electricity demand. It needed a solution it could quickly deploy. Gas peaker plants were out of the question. Traditional solar and wind were also off the table due to their intermittent nature. The solution had to be compact, since it would be servicing densely populated areas around San Diego and Los Angeles.

At the time, grid-scale battery storage was still very new. The California Public Utilities Commission (CPUC) was fearful of blackouts. It mandated several measures in order to find a quick solution to the problem, one of which was quick approval of an energy storage solution. The CPUC told SDG&E and Southern California Edison to find a battery storage system supplier that could deliver and put a system into operation in a few months.

SDG&E decided to make this a major test case for its service area. So in August 2016, SDG&E chose AES Energy Storage to build the two energy storage projects. Together, they are 37.5 MW, and can store a total of 150 MWh of electricity. They are located at several sites, one of which is a substation in Escondido, a northern suburb of San Diego. The Escondido system contains 24 containers that house numerous racks of lithium-ion battery packs.

Because of the tight schedule as dictated by the CPUC, AES was at an advantage. It was and is the world's largest energy storage system installer. AES's contract with SDG&E stipulates that AES must maintain the nameplate capacity of the system (37.5 MW for four hours) for 10 years. After that, maintenance is the responsibility of SDG&E. In order to meet capacity for the full 10-year timeframe, AES oversized the project upfront.[28] The system is used to meet peak loads, and therefore is discharged and charged almost completely on a daily basis. This is a strain on lithium-ion cells, hence the oversizing of the project.

Even prior to the Aliso Canyon disaster, SDG&E was taking a serious look at energy storage. James Avery, the chief development officer for the utility, raised some eyebrows at the 2015 Energy Storage North America conference when he dreamed out loud to the audience, "I see a future where there will be no more gas turbines. Two years ago, we were only looking at gas turbines." Avery believes that we are living through the energy storage tipping point. Soon he thinks it will be commonplace to use energy storage in place of gas peaker plants and even baseload plants.[29]

It's clear that energy storage is going to be a benefit to electric utilities, especially as their grids have more and more solar and wind energy generation systems tied to them. The combination of renewables and energy storage is going to eventually replace most other conventional forms of power generation. In the next chapter, we are going to look at the effects that electric vehicles (EVs) are going to have on the world's power grids, and how someday, they may turn into sources of grid power when not being driven.

NOTES

1. s2.q4cdn.com/601666628/files/doc_presentations/2017/Everoze-Batteries-Beyond-the-Spin.pdf
2. aesukireland.com/our-business/energy-storage/kilroot-energy-storage/default.aspx

3. ieefa.org/wp-content/uploads/2018/02/Cheap-Renewables-Transforming-Global-Electricity-2018.pdf

4. ieefa.org/wp-content/uploads/2018/02/Cheap-Renewables-Transforming-Global-Electricity-2018.pdf

5. ieefa.org/wp-content/uploads/2018/02/Cheap-Renewables-Transforming-Global-Electricity-2018.pdf

6. www.nexteraenergy.com/sustainability/environment/renewable-energy.html

7. www.nexteraenergy.com/company/work/battery-storage.html#

8. www.bizjournals.com/phoenix/news/2018/05/16/srp-nextera-unveil-states-largest-60-million-grid.html

9. marcellusdrilling.com/2018/01/new-englands-lack-of-pipelines-most-expensive-gas-in-the-world/

10. www.renewableenergyworld.com/articles/2018/05/report-renewables-energy-efficiency-in-new-england-will-replace-the-need-for-gas-pipelines.html?cmpid=enl_rew_solar_energy_news_2018-05-26&pwhid=2bb71543f97d6dc6da41d4b5652a6a6a735c8dabc6f15061235368f662666b5ebd83032edcfe697279767714bcfc1f90ae0bf66ea4b40c1b4aadb176d3a9caa1&eid=288141552&bid=2116814

11. Ibid.

12. www.reuters.com/article/us-toshiba-accounting-westinghouse-bankr/group-says-georgia-nuclear-plant-costs-rise-to-29-billion-idUSKBN1962YH

13. seekingalpha.com/article/4151561-southern-companys-complete-commitment-completing-plant-vogtle

14. www.world-nuclear.org/information-library/country-profiles/countries-t-z/usa-nuclear-power.aspx

15. www.beyondnuclear.org/reactors-are-closing/

16. www.latimes.com/business/la-fi-diablo-canyon-nuclear-20180111-story.html

17. https://stateimpact.npr.org/pennsylvania/2018/03/29/firstenergy-says-its-closing-three-nuclear-plants-seeks-federal-help/

18. https://www.forbes.com/sites/michaelshellenberger/2018/08/01/nuclear-plant-closures-show-why-when-it-comes-to-energy-small-is-expensive/#3ef8e9c771a2

19. https://www.greentechmedia.com/articles/read/key-backer-of-trumps-coal-and-nuclear-bailout-effort-is-nominated-to-ferc#gs.kOzfuxQ

20. www.powermag.com/exelon-cuts-jobs-ahead-of-oyster-creek-closure/

21. www.eba-net.org/assets/1/6/6-279_-_frye_nukes-clean_final_print_11-2-08.pdf

22. www.utilitydive.com/news/scana-ceo-white-house-did-not-respond-to-pleas-for-summer-nuke-support/448498/

23. www.greentechmedia.com/articles/read/aes-buys-energy-storage-for-less-than-half-the-cost-of-a-wires-upgrade#gs.tGKCsT4

24. www.socalgas.com/regulatory/documents/a-14-11-004/SCG-06_P__Baker_Testimony.pdf

25. ftp://ftp.consrv.ca.gov/pub/oil/Summary_of_Operations/1959/Vol45No1.pdf

26. www.scpr.org/news/2016/02/10/57348/sorting-out-porter-ranch-facts-vs-rumors/
27. science.sciencemag.org/content/351/6279/1317
28. www.utilitydive.com/news/inside-construction-of-the-worlds-largest-lithium-ion-battery-storage-faci/431765/
29. www.utilitydive.com/news/esna-2015-why-energy-storage-is-key-to-a-future-with-no-more-gas-turbines/407409/

CHAPTER SIXTEEN

EVs as an Energy Source

With a little software and a few more electronic circuits, utilities can easily turn a homeowner's EV into a backup or evening source of stored power. I will discuss the potential ramifications of this, as it will eventually be a standard or optional feature on every EV sold. First, let's look at the effects that an increasing level of electric vehicles is going to have on the world's oil markets.

PEAK OIL ... AGAIN

In 2010, I wrote and spoke about the concept of "peak oil." Simply put, this theory states that global oil *production* will hit a maximum (peak) level before declining.[1] Oil prices had hit a record high of $147 a barrel in July 2008, and many analysts focused on the supply-demand equation and the topic of peak oil. Back then, peak oil was all about peak *supply*. The introduction of hydraulic fracking and horizontal drilling has since blown the peak oil supply argument right out of the picture. Producers have developed so much new supply during the last decade that the United States is now the world's top crude producer.

Fast-forward to 2018. Fuel efficiency is increasing as new technologies are reducing the amount of fuel needed in fossil fuel–powered vehicles. New carbon emission rules are continuing to go into effect in nations other than the United States. But there's one important change happening that could start to lower the amount of oil the world consumes every day. And that's the switchover to EVs from fossil fuel-powered cars and trucks.

EV adoption is close to its tipping point. When that happens, EVs will quickly become the dominant type of vehicles offered for purchase at car dealerships around the world. In Norway, every second car sold is an EV.[2] And that means we will approach "peak oil" once again. But this time, "peak oil" will mean something entirely different.

I'm talking about peak oil *demand*. With the introduction of EVs, we'll slowly start to see a reduction in the demand for gasoline and diesel. We'll also see a corresponding decrease in the demand for crude. A drop in oil demand and the timing of the peak will depend on when mass adoption of EVs starts. This will have far-reaching ramifications for the oil industry. In fact, hitting peak oil demand while the world economies are in growth mode will be the first time oil demand has dropped since the first well was sunk by Colonel Edwin Drake back in the 1850s in Titusville, Pennsylvania.

All the major oil companies are focused on getting the peak oil prediction right. They are sitting on trillions of dollars' worth of oil reserves. The big problem is that the peak of oil demand is due to disruptive forces. As a result, when the peak comes, it's going to be much more rapid than anyone realizes. And that's what makes it very difficult to predict. When the peak arrives, the global oil market will likely remain volatile for months or even years as the adjustments to the oil market take place. Prices will plunge because supply will exceed demand for some period. Many of the smaller independent producers will go out of business trying to resize.

In the 2018 edition of BP's *Energy Outlook*, the oil giant sees crude demand slowing and then plateauing in the late 2030s. It expects global passenger vehicles to double to two billion by 2040. That fleet would include over 320 million EVs. That's a 100-fold increase over today's EV numbers. In BP's latest (2018) scenario, it expects 190 million EVs by 2035. (That's almost double what BP predicted in 2017's *Energy Outlook*.)[3] BP thinks US oil demand will peak around 18.7 million barrels per day (Mb/d) and finally start declining by the end of the next decade.[4]

Even back in 2017, shareholders of Occidental Petroleum Corporation voted in favor of making the company look at the long-term effects of climate change on its future business. That was the very first time shareholders of one of the big oil companies undertook this kind of vote.[5]

Some oil executives are kidding themselves. Most notably, the CEO of Saudi Aramco. Amin Nasser doesn't see EVs as a threat for at least several decades. Chevron and Exxon Mobil don't foresee a peak in oil demand at all. Shell seems to be getting the message. The company, which sees a peak in oil demand occurring in the years between 2025 and 2030, remains increasingly focused on natural gas as it moves away from oil. Total is doing the same thing, forecasting an oil demand peak in 2040. The exact date of peak oil demand isn't easy to predict. The important thing is that it's coming.[6] And that means a lot of the world's oil is going to stay right where it is: in the ground. Expensive-to-get, offshore deep-water fields are particularly vulnerable.

But that's only part of the story. By 2040, autonomous vehicles will be widespread, and most of them will be EVs. That's because EVs have much lower maintenance costs than internal combustion engine (ICE) vehicles. Today EVs are only racking up about 2 percent of all passenger vehicle miles. Fast-forward to 2040: Autonomous EVs will account for at least 30 percent of passenger miles.[7]

I think crude oil demand is going to peak lower and decline sooner. Fessler's second law of technology states, "When it comes to technology, changes happen much faster than anyone expects they will." All you have to do is look at how rapidly smartphones have become widespread. It took a decade or less for half the world's population to have one in their pocket. Why would the widespread adoption of EVs by the car-buying public take any longer?

Battery pack energy densities are rapidly increasing, and their costs are quickly dropping. I think we could hit peak oil demand by 2025. I think half the vehicles on our planet's highways could be EVs by 2040. That will bring down crude demand much faster than current projections. And it will be much faster than most of the scenarios being looked at by the big oil companies. But the decline of oil and the widespread adoption of EVs is good news for another group of companies: electric utilities.

EVs: THE STRATEGIC OPPORTUNITY OF THE TWENTY-FIRST CENTURY FOR UTILITIES

There's no question that Steve Jobs was a true visionary. His forward thinking started Apple, Inc. on its way to becoming the biggest company in the world. He had a knack for knowing what the public wanted before it did. He and his design teams went on to create and change thousands of different businesses, from music to personal communications.

Another visionary equal in brilliance to Jobs is Elon Musk. On April 8, 2016, one of his companies, SpaceX, successfully stuck the landing of a used Falcon 9 first stage rocket on a drone ship parked in the Atlantic. As if that wasn't difficult enough, high winds and heavy seas added to the drama. But SpaceX did it anyway. It was a fantastic display of technology. The second stage boosted the Dragon spacecraft into orbit to rendezvous with the International Space Station. But space isn't the only place Musk is displaying his advanced technology. He's also the Chairman and CEO of Tesla, Inc., the biggest EV company in the world. But Musk describes it as a sustainable energy company.

Now utilities are slowly starting to embrace EVs, and for good reason. For years, utilities were stable, income-producing machines for their shareholders. But with the advent of distributed energy resources (DERs), like solar and cheap battery storage systems, utilities are facing declining revenues. Enter the electric vehicle.

At first, utilities, along with many auto industry pundits, dismissed EVs as another passing fad. The thought was EVs would disappear as soon as oil prices dropped. But oil prices did drop, and EVs continued to sell. As of 2018, oil prices are double what they were just a year or so ago, and EV sales are strong and getting stronger.

On March 31, 2016, Tesla unveiled its long-awaited Model 3. Tesla billed it as its "EV for the masses." It looks like Elon Musk had another home run on his hands. According to a shareholder letter issued in May 2018, Tesla had over 450,000 Model 3 reservations worldwide as of the end of Q1 2018.[8] The expected sales price ranged from $35,000 to $42,000. The part that sold the car though is the range, estimated to be 210 miles per charge (standard battery) to as much as 310 miles (long-range battery).[9]

Tesla got the ball rolling with EVs, and its inexpensive Model 3 is receiving widespread adoption. Now manufacturers such as Ford, GM, BMW, and nearly all the other car and truck manufacturers, have EV models either in production or design. But why are utilities so interested in EVs? As I mentioned, utilities are now coming around to the fact that EVs are here to stay. EVs use a fair amount of electricity to recharge, and therefore represent an additional monthly income stream.

How much will an EV add to the average monthly utility bill? The number will vary widely and will depend on the cost of electricity where the driver lives, how many miles a month he or she drives, and the EV's energy consumption rate. The average cost of power in the United States is 12 cents per kilowatt-hour (kWh).[10] Let's assume the EV owner drives 15,000 miles per year. His car is a Tesla Model S P90D with an energy consumption rate of 32.33 kWh per 100 miles.[11] To determine his monthly EV charging bill, we must calculate the total number of kWh used monthly: $((((15,000/100) \times 32.33) \times .12)/12)$. In the case of this example, the monthly EV charging costs are $48.50. For smaller cars with smaller motors and battery packs, monthly energy costs will be less.

The potential of wringing another $30, $40, or even $50 per month out of each of its customers is attractive to American utilities. That's "found money" for them. Right now Americans spend about the same amount for electricity as they do for fossil fuels, about $400 billion per year on each. Shifting $400 billion from the fossil fuel industry over to the electric utility industry will mean massive changes. Let's say utilities could capture all of the electricity used to charge light-duty EVs through the EV charging stations in their territories. That would increase electric sales by about $100 billion annually. EV drivers would save about $300 billion per year in fossil fuel costs. That's because EVs are four times as efficient as fossil-fuel vehicles.

Higher electricity sales will increase the pressure on utilities to lower rates. That would benefit all utility customers. Most EV charging takes place in the wee hours of the night when electricity use is at its lowest levels. Utilities can rake in more revenues without building new generating plants. By flattening out electricity demand curves, utilities can get more revenue to cover existing assets. That means they can charge less to recoup their costs.

A NEW SOURCE OF POWER GENERATION FOR UTILITIES: V2G

While it's not in place yet, the ability for a utility to control its DERs means it potentially has a large, dispatchable, and growing baseload source of power. This is the concept of vehicle-to-grid (V2G) power. The idea is that EVs can provide power back into the grid when not in use. It can then recharge its battery pack during periods of low electricity demand.

A V2G system must have three components: (1) a connection (through its charging system) to the grid, (2) a control connection necessary for communication with the grid Independent System Operator (ISO), and (3) EV onboard software for control and power metering. Figure 16.1 shows the connection between fleet EVs, an individual EV, and the power grid. Electricity flows one way from large generators through the transmission and distribution grids to customers. Electricity can flow back into the grid via individual EVs or fleet EVs. Also depicted is the ISO that is broadcasting control signals (request for power) to numerous EVs available to provide power to the grid.

At today's adoption rates, it's not unreasonable to assume that within 20 years, 25 percent of today's US fleet of 253 million[12] cars and trucks will be electrified (63.25 million). The average EV battery pack is 75 kW. These battery packs are capable of producing peak bursts of power in the 50 to 100 kW range. But I'm going to conservatively assume the average EV is capable of sourcing just 15 kW of power, taking into account building wiring capacity limits. Owners use their EVs an average of 17,600 minutes per year, or 48 minutes per day, just like fossil fuel vehicle owners.[13] That's only 3.3 percent of the time. That means 96.7 percent of the time an EV can plug into a charging port.

FIGURE 16.1   HYPOTHETICAL V2G SCHEMATIC

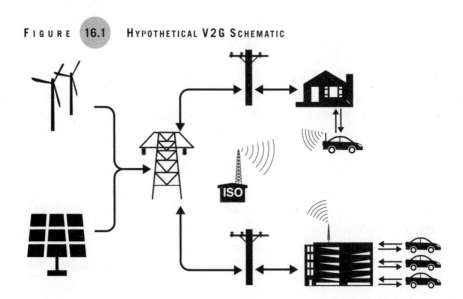

The total amount of available system power from the US EV fleet is 948.75 GW (63.25 million × 15 kW). With proper control software, all of that power would be available to utilities within milliseconds to seconds. Compare that to the total system power of America's conventional power generation system. It consists of 1,080 GW of utility-scale power[14] generation from all sources. Note that at a 25 percent EV penetration rate, the amount of power available from them to US utilities is nearly equal to the entire capacity of today's generating fleet. The capital necessary to tap EVs as a power source is one to two orders of magnitude less than building new fossil-fuel power plants. Add another order of magnitude or two if we're comparing EVs to nuclear power plant costs.

There are four power markets in which V2G could participate. They are baseload, peak, spinning reserves, and frequency regulation. Baseload power is "on" all the time. Baseload provides the bulk of all power generated. Peak power is necessary for periods of high demand, and usually occurs in the morning and evening hours. Peak power is also needed during periods of high temperatures when maximum air conditioning load is present. Spinning reserves (sometimes referred to as operating reserves) are synchronous generators in standby mode. They are ready to connect to the grid at a moment's notice in case of an existing generator fault. Spinning reserves are generally only required one or two times per month and then only for 10 minutes to one hour. Frequency regulation is only necessary for a few minutes at most but may be needed 400 times in any given day.[15]

Both spinning reserves and frequency regulation providers are paid just for being available to use, whereas baseload and peak are paid based on the number of kWh generated. V2G is not suitable for baseload requirements. The length of time it's available is too short. It is, however, usable for peak power generation in some circumstances. V2G is very competitive for spinning reserves as well as frequency regulation.

The central issue that planners need to address for a viable V2G environment is balancing the requirements Of EV owners/drivers and the utility grid operator. EV drivers must have enough battery power available to meet their daily driving requirements. The grid operator must have a power source that is available at precise times during the day. There are three ways to mitigate potential conflicts: (1) increase vehicle battery pack size, (2) use power from EV fleets with scheduled usage (municipal EV buses, etc.), and (3) use intelligent control software that compliments both parties.

Increasing the EV battery size adds cost and weight to the vehicle and would not generally be acceptable to the EV owner. The reason V2G is viable in the first place is that the EV sits idle 96.7 percent of the time. Using fleet vehicles for V2G is a perfect example. A fleet of electric UPS trucks that are in use from 8:00 a.m. to 5:00 p.m. can predictably be used for V2G power purposes for the other 15 hours of the day during the week, and all day Saturday and Sunday. The entire V2G market, however, is much larger than that which could be realized with just fleet vehicle participation.

That brings us to the third strategy: using intelligent software to complement the needs of both parties is the primary V2G application. It turns out that the needs of EV drivers and grid operators complement each other. They need the power of the battery pack at different times, and these times are predictable. Their needs also differ in one other respect: one needs energy and the other needs power. Most driving times are predictable. But spinning reserve and frequency regulation power requirements are unpredictable. EV drivers need the stored energy in their particular vehicles at the start of a trip. The grid operator, on the other hand, needs power, possibly at numerous times. And that power is generally required instantaneously. The grid operator could care less what EV or EVs the power comes from.

How can the V2G needs of the EV driver and grid operator be managed? With today's increasingly smart artificial intelligence (AI) software, the vehicle could easily "learn" the driving patterns of the owner. After a short time, the software could allow the EV to offer V2G services to the local utility. Drivers could have a single button on a touch screen menu that would override V2G participation at any given time.

A second complementary scenario is between the grid operator and the owner of the home where the EV resides. When the grid operator doesn't need spinning reserves or frequency regulation and the grid power goes down, the homeowner is generally in need of backup power. Traditionally, backup generators provide this. The lag time of getting a seldom-used generator running and connected to the home "grid" must be considered.

Backup power from an EV is available nearly instantaneously (within a few milliseconds) and could serve the homeowner for a few hours or even a few days if restricted to just lighting and refrigeration.

Powerful software can look at the status of all the EVs in a utility's territory. Additionally, it would create a database listing the available EVs at any given instant. When additional power is required, the utility could instantly tell any number of available EVs to start sourcing power onto the grid to meet that specific need. Automatic billing would compensate the EV owners. They would then receive credit for the power used by the utility. For utilities, it's a huge cost avoidance, in the form of not having to build, operate, and maintain a new power generating plant.

Now utilities are just starting to consider all of this in a favorable view. Let's face it: This is entirely disruptive to the 100-year-old way of doing things, from a utility's perspective. But utilities and the bodies that regulate them are both like a big ship. It takes time to turn it around. This is the direction in which we are going, however. And as with most advances in renewable energy, California is leading the way in the United States.

In 2015, the electric grid in California needed 10,091 MW of quick-responding generating resources to satisfy a load spike that lasted as long as three hours. It typically started in the late afternoon and continued well into the evening. Getting power during the day isn't a problem in the Golden State, as its abundant rooftop solar keeps demand flat during the day. By 2019, however, continuing widespread adoption of EVs in California could send its power demand spike to 14,000 MW.[16]

Natural gas peaker plants could easily meet that demand. But that flies in the face of California's plan to greatly reduce its greenhouse gas emissions. And utility-scale battery storage would not provide enough electricity. Enter EVs. California utilities have long known about the benefits of EVs as a revenue source. But now they are looking at them as a potential source of power that could help deal with California's growing afternoon/evening power demands. According to the California Public Utilities Commission (CPUC), EV battery storage could be the answer.

Its proposed framework looks at what it refers to as Vehicle-Grid Integration (VGI). It expects customer vehicles would be compensated for VGI benefits provided to the utility for several different charging and sourcing arrangements. As was mentioned earlier, California's afternoon/evening peak demand could spike to 14 GW by 2019. If all EV owners were to charge during California's evening peak demand, additional generating capacity and major grid upgrades would all be necessary. But most EV owners are asleep in the early morning hours. That's when EV charging can take place if programmed to do so. In the afternoon/evening peak demand time, EVs could be programmed to source power back onto the grid. VGI changes EVs from a problem that utility grid operators have to deal with to a generating asset that can be used to mitigate afternoon/evening peak demand.

It's clear that EVs connected to charging stations that have the ability to both charge an EV battery and source power back onto the grid are a valuable resource for utilities. Utilities can use EVs' flexibility as a group in lieu of natural gas peaker plants to meet peak power demands. We have the technology, and it's a simple matter of implementation. My bet is California will solve the problem first. This will provide the model for other states to follow.

NOTES

1. David C. Fessler, "Forget 'Peak Oil'... Let's Talk About 'Peak Energy,'" Investment U e-Letter, no. 1245, April 23, 2010.

2. www.mckinsey.com/industries/automotive-and-assembly/our-insights/the-global-electric-vehicle-market-is-amped-up-and-on-the-rise?cid=other-eml-alt-mip-mck-oth-1805&hlkid=967d8c9e6ffd4733b6215db3bac35072&hctky=1657310&hdpid=7614e4eb-6c11-4d8e-85fb-0f415f6005d1

3. https://www.bp.com/content/dam/bp/en/corporate/pdf/energy-economics/energy-outlook/bp-energy-outlook-2017.pdf

4. https://www.bp.com/content/dam/bp/en/corporate/pdf/energy-economics/energy-outlook/bp-energy-outlook-2018.pdf (p. 113)

5. www.wsj.com/articles/get-ready-for-peak-oil-demand-1495419061?mg=prod/accounts-wsj&mg=prod/accounts-wsj

6. www.wsj.com/articles/get-ready-for-peak-oil-demand-1495419061?mg=prod/accounts-wsj&mg=prod/accounts-wsj

7. oilprice.com/Energy/Energy-General/Bank-Of-America-EVs-To-Lead-To-Peak-Oil-Demand-In-2030.html

8. https://techcrunch.com/2018/06/28/tesla-opens-model-3-reservations/

9. www.tesla.com/model3

10. www.edmunds.com/fuel-economy/the-true-cost-of-powering-an-electric-car
    .html
11. en.wikipedia.org/wiki/Tesla_Model_S
12. www.latimes.com/business/autos/la-fi-hy-ihs-automotive-average-age-car-
    20140609-story.html
13. aaa.com/2016/09/americans-spend-average-17600-minutes-driving-year/
14. www.eia.gov/electricity/monthly/epm_table_grapher.php?t=epmt_6_01
15. citeseerx.ist.psu.edu/viewdoc/download?doi=10.1.1.186.8557&rep=
    rep1&type=pdf
16. www.utilitydive.com/news/how-california-utility-regulators-are-turning-
    electric-vehicles-into-grid-r/430314/

CHAPTER SEVENTEEN

Greenhouse Gases Disappear

The effect of not building more coal-fired utility generating stations and removing internal combustion engine cars from the road is already having a profound positive effect on lowering greenhouse gases (GHG). In this chapter, I'll look at some GHG projections into the future.

Of all the nasty things humans have done to damage the earth, creating a giant hole in the ozone layer is near or at the top of the list. The ozone layer protects our planet from receiving too much **ultraviolet (UV)** radiation. Excessive UV radiation is known to cause cataracts, skin cancer, plant damage, and immune system suppression. Two years after the reports of the scientists who discovered the hole were confirmed, several nations reacted quickly to solve the problem by signing the Montreal Protocol in 1987. The protocol ultimately banned **chlorofluorocarbons (CFCs)**, nasty chemicals that deplete ozone.

However, a new study done by NASA confirms that the hole in the ozone layer is finally closing. The hole is now the smallest it has been since 1988. This data comes from the Aura satellite, which has been measuring the levels of the nasty chemicals that created the hole in the first place. The study was published in January 2018 in *Geophysical Research Letters* and shows that a drop in ozone-depleting chemicals has translated into a depletion that is 20 percent less than it was in 2005.

Susan Strahan, who works at NASA's Goddard Spaceflight Center and is an atmospheric scientist, was the lead author of the study. In a press release, she commented, "We see very clearly that chlorine from CFCs is going down in the ozone hole, and that less ozone depletion is occurring because of it."[1] The CFCs that Strahan was talking about are depleting the ozone. They were contained in refrigerants, aerosol sprays, and blowing agents used to make foam and packing material. The sun's ultraviolet radiation alters the CFCs and in the process creates chlorine, which causes a depletion of ozone.

The ozone hole was first detected back in the 1980s over Antarctica. It turns out that the extremely cold temperatures of the Antarctic stratosphere facilitate reactions that happen in polar stratospheric clouds. Those clouds form most readily around the poles. The Antarctic winters (July to mid-September) are the best time to measure changes in ozone. That's because temperatures are the coldest and the most stable during that time, allowing for extremely accurate measurements of ozone. The problem is, it's completely dark during winter in Antarctica, and most satellites need sunlight to measure gas levels in the atmosphere. However, the Aura satellite uses microwave technology, allowing measurement without sunlight. This enabled scientists to accurately measure ozone-depleting chlorine gas levels during Antarctic winters.

The good news is the level of chlorine has been declining 0.8 percent per year between 2005 and 2016, the last year for which data is available. The recovering ozone layer is a perfect example of humanity taking action to solve a global issue. Anne Douglass, a coauthor of the NASA study, said, "CFCs can remain in the atmosphere for 50–100 years. As far as the complete closure of the ozone hole, we're looking at 2060 or 2080, and even then there might still be a small hole."[2] However, we are clearly on the right track.

GLOBAL WARMING'S BIGGEST SKEPTIC

President Donald Trump has been a prominent vocal skeptic of global warming. For instance, on October 31, 2016, then-candidate Trump was speaking at a campaign rally in Warren, Michigan. Regarding climate change, he said, "It's time to put America first. We're going to put America first. That includes a promise to cancel billions in climate change spending for the United Nations."[3] His flurry of actions during his first year is intended to roll back many of President Obama's policies that curbed climate change and reduced limits on environmental pollution. Other efforts are focused on reducing federal environment and science funding.

Worried that incoming Trump administration officials might try to delete or alter US climate information databases, academics and scientists created the Environmental Data and Governance Initiative. It comprises an international network of nonprofit organizations and scientists who are concerned about "potential threats to federal environmental and energy policy and to the scientific research infrastructure built to investigate, inform, and enforce them. Dismantling this infrastructure – which ranges from databases to satellites to models for climate, air, and water – could imperil the public's right to know, the United States' standing as a scientific leader, corporate accountability, and environmental protection."[4]

Here's a partial list of environmental and climate change-focused actions Trump took and when he took them:

- January 24, 2017: President Trump issued a document aimed at fast-tracking the remaining permitting issues facing the Dakota Access and Keystone XL oil pipelines.
- January 25, 2017: All references to "climate change" are removed from White House website.
- February 16, 2017: Congress passes, and the president signs, a joint resolution weakening the US Department of the Interior's "Stream Protection Rule." The rule, passed under President Obama, would have placed even stricter limits on the dumping of wastewater from underground mines into surface waterways.
- February 17, 2017: Congress confirms Scott Pruitt as head of Environmental Protection Agency (EPA). Pruitt had a history of suing the EPA over a number of its regulations, most notably the Clean Power Plan.
- March 9, 2017: In an interview on CNBC's *Squawk Box*, Scott Pruitt says that it's unclear that carbon dioxide plays any role in climate change. This is completely opposed to world scientific consensus.

- March 13, 2017: The Trump White House releases its first preliminary budget. It proposes sharp cuts to EPA and National Oceanic and Atmospheric Administration (NOAA) budgets.
- March 24, 2017: President Trump's State Department green-lights the Keystone XL pipeline, granting it a federal permit to begin construction.
- March 28, 2017: President signs an executive order to begin rescinding the Clean Power Plan.
- April 14, 2017: EPA's Pruitt voices his opposition to the Paris Climate Agreement, calling it "a bad deal for America."
- April 19, 2017: The Interior Department deletes much of the climate change information from its website. The new page mentions "climate change" just once with no explanation of what it is, how it affects the earth, and what the Interior Department is doing to combat it despite the department having eight Climate Science Centers,[5] "to help resource managers cope with a changing climate."[6]
- April 28, 2017: The EPA removes the section that explained climate change from its website.
- May 23, 2017: Trump's 2018 final budget slashed the EPA's budget by 31 percent, the steepest cut of any federal agency. The cuts could equate to a $2.7 billion reduction in spending. In the crosshairs were cuts to Superfund cleanup funds, radon detection programs, and lead-risk reduction programs. Also, programs working to restore cleanliness of Puget Sound, the Great Lakes, and the Chesapeake Bay were all axed.
- June 1, 2017: President Trump tells the world that the United States is pulling out of the Paris Climate Agreement, a position in complete opposition of 194 other countries. By signing up to the agreement, those countries made promises to the world to help curb greenhouse gas (GHG) emissions.
- August 22, 2017: Mining health study stopped, and climate advisory panel disbanded.
- October 9, 2017: President Trump's EPA gets ready to scrap Clean Power Plan, the centerpiece of President Obama's climate change efforts.
- October 23, 2017: Interior Department proposes 77 million acres of oil and gas leases within the Gulf of Mexico for auction.

- December 18, 2017: President Trump announces "climate change" will no longer be regarded as a threat to national security.
- January 25, 2018: President Trump's EPA gets rid of "once in, always in," a President Clinton–era policy created by Clinton's EPA. Its purpose was to "lock in" any reductions of hazardous air pollution levels from industrial sources.
- January 31, 2018: The *Washington Post* reported that Trump's 2019 budget seeks to heavily slash Department of Energy funding for energy efficiency and renewable energy initiatives by a whopping 72 percent. If passed, spending would be cut from 2017's level of $2.04 billion to just $575.5 million in 2019. Staff would be cut from 2017's level of 680 to 450 in 2019.
- February 12, 2018: Trump's FY 2019 budget addendum proposes yet more cuts and sweeping rollbacks to US government programs that study and help reduce climate change effects. Also included were additional cuts to fund renewable energy research.
- March 16, 2018: The US Federal Emergency Management Agency struck "climate change" and related language from its strategic plan.
- April 2, 2018: President Trump's EPA begins the rollback of Obama-era fuel efficiency standards for light-duty trucks and automobiles. Tightened fuel standards were one of our country's most significant efforts to curb US carbon emissions. Roughly one-sixth of all US GHG emissions come from cars and light-duty trucks.
- May 9, 2018: According to *Science* magazine, Trump's administration ended NASA's Carbon Monitoring System. Costing just $10 million annually, the system helps improve global carbon emissions monitoring.[7]

The above is by no means a comprehensive list but is believed to be accurate up to the time of this writing. It's a sad but stark example of how one man with almost no knowledge of climate or environmental science can singlehandedly reverse years of heading in the right direction, at least as far as 99 percent of scientists are concerned.

HOW CHINA IS HANDLING CLIMATE CHANGE AND GHG EMISSIONS

Today, the United States as a nation stands alone in its rejection of climate change science. That's unfortunate, since the United States is second only to China in the volume of greenhouse gasses it spews into the atmosphere every year. Fortunately, nearly every other country in the world has a mechanism or plan as to how it intends to reduce GHG emissions. Perhaps the most critical plan is that of China, the world's largest emitter of GHGs. China's power generation sector pumps out a massive 3.3 billion tons of carbon and other GHGs every year.[8] The number of reductions and the speed with which the Red Dragon can make them could potentially be one of the most significant GHG reduction efforts in the world.

On December 19, 2017, China launched an emissions trading system (the world's largest) to reduce carbon emissions.[9] It will initially target the country's biggest polluters: its coal-fired power generation plants. It will eventually expand to cover the rest of the Chinese economy.

China has ambitious plans to see that its GHG emissions reach a peak no later than 2030. China's GHG reduction plan is being seen as a game-changer. "It shows global leadership on the part of the Chinese government," says Nathaniel Keohane, vice president of the US-based Environmental Defense Fund. In fact, says Keohane, China's emissions trading system could enable China's GHG emissions peak to occur even earlier than 2030.[10]

Here's how China's new system is going to work. Each power plant will receive an allowance to emit a level of carbon dioxide (CO_2) commensurate with its size. This will be the plant's target emissions level. Any plant that comes in under its target will be able to sell its extra emissions permits to other plants that overshoot their levels. Those plants will be ordered to seek higher efficiency instead of paying for excess emissions.

China's bold plan will almost immediately put a price on carbon emissions in China, at least as it pertains to Chinese power generation. China has been working on the design of the plan for over a decade. It could take all of 2018 to create the structure and regulations to bring the plan to operational status.[11] So far, the exchanges that will trade carbon allowances/permits have been set up, although specific permit allocations and the total allocation have not been announced. Once they happen, initial prices for carbon will quickly become known.

After China's power sector fine-tunes the plan, the carbon system will be expanded over the next several years to cover a total of eight sectors: power generation, civil aviation, iron and steel manufacturing, building materials, non-ferrous metal production, paper manufacturing, and chemical and petrochemical manufacturing. The Chinese government views the power sector as the low-hanging fruit of this massive undertaking. The initial system, covering the power sector, should be functional by early 2019. China's carbon trading system for its power sector will be 1.5 times as large as the European Union's system, which is the largest in the world as of this writing.[12]

The UK-based **Carbon Disclosure Project (CDP)** is helping the Chinese get its massive project underway. Paula DiPerna is a CDP special adviser and a key individual in the Chinese project. Here is what she had to say about China's efforts to reduce carbon: "The world should welcome the announcement of a national cap-and-trade in China, which will set new standards for global carbon pricing, address climate change head-on, and help integrate environmental finance with general financial best practices."[13]

Hopefully, the success of the Chinese emissions trading system will prompt other countries to set up their own. Could the United States eventually do the same? It's doubtful that an administration that "digs coal" would even consider it. But as we've seen with other sustainable initiatives detailed earlier in the book, the United States has many companies that realize the importance of cutting GHG emissions.

HOW MAJOR INFRASTRUCTURE COMPANIES ARE CUTTING GHGs

The steel-making business is a carbon-intensive industry. The steel industry is responsible for about 3 percent of the world's CO_2. That is a small amount compared to that produced by coal-fired power generation. But the industry has already seen a 33 percent reduction in GHG emissions since 1990.[14] So it should come as no surprise that throughout history it's been notoriously bad when it comes to GHG emissions.

In its most recent sustainability report, US Steel talks about its goal of cutting GHGs by the end of 2019.[15] Based in Pittsburgh, Pennsylvania, US Steel has operations in Gary and Portage, Indiana, and East Chicago, Illinois. It's one of the largest employers in Indiana. US Steel has a number of initiatives underway to reduce GHGs. One of the easiest ways for steel plants to reduce GHGs is to reduce the amount of power they consume. Switching to LED lighting and co-generation plants help to reduce power needs for steel making.

In the case of US Steel, it's investing in new technology to head the steelmaking process in an environmentally conscious direction. The best way to reduce power draw during the steelmaking process is to use the latest control technology. That's precisely what US Steel is doing at its Mon Valley Works' Clairton coke plant. At its Minnesota Ore Operations, US Steel engineers and operators work together with the designer and manufacturer of a kiln burner to increase its efficiency and significantly reduce nitrous oxide (NOx) pollutants.

ELECTRICITY IS THE NEW OIL

At least that's what Lutz Bandusch, CEO of ArcelorMittal's Hamburg, Germany, steel plant, believes. The Luxembourg-based company is on a mission to show other manufacturers around the globe how to transition to renewable energy. The Hamburg plant has initiated "NEW 4.0," ArcelorMittal's "energy system of the future" pilot project.

NEW stands for Norddeutsche Energie-Wende (Northern Germany Energy Transition). The "4.0" refers to the fourth industrial revolution, which involves artificial intelligence and smart system networking. NEW 4.0's intention is to show that when industry, government agencies, power distributors, and power generators coordinate their efforts, only eco-friendly power sources are necessary. It hopes to make this cooperation a reality in the states of Hamburg and Schleswig-Holstein by 2035. ArcelorMittal and the other partners believe carbon emissions can be reduced by 50 percent. Bandusch remarked, "We have to work on renewables: Fossil fuels will not last forever, so it's very important to look for solutions beyond oil now."[16]

For its part, ArcelorMittal is making its production flexible to accommodate variations in wind speed (which affect wind-generated power) and cloudy days (which affect power from solar arrays). Renewable energy dictates that big users of power like ArcelorMittal think differently. And they do. They now pay close attention to the weather forecast when putting together production schedules.

One of its projects is called Timeshift. In its massive electric arc furnaces used for melting steel, engineers adjust power input levels to accommodate available power. It's a huge benefit for power generators that, before this project, had to shut down windmills or solar arrays if there were no customers to take the power. Now, ArcelorMittal itself can take the power and use it to melt scrap metal in its arc furnaces. The energy isn't wasted. It's a big demand-side management project involving several partners. And the bottom line is, ArcelorMittal can use renewable energy, instead of natural gas, to heat up its steel in order to melt it.

In another project, named Power2Steel, ArcelorMittal engineers want to use excess renewable energy to inductively preheat iron billets, which are lengths of metal produced via continuous casting or extrusion and later used in finished products such as wire rod. Today, the company uses natural gas to heat them. Having the ability to use both fuels, either renewable energy or natural gas, will give ArcelorMittal fuel flexibility, while only using as much natural gas as necessary.

ONE TRILLION TONS

That's how much carbon-climate scientists believe the human race can safely emit into the atmosphere. Emitting one trillion tons of carbon equates to a 2°C (roughly 4°F) increase in the mean global temperature. Above that, scientists believe the chances of "highly adverse consequences" increases significantly. If that's the total carbon budget, how much have we "spent" so far? How quickly will we reach the total, given our current emission trends? And, most importantly, what can be done to make sure we stay under the one trillion ton budget?

The elimination of fossil fuels from energy production and the transportation sector is paramount in our efforts to not bust our carbon budget. But the coal, oil, and natural gas economies are well entrenched in our society. Changes in the generation of electricity take a lot of time. For instance, the United States fossil fuel infrastructure is vast and expensive. Developed over the last century, the exploration, mining, and transportation of coal cost hundreds of billions of dollars. The same is true for oil and natural gas. The exploration, drilling, transport, production, and refining of oil and natural gas each took many decades to build and again, the price tag was in the hundreds of billions of dollars for each segment.

We've already sent 500 billion tons (half of the total) into the atmosphere. Absent any changes in our current usage trends, we will slam into the one trillion ton number by 2050.[17] A big part of our problem is inertia. China is just starting to slow the number of coal-fired generating plants it's deploying there. The reality of locking in energy infrastructure into fossil fuel-based generators is a big part of the problem. In the United States, we are rapidly moving away from coal-fired generators and replacing them with cheaper natural gas and renewables. But in a ridiculous attempt to save a few thousand coal-mining jobs, President Trump is on the verge of ordering utilities to buy power from the remaining uneconomical coal-fired generating plants. In the end, I believe technology and cheap prices will trump Trump.

As I alluded at the beginning of this chapter, carbon emissions are starting to flatten and even decline in some areas of the industrialized world. China and India are still rapidly industrializing. China is trying to ramp up industrially and to slow carbon emissions at the same time. It's possible that China and India alone could bust the world's one trillion ton carbon budget before the end of this century. The solution to the problem is to make sure we don't lock in a carbon-emitting infrastructure. That's the problem with something like a coal-fired generating plant, which has a useful life of 50 years or more. Today's oil and gas pipelines can have a useful life of 50 to 100 years. The problem is that once a company invests in an oil or gas pipeline, it is economically incentivized to use it in order to pay for it.

Even with the best intentions, staying below the one trillion ton carbon emissions budget won't happen without some serious, focused government policy interventions. Strict building standards that limit carbon emissions and favor dense, urban living are a good start. Low or zero-carbon emission vehicles (EVs) combined with zero-carbon public transit will make a huge dent in global carbon emissions. There's no question that the infrastructure decisions we make today are of paramount importance regarding long-term climate change and greenhouse gas emissions. And it's far less expensive to build the correct infrastructure the first time rather than have to go back and replace or retrofit it.

Another part of the solution of low-carbon emissions is energy efficiency. One of the best examples so far is the ongoing replacement of incandescent and other inefficient light sources with LED replacements. I've personally done it at my farm and save over $800 annually. I've already paid for the more expensive LED bulbs, although if I were doing it again today, my bulb costs would be about 50 percent less than they were when I bought most of them in 2016. Another example of energy efficiency at work is in today's appliances. We have a refrigerator that was manufactured in 1991. There's absolutely nothing wrong with it, except that it draws about 1,200 watts of power on a continuous basis. Replacing it with a similar model manufactured today would result in energy savings of 91.7 percent. Today's models draw just 100 watts, one-twelfth of the power of my old fridge. The new unit will pay for itself in less than six years. I expect to undertake that replacement soon.

Energy efficiency solutions take advantage of new advances in engineering, technological innovation, and thermodynamics. They always yield reductions in energy use. Here's a simple example: Let's assume a coal-fired generating plant is 33 percent efficient, which happens to be the average in the United States. Let's hook that up to an incandescent light bulb, which is 5 percent efficient. The net efficiency of converting energy to light, in this case, is roughly 1.65 percent. But we're getting rid of coal plants and replacing some of them with combined-cycle, gas turbine power plants (60 percent efficient). Powering that same incandescent bulb, we now have a net energy conversion of 3 percent. But now, let's take the average utility-scale, solar power plant, which has an efficiency of 20 percent.[18] We're going to power an LED light bulb, which has an energy efficiency of 90 percent.[19] Now our net energy conversion is 18 percent or nearly *11 times* that of coal plants combined with incandescent bulbs. That's the power of "Technology marching on," as my First Law of Technology states.

It should be clear that staying below our one trillion ton carbon limit is going to require many disciplines focused on one goal: a sustainable energy future. It's something that Elon Musk talks about constantly. Getting there is going to mean eliminating most fossil fuel use (we still haven't figured out how to fly economically on solar power or using batteries). But it also means continued focus on energy efficiency, renewable energy generation combined with storage, and an electrified ground transportation sector. Putting that all together gets us to a sustainable energy future, and one with manageable carbon emissions.

NOTES

1. www.newsweek.com/nasa-hole-earths-ozone-layer-finally-closing-humans-did-something-771922

2. www.newsweek.com/nasa-hole-earths-ozone-layer-finally-closing-humans-did-something-771922

3. www.c-span.org/video/?417729-1/donald-trump-campaigns-warren-michigan

4. envirodatagov.org/about/

5. nationalgeographic.com/2017/03/how-trump-is-changing-science-environment/

6. archive.org/web/20170225220625/www.doi.gov/climate

7. nationalgeographic.com/2017/03/how-trump-is-changing-science-environment/

8. www.theguardian.com/environment/2017/dec/19/china-aims-to-drastically-cut-greenhouse-gas-emissions-through-trading-scheme

9. www.theguardian.com/environment/2017/dec/19/china-aims-to-drastically-cut-greenhouse-gas-emissions-through-trading-scheme

10. www.theguardian.com/environment/2017/dec/19/china-aims-to-drastically-cut-greenhouse-gas-emissions-through-trading-scheme

11. www.theguardian.com/environment/2017/dec/19/china-aims-to-drastically-cut-greenhouse-gas-emissions-through-trading-scheme

12. www.theguardian.com/environment/2017/dec/19/china-aims-to-drastically-cut-greenhouse-gas-emissions-through-trading-scheme

13. www.theguardian.com/environment/2017/dec/19/china-aims-to-drastically-cut-greenhouse-gas-emissions-through-trading-scheme

14. www.ussteel.com/posts/reduction-emissions

15. www.nwitimes.com/business/jobs-and-employment/u-s-steel-aspires-to-reduce-greenhouse-gases/article_bd89a8cd-4d94-5e27-8703-1ef18d132dd3.html

16. advancedmanufacturing.org/steelmaker-looks-beyond-oil-part-renewable-energy-program/

17. Myles R. Allen et al., "Warming Caused by Cumulative Carbon Emissions Towards the Trillionth Tonne," *Nature* 458, 1163–1166, April 30, 2009. See also Catherine Brahic, "Humanity's Carbon Budget Set at One Trillion Tonnes," *New Scientist*, April 29, 2009. But compare Meinshausen et al., "Greenhouse-Gas Emission Targets for Limiting Global Warming to 2° C," *Nature* 458, 1158–1162, April 30, 2009.

18. www.huffingtonpost.com/entry/the-truth-about-efficiency-in-solar-power-generation_us_5a028d5fe4b02f3ab3377e60

19. www.mrsec.psu.edu/content/light-bulb-efficiency

CHAPTER EIGHTEEN

Getting to Net Zero: US Energy Independence

In this chapter, I'm going to look at the move toward US energy independence. Renewable energy generation, combined with cheap battery storage, is a huge disruptor in terms of reducing US dependence on fossil fuels. As more storage is combined with solar, the amount of fossil fuels we use will start to drop. As our renewable energy generation continues to increase, all fossil fuels will become stranded in the ground. Over the next century, the fossil fuel industry will transition to a much smaller sector. It will primarily cater to the airline industry and government use. Other countries will also be able to vastly reduce or eliminate the need for most fossil fuels. The process of stranding fossil fuels is already underway. It started with the retirement of old, dirty, coal-fired power plants. As a result, coal mining is a dying business. I believe oil will be next, driven by the growth in EV sales. Finally, natural gas will not only help the United States gain energy independence but will also be the transition fuel that leads humanity to a sustainable energy future.

THIS HIDDEN ENERGY "SOURCE" IS GROWING
FASTER THAN RENEWABLES

I get puzzled looks when I ask a younger person to "dial" a number for me. I'm old enough to remember telephones with a rotary dial on the front. We had one in our house and we were even on a party line with another customer. It wasn't until the mid-1960s that we had our own dedicated telephone line. And even when touch-tone dialing was available, my parents were slow to switch over. They grew up during the Great Depression, when every penny counted, so they were reluctant to spend another $2 per month for touch-tone dialing service. But what a timesaver. It's another example of "Technology marching on."

The switchover from incandescent lighting to LED lighting is not unlike the switch from rotary to touch-tone dialing. About three years ago, I bought my first LED light bulb. It replaced a 60-watt incandescent bulb that was in a hard-to-reach spot in our house. Since then, I've replaced all of the lighting on our farm in Pennsylvania with LED bulbs. Even four- and eight-foot fluorescent bulbs have been tossed and replaced with high-output LED versions. My annual electricity savings? About $840 per year. Even though it cost me about $2,000 for the LED bulbs, they paid for themselves in less than three years.

LED bulbs last far longer (usually 25,000 hours or more) than incandescent and fluorescent ones. In unheated garages, LEDs work far better than even cold-start fluorescents. I'm not the only one making the switch to LEDs. According to the US Department of Energy, Americans have installed more than 450 million LED bulbs through 2017. That's up from less than 500,000 in 2009. In fact, almost 70 percent of Americans have purchased one LED bulb. I'm not surprised. Prices for LED bulbs have dropped 94 percent since 2008. You can now buy a 60-watt equivalent LED bulb for under $2.00.[1]

This is a classic example of my Three Laws of Technology, which I talked about in the early part of my book and repeat here:

1. Technology marches on.
2. When it comes to technology, changes happen much faster than anyone expects they will.
3. New technology is almost always disruptive and transformative.

Ten years ago, who would've thought the lowly light bulb would have such a disruptive and transformative effect on US energy? No one predicted the eventual adoption of LED bulbs. They were too expensive. But here we are, a decade later, and consumers are rapidly replacing their old, energy-hogging, short-lived incandescent bulbs. They are doing it faster than anyone would have predicted. It's what's responsible for the rapid growth of the hidden energy "source" I referred to earlier.

ENERGY EFFICIENCY: AMERICA'S FASTEST GROWING ENERGY SOURCE

So, what is the hidden source? It's energy efficiency. Experts often refer to energy efficiency as the "first fuel" of our global energy system. Increasing energy efficiency is the most important step we can take in order to move toward a sustainable energy future. Few think of energy efficiency as a source of energy. But it is in fact a source, and it's the fastest growing one we have.

It's the most important one, too. Look at the chart in Figure 18.1.

The figure shows that GHGs related to energy production have been steadily increasing for decades. It wasn't until 2014 when GHG emissions finally held steady at roughly 32 billion tons of carbon dioxide equivalent (CO_2-eq). This is due to two major factors. The first is a change in our energy mix away from coal and toward renewables and natural gas. The second and largest factor is due to gains in energy efficiency. It's played a major role in steadying our CO_2 emissions.

FIGURE 18.1 GLOBAL ENERGY RELATED GHGS SINCE 1990

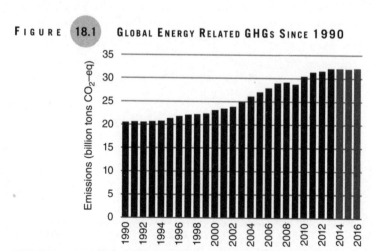

Data source: International Energy Agency. Accessed June 27th, 2018. Graph redrawn by author.

As a direct result of efficiency gains, energy demand is about 1 percent below levels reached back in 2000. That means today's energy use is less than half of what it would be without those efficiency gains. In the United States, energy efficiency is alive and well. US homeowners have installed about 450 million energy efficient, LED light bulbs.[2] In 2017, the global LED bulb market was $2.37 billion. By 2025, it's expected to reach $3.99 billion, growing at a compound annual growth rate of 6.7 percent.[3]

But what does that really mean? If we assume each bulb operates three hours per day, we have an implied savings of 50 million megawatt-hours per year. That's equal to about 0.16 megawatt-hours per capita. It's also equal to 2.4 percent[4] of the output of all of America's coal-fired power plants.[5] It shouldn't be surprising that utilities are retiring them. Many just aren't needed anymore. And increasing energy efficiency is one of the reasons.

As you can see from Figure 18.2, US residential energy consumption was lower in 2015 than it was in 2010. And that is in the face of an economy that's seen significant growth and improvements over the last eight years.

FIGURE 18.2   ELECTRICITY USE PER CAPITA

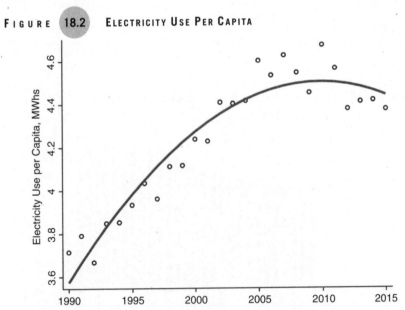

Data sources: EIA and the US Census Bureau blogs.berkeley.edu/2017/05/08/evidence-of-a-decline-in-electricity-use-by-u-s-households/. Accessed June 27, 2018. Graph redrawn and modified by author.

Energy efficient appliances certainly deserve some credit for the reduction in energy use. Data from the Natural Resources Defense Council suggests that Americans are spending far less to power their homes than they did two decades ago. From 2000 through 2015 US GDP increased 30 percent. However, during that same timeframe US energy consumption didn't grow at all. And today, the average American consumer is saving $500 annually on utility bills, due to more efficient appliances.[6]

But it's the replacement of the lowly incandescent light bulb with LEDs that has made the difference. It's not just a few states seeing decreases in electricity use. As you can see from Figure 18.3, 48 out of the 50 states and Washington, DC, saw residential consumption decline.

F I G U R E 18.3 DECLINE IN ELECTRIC USE

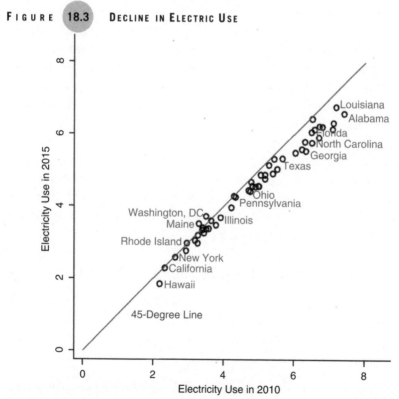

Data sources: EIA and the US Census Bureau blogs.berkeley.edu/2017/05/08/evidence-of-a-decline-in-electricity-use-by-u-s-households/. Accessed June 27, 2018. Graph redrawn and modified by author.

Could there be another reason for the decrease in the electricity use? Let's look at a few alternative explanations. It can't be any of the traditional economic factors like income and electricity prices. Household incomes have increased about 3.6 percent since 2010.[7] So everything else being equal, one would expect income effects would have resulted in higher electricity use. After all, when consumers have money to spend they often spend it on electronics: new computers, TVs, gaming consoles, appliances, and so forth, with the potential from additional use alone to draw more electricity. And it's not the price of electricity, either. Residential electricity prices have been virtually the same since 2010.[8] The bottom line is the decrease in electricity use is primarily due to gains in energy efficiency.

The real question is what will happen to efficiency gains as electric vehicles (EVs) continue to make inroads? I believe their adoption will happen much quicker than most experts predict (see Fessler's Second Law of Technology above). There are still plenty of efficiency gains to be had from all those consumers who *haven't* switched to LED bulbs or today's super energy-efficient appliances. Now that LED bulbs are making lighting cheaper per lumen (measure of quantity of light emitted from a source), homeowners may start using more lighting, especially outdoors. That could negate some efficiency gains, but I don't believe that will make a big difference.

There's no question that strong, energy efficient policy initiatives need to be the core of every government's energy policy. Energy security, lower energy bills, lower air pollution, and decarbonization of our energy supply are all made much easier with strong energy efficiency policies. Are there other energy efficiency gains we can make in the future? Plenty is the simple answer.

HERE'S HOW TO LOWER *YOUR* ENERGY BILL

In the next few paragraphs, I'll reiterate some things you can do (and others to keep in mind) to help reduce your energy bill. Most are simple, some cost money, but all will pay for themselves in a relatively short time.

- **Get rid of your old appliances and replace them with newer, more efficient "Energy Star-Rated" ones.** Today's appliances are far more stingy than those made a decade or more ago. They use far less water and electricity. For example, today's refrigerators and freezers can save 50 to 80 percent on electricity compared to models made in 2000 or earlier. Older dishwashers should be replaced as well, as newer models get dishes cleaner (no pre-rinsing with hot water necessary) and use less water and electricity in the process. New clothes washers use 70 to 75 percent less water than 20-year old agitator washers did. Remember that appliances represent roughly 9 percent of the average home energy bill, whereas 16 percent goes to heat and water, and 43 percent keeps the house warm or cool.[9]

- **Replace your existing thermostat with a new electronic one.** If you're not dialing back your thermostat when you're not home, you're missing out on an opportunity to save as much as 10 percent of your annual energy bill. You can buy these thermostats for well under $100. Most can easily be installed with just a screwdriver.
- **Making small changes can add up.** Power strips with electronic device chargers plugged in can be as much as 12 percent of the average home energy bill. Turning them off when not home during the day or when on vacation could save you as much as $100 annually.
- **Lower your hot water tank upper-temperature limit.** Is your home hot water scalding to the touch? Turning down the temperature could save 4 to 22 percent on your water-heating bill. Another energy-saving action is to purchase an insulating blanket for your heater's size. This could potentially save an additional 7 to 16 percent on your water-heating bill. These blankets are available at home improvement centers.
- **Use sleep mode on your computers.** Using the power management features of your computer and laptop could save you as much as 4 percent on your electric bill. Make sure you let your computer go to sleep quickly for maximum savings.[10]

These are just some things you can do to easily save money on your energy bill. Insulating hot water pipes, fixing leaky faucets, weather-stripping windows and doors, sealing other air leaks, and planting shade trees are some other examples of things you can do to maximize your energy savings. To get the biggest bang for your buck, consider getting a professional home energy audit. This will pinpoint your biggest energy losses and prioritize the things you can do to remedy them.

THE COMPELLING ECONOMICS OF CLEAN ENERGY

Right now in the United States, utilities are in the midst of a mad rush to build natural gas–fired power plants. But this could lock utility ratepayers into $1 trillion of avoidable grid costs between now and 2030. As I mentioned earlier in this book, the US power grid is the oldest, most technologically complex, and longest running machine in the world. The problem with the grid is due in part to its complexity and its age. It is in constant need of maintenance and repair. It's not aging gracefully.

The grid has powered the US economic engine for more than 100 years. To provide customers with the same high level of reliability and service for the next 100 years, significant upgrades are needed. This is going to cost a lot of money. The most significant part of the grid that needs replacement is its fleet of fossil fuel–powered generating plants. Half of them have passed their 30-year anniversary. That means they'll be retiring by 2030.

"Technology marches on," as I like to say, and fossil fuel-powered generating plants have been touched by the magic wand of new technology, too. While clean coal technology has so far failed to pan out, the same is not true with natural gas–fired plants. New combined-cycle, natural gas–fired turbines (CCGTs) are very efficient. And the power plants they go into are quick to build and cost much less than the previous generation of **thermal power plants**. Starting about five years ago, in conjunction with America's newfound natural-gas bounty, utilities began a "rush to natural gas."

Both independent power producers and utilities have announced plans to spend more than $110 billion between now and 2025 on new natural gas–fired power plants. Extrapolating that spend rate through 2030 suggests that more than $500 billion would be necessary to replace 500 gigawatts (GW) or about half of the existing thermal power plant fleet (coal, nuclear, and old natural gas–fired power plants) with new ones fueled by natural gas. Throw in another $480 billion in fuel to power those plants through 2030. That gets us to our lock-in of $1 trillion in expenditures. Even worse, it locks-in another 5 billion tons of CO_2 emissions through 2030 and 16 billion tons emitted through 2050.[11]

There's no question that the new natural gas plants will be cleaner, cheaper to install and run, and more efficient than the ones they are replacing. But they aren't the only option available to replace retiring thermal capacity. Renewable energy generation sources (solar, wind, and other distributed energy resources, including battery storage) are far cheaper than they were a decade ago. In most areas, they are now the least expensive option for system developers and utility operators. These up-and-coming, twenty-first-century power grid resources have demonstrated they can provide most, if not all of the services their predecessors did. All these new technologies combined can run circles around old, thermal plants and often at a lower cost.

The Rocky Mountain Institute (RMI) looked at the costs of four natural gas–fired generating plants that utilities are presently proposing in four different states across the United States. They compared those costs against region-specific, renewable energy and distributed energy resources that can provide comparable services. Two systems were combined-cycle gas turbine power plants, and two were combustion turbine power plants. In three of the four cases, the portfolio of clean energy resources was less expensive than the natural gas–fired power plants by 60 percent, 47 percent, and 8 percent. In the fourth case, the clean energy portfolio cost 6 percent more than the proposed natural gas plant. When RMI factored in additional cost reductions of $7.50 per ton price of CO_2 emissions and distributed solar, all four systems were lower risk and more cost-effective than the natural gas plant proposed.

But it turns out that clean energy resources aren't just competitive with proposed natural gas-fired power plants. They are an increasing threat to existing power plants. RMI compared the future operating costs of two CCGT power plants through 2040 against a portfolio of clean energy resources. It found that even with natural gas priced at $3 per million Btu, the clean energy portfolio is less expensive in one case and comparable in cost in the other. With gas at $5 per million Btu, both CCGTs are far more costly to operate than the clean energy portfolio would be.[12] The bottom line is that the same technology making renewable resources cheaper than new natural gas–fired power plants also has renewable energy threatening to strand existing investments in natural gas power plants and related infrastructure like pipelines, gas treatment plants, and so on.

Based on RMI's findings, regulators and system investors alike need to carefully weigh any future investments in natural gas–fired generators and accompanying pipeline and other infrastructure. Many of today's proposed projects, some already under construction and some planned, are at risk of becoming stranded assets. Unfortunately, ratepayers often end up footing the bill for failed utility investments. In the case of independent power producers, shareholders usually end up with the bill. Utilities should consider redirecting all future proposed capital expenditures for natural gas–fired power plants toward renewable energy assets that can provide clean energy at a significant cost savings compared to natural gas. Think about the avoided cost that utilities could realize. The renewable energy assets would be far less expensive to build than the $500 billion worth of natural gas–fired power plants, and the utilities wouldn't have to spend another $500 billion on natural gas to run them. The sun and wind are free energy sources. And don't forget the 5 billion and 16 billion tons of CO_2 not emitted through 2030 and 2050, respectively. All that clean energy helps us stay on the road to a sustainable energy future.

GETTING TO "NET ZERO"

It should now be clear that renewable energy sources aren't the "enemy" of utilities, the government, or any other entity. They are part of moving humanity toward a sustainable existence. A decision to purchase a power plant is no different than buying a car. A fossil fuel–powered car and an EV both get the occupants from point A to point B. One runs on fossil fuels, and the other runs on electrons. One emits CO_2, and the other doesn't. And today, buying an EV costs about the same as buying a fossil fuel–powered vehicle. All of the same comparisons are true for fossil fuel–fired power plants compared to renewable energy resources.

Net zero, when we are talking about energy, can mean several things. Most large corporations now have a significant focus on lowering their energy costs. In 2017, the residential and commercial sectors in the United States consumed 39 percent of all US energy.[13] And despite the Trump administration's claim that the adoption of solar, wind, and other clean energy technologies are driving *up*

US energy costs, the exact opposite is true. It's all due to America's rapid adoption of energy efficiency measures and the clean energy technologies I've been writing about in this book. It all means that US consumers and businesses drove their energy costs *down* to record lows in 2016.[14]

Renewable deployment continued in 2017, close to a record pace. Both US GDP and energy productivity accelerated. When energy *productivity* grows, our economy can grow even though our use of energy declines. And our GHG emissions dropped to a 25-year low, in spite of a distinct lack of policy support from the Trump administration. Renewable power generation (including hydro) jumped 14 percent in 2017 to 717 terawatt-hours (TWh) from 628 TWh in 2016. That growth means renewables are now providing 18 percent of all US power generation, *double that of just a decade ago*. Almost 23 GW-worth of solar and wind projects came online in 2017. This big jump in renewables means they are no longer classified as "other" forms of generation. Solar and wind are now a large and growing segment of all new US installations, reaching 62 percent in 2017.[15]

And utilities are getting the message when it comes to deploying new natural gas–fired generators. Their share of new installations dropped by 8.1 percent. That means natural gas's overall share of US generation dropped to 32 percent in 2017 from 34 percent a year earlier. Regardless, natural gas is still the number one generator of electricity in the United States. Coal slipped further, and owners of coal-fired generating plants announced 12.5 GW of plant retirements for 2018. And consumers are spending less money on energy, too. In 2017 the average consumer spent 1.3 percent of consumption on electricity, a drop of 0.1 percent from 2016.[16]

In 2017, wholesale purchasers of energy (utilities and energy cooperatives) were able to secure renewable energy contracts at even lower price points than in 2016. Just imagine a power purchase agreement (PPA) coming in at slightly over $17 per megawatt-hour (MWh) for wind and around $20 per MWh for solar. Building a solar plant has become more economical, too. Since 2012, utility-scale solar PV costs have dropped a staggering 49 percent to $1.1 million per MW from $2.2 million per MW. Wind turbine PPA prices are below the symbolic "dollar-per-watt" level, reaching $0.99 million per MW, a decrease of 21 percent since 2012.[17]

And even as the United States slowly transitions to a sustainable economy, it's managed to remain energy-competitive on the global industrial scene. In the United States, industrial power prices averaged just 6.76 cents per kWh in 2016. Out of all the G-7 countries, only Canada has cheaper industrial power (5.46 cents per KWh in 2016). The United States beat out Japan, China, Mexico, and India.[18] Clean energy technologies are making traditional energy generation, primarily coal and oil, more expensive and less competitive than ever. Clean energy is a win for American consumers, American manufacturers, and American businesses.

Our demand for fossil fuels continues to decline with every new wind or solar plus storage generation system that gets installed. EVs continue to be purchased at record rates, jumping 23 percent in 2017 from 2016. Reports estimate that there were roughly 749,000 EVs on US highways as of the end of 2017. The EV tipping point is getting closer here in the United States. Over the next couple of years, more EVs will be sold than fossil fuel-powered models. Around the world, nearly every new model sold by 2020 will be a hybrid or battery EV. The move to sustainability and "net zero" energy is underway. And within few years after that, average homeowners will have the ability to generate and store energy. They will have complete control over their home's energy usage profile, keeping overall energy usage at or below what is produced by the home's solar array.

As we continue to transition to clean energy sources, we continue to approach the elusive "net zero" of energy use. In the midst of all this change in our energy landscape, Americans' energy bills have never been lower. They are spending less after-tax income on energy than ever. And more major US corporations have jumped on the renewable and sustainable energy bandwagon. They are individually committed to getting to "net zero" energy demand by installing solar and wind at their facilities or purchasing sustainably generated power. And they are embracing energy efficiency as part of their sustainable energy plans.

What else is needed? We need additional infrastructure investment. Utilities need to build more transmission lines to carry renewable power from where it's generated to major metropolitan areas. And yes, in spite of the current administration and its open disdain for anything renewable, government policy needs to embrace a sustainable energy future for America. Governments at the local and state level are continually getting on board with renewable energy. Without the engagement of the federal government, renewable energy players face uncertainty regarding investments in new factories and new jobs. And it's clear from the more than three million jobs that already exist in the clean energy sector in the United States that clean energy is a viable and thriving sector of the country's economy. While I believe the move toward a sustainable energy future is already well underway and unstoppable, as a country, we could reach "net zero" much faster if sustainable energy were a national priority.

NOTES

1. www.theenergycollective.com/lucasdavis/2404090/evidence-decline-electricity-use-u-s-households
2. www.bloomberg.com/view/articles/2017–05–09/the-economy-changing-power-of-the-led-bulb
3. www.openpr.com/news/1098490/Global-LED-Light-Bulbs-Sales-Market-is-expected-to-reach-32200–15-M-USD-in-2021.html
4. https://www.eia.gov/electricity/monthly/epm_table_grapher.php?t=epmt_1_01. Data taken from table 1.1, 2016 Coal generation annual totals. 2.4% number is 50 million megawatt hours divided by 1.207 billion megawatt hours.
5. www.eia.gov/electricity/annual/html/epa_04_01.html
6. www.consumerreports.org/energy-efficiency/why-new-major-appliances-use-less-energy/
7. stlouisfed.org/series/MEHOINUSA672N
8. www.eia.gov/totalenergy/data/monthly/
9. www.consumerreports.org/energy-efficiency/why-new-major-appliances-use-less-energy/
10. www.energy.gov/energysaver/articles/how-much-can-you-really-save-energy-efficient-improvements
11. www.rmi.org/wp-content/uploads/2018/05/RMI_Economics_Of_Clean_Energy_Portfolios.pdf
12. www.rmi.org/wp-content/uploads/2018/05/RMI_Economics_Of_Clean_Energy_Portfolios.pdf
13. www.eia.gov/tools/faqs/faq.php?id=86&t=1
14. www.scientificamerican.com/article/energy-costs-at-record-lows-thanks-to-natural-gas-and-clean-energy/
15. http://www.bcse.org/wp-content/uploads/2018-Sustainable-Energy-in-America-Factbook.pdf
16. http://www.bcse.org/wp-content/uploads/2018-Sustainable-Energy-in-America-Factbook.pdf
17. http://www.bcse.org/wp-content/uploads/2018-Sustainable-Energy-in-America-Factbook.pdf
18. http://www.bcse.org/wp-content/uploads/2018-Sustainable-Energy-in-America-Factbook.pdf

CHAPTER NINETEEN

Energy 2118: A Look Ahead

W hat will the world's energy picture look like a century from now? I'll explore possible and probable energy scenarios. Of course, much of this will be based on current technology and where I see that going. Let's once again review my Three Laws of Technology:

1. Technology marches on.
2. When it comes to technology, changes happen much faster than anyone expects.
3. New technology is almost always disruptive and transformative.

I believe these statements are especially relevant when we look at what's ahead for the energy sector. The third law, "New technology is almost always disruptive and transformative," is perhaps the most relevant. There are plenty of technological developments that have already had an impact on the energy sector. LED light bulbs and affordable solar and wind, just to name a few. But those and new developments will further change the system. Tomorrow's power grid won't look anything like it does today. The energy system of the future is no longer just utilities as energy providers and businesses and homeowners as customers. Here's an overview of what I believe are some of the top trends that will drive the evolution of the energy sector.

RENEWABLE ENERGY COSTS ARE PLUMMETING

When it comes to PV solar, wind, and energy storage, falling costs are driving rapid acceptance and deployment of these systems at the utility-scale, commercial, and residential levels. Rapidly falling prices are encouraging businesses and homeowners alike to move toward real energy independence. They are installing enough PV solar combined with storage to generate and manage the use of their own electricity. The rapidly falling costs of LED lighting, and its design into commercial and industrial form factors, is quickly reducing building energy loads. Homeowners are also installing Energy Star-rated appliances as another means of reducing electricity and water bills.

Utility-scale PV solar saw 1.4 GW installed in the first quarter of 2018 and was 57 percent of all solar installation during the quarter. Q1 2018 was the 10th quarter in a row with more than 1.0 GW of utility-scale solar installed. The forecast for 2018 is 6.6 GW. Even with Trump's recent Section 201 tariffs on cell and solar modules, PV solar is still an economical alternative to fossil fuel-powered generation. The utility-scale PV solar forecast for 2019 stands at 7.0 GW, and 2020 and 2021 are each 8.1 GW. The overall PV solar estimate shows an annual forecast of about 8.1 GW by 2023.[1]

The solar investment tax credit (ITC) is scheduled to step down to 10 percent in 2023. I think we'll see additional developers and individual corporations rush to procure systems or power procurement agreements before the ITC drops. I believe those numbers could increase as the Section 201 tariffs are reduced in a year or two.

Lower costs benefit both the utility-scale customer (utilities) and the small commercial and residential customer. The falling system costs will increasingly leave small, residential customers with two choices. In one scenario, a PV solar system is installed, and the customer remains connected to the utility. In the second scenario, the customer installs both PV solar and energy storage and completely defects from the utility. These two seemingly opposite scenarios need to be reconciled to pay for massive stranded costs that utilities will otherwise incur.

ADVANCES IN GRID INTELLIGENCE, OPTIMIZATION, AND DATA MANAGEMENT

The rapid deployment of Internet of Things (IoT) sensors throughout the grid is beginning to introduce a massive wave of operational and market data for grid operators to interpret. It's a fantastic opportunity for grid optimization of America's largest machine, its power grid. It's especially important in the twenty-first-century grid, which is rapidly evolving into one with increasing quantities of distributed energy resources (DERs). Without some form of management, DERs could quickly overwhelm network operators and potentially reduce overall grid reliability.

Today, energy technology is quickly becoming dependent on information technology. With more sensors, smart switches, and smart actuators being deployed and relaying information back to control computers, grid operators have an increasing situational awareness of the grid. Before the smart grid, the only way a grid operator knew a part of the grid was nonfunctional was if a customer called in and said they had no power. Those days are rapidly disappearing. Today's smart grid, with its increasing granularity of performance data, can tell system operators of a problem before it becomes one. For instance, as a particular segment of distribution line nears its capacity limit, current sensors will report that to grid operators. Line crews can be dispatched well ahead of any line overload failure to install larger conductors. The entire grid can be analyzed, and investment needs prioritized for grid enhancement.

There is another side to twenty-first-century grid management. With real-time access to customer power requirements at all points on the grid, operators will know the immediate value of power necessary at all points on the grid network. With real-time monitoring of DERs and EVs, the locational value of those DERs and EVs is available. Being able to source power from many small PV solar and energy storage installations will allow grid operators to postpone or completely eliminate large, centralized generating plants. What a difference from the grid of just 10 or 20 years ago.

GRID RESILIENCE, RELIABILITY, AND SECURITY

The Arab Oil Embargo of 1973 created long gas lines. I remember this because it was just five years after I started driving. I used to wonder why we couldn't use less gas or find more crude oil. That embargo has influenced US foreign policy to the present day. Since the 1970s, every US president has campaigned about and promised US energy security and/or independence.

Today, US energy production has never been stronger. The United States is an exporter of both natural gas and crude oil. It's not unreasonable to think that the country could become completely energy independent (no more imports of crude oil) in another decade or so. The more rapid the uptake of EVs, the quicker the United States (and the rest of the world) will wean itself off of crude.

In the meantime, another oil embargo by OPEC could leave the United States with long gas lines once again. However, it would give EV sales a huge boost. In the short term, another oil embargo is probably the biggest energy security issue we have. With natural gas, a 200-year supply offers a low-cost fuel for use in residential and commercial heating, as well as power generation. To date, natural gas has helped the United States reduce its GHG emissions by replacing old coal-fired generation plants with new, efficient, and less polluting gas-fired ones. Natural gas is widely viewed as the twenty-first century's transition fuel to a completely sustainable energy future.

The potential for renewable energy to reduce or completely eliminate energy security issues varies by country. The primary determining factors are an abundance of solar and wind resources and their distance from the electrical load. Mexico and India have resources located close to major load centers. China and the United States have abundant wind and solar, but long transmission lines are necessary to bring that electricity to major metropolitan loads.

Over the last five years or so, the size and frequency of extreme weather events have increased. Whether due to global warming or the law of averages, extreme weather events can raise havoc on even the most up-to-date power grids. But as we all saw in Puerto Rico in 2017, an older out-of-date power grid is extremely susceptible to failure. Instead of rebuilding and reinforcing existing hub-and-spoke grid structures (today's predominant grid architecture), resilience planners need to increase system flexibility. This allows critical grid sectors to restart quickly without permission from central grid control, in the event of an outage. Increased resilience to natural disasters has to be a top priority for grid planners. Critical infrastructure and associated control systems should be able to easily restart in the event of a natural disaster-induced outage.

CUSTOMER GRID INTERACTION

Customers are engaging power grids more now than ever before. During the last 100 years, the only interaction customers had with their electric grid was to plug in an appliance, flip a light switch, and pay their monthly bill. Today, that's completely changed. Customers are now focused on how much energy they're using. The purchase of energy-efficient appliances, EVs, PV solar, and now energy storage is becoming a reality for many energy users. Today's homeowners are taking that one step further, and are looking at the value of the services that are energy hogs: HVAC, lighting, appliances, entertainment, and other electronic devices. Today's technology is allowing customers to play an ever-increasing role in energy supply and demand. Today, utilities are faced with an increasing number of renewable energy sources on the supply side of the grid. Making intelligent demand a dispatchable resource will help utilities balance supply variability. Matching supply and demand will become much more a customer function as grids and control software become increasingly more intelligent.

A BIFURCATED ENERGY LANDSCAPE

Looking at today's global energy landscape from 50,000 feet, it quickly becomes apparent that we are witnessing a fork in the road. In developed countries, like South Korea, Japan, the United States, and the European Union, energy demand *growth* is slowing down. Areas of decreasing demand are largely due to slower economic growth and the rapid growth of energy efficiency programs and policies. Adding distributed energy resources also helps to reduce peak energy demand. While this benefits customers with lower energy bills, it raises regulatory issues over the cost recovery of existing grid infrastructure.

The other fork in the energy landscape is in emerging economies. In many of those, we are witnessing urbanization, strong growth, and industrialization. In some of these settings, planners have the opportunity to bypass or leapfrog old technologies in favor of an abundance of renewable energy resources and a distributed smart grid. Large, centralized generating plants, expensive transmission lines, and associated substations can all but be eliminated during the grid-planning phase. This is not unlike what has happened with telephones in many small countries. Expensive wire-line telephony was instead implemented with cellular towers and infrastructure. In the long run, it's a lot less costly and far more reliable.

THE ROLE OF FINANCE AND INVESTMENT IN TOMORROW'S GRID

The twenty-first-century power grid is one of disruption of the status quo. Nowhere is that more apparent when it comes to the role of finance and investment. As renewable energy becomes an increasingly larger part of legacy, global power grids, the downward pressure on revenues is a real problem. This is especially true at the wholesale level. As additional solar and wind energy connects to the grid, it reduces utilization of legacy thermal generating assets (primarily coal, nuclear, and natural gas generators). We are already seeing this across the United States as well as Western Europe and India. Utilities are spinning off thermal generating units into separate operating companies to keep their costs off corporate balance sheets. Disruptive renewable energy sources are rapidly displacing old, thermal assets. Energy-efficiency measures and renewable energy reduce utility electricity revenues, the main source of a utility's income. As a result, some utilities are faced with the perception of being risky investments. The costs of retiring and dismantling legacy assets must be borne by the new assets replacing them. The same thing is happening with the delivery of electricity. Many utilities have spun off the transmission assets into separate companies. Increasing distributed generating assets are squeezing revenues of legacy transmission companies. This is all happening at a time when additional investment is needed to maintain and repair this aging infrastructure.

THE RISK OF DOING NOTHING

It's clear that energy systems of the twenty-first century aren't going to look anything like those of the twentieth century. As I detailed above, there are major trends that aren't going away. In fact, they are becoming status quo. Utilities, governments, and other private companies that are in denial of these trends risk falling behind other states and countries. Remember, economies, regardless of where they are, run on electricity. And with most of the world on board with the potentially devastating effects of greenhouse gas emissions and global warming, the move to a sustainable, pollution-free energy model is underway. The remaining, futile attempts by the Trump administration to support fossil fuels are, at best, a last-ditch effort to satisfy a few old industry cronies.

Solar and wind installations are on the rise, just about everywhere. Even the United States is finally getting on board with offshore wind. Most US corporations are taking a hard look at their energy bills. They are rapidly implementing wholesale lighting swap-outs in favor of energy-saving LED versions. Moving to solar plus storage can reduce energy use. Energy-intensive activities can be scheduled during the daytime when solar energy is available. Energy storage is able to time-shift excess energy to periods when it's needed. It's a great way for companies and individuals to reduce energy use and carbon footprints at the same time.

The energy disruption triangle is happening right now. The smart grid is here and getting smarter. It's not a question as to *if* distributed energy resources (DERs) like solar, wind, and energy storage are going to be deployed on the power grids of the twenty-first century. The real question is how much DER will deploy, how quickly it will deploy, and what the cost will be, including the cost of the stranded assets DERs leave behind. Decision makers need to quickly get on board or risk missing opportunities to move forward and reduce energy costs, thus ending up with unhappy customers. Lack of action by major power grid stakeholders could result in low levels of investment, huge stranded capital assets with no way to pay for them, and outdated, greenhouse gas-producing generation infrastructure that's locked in for decades.

The good news is that most utilities, governmental agencies, and large corporations *are* getting on board. Our energy system is right at the disruptive tipping point. New, energy-saving technology is rapidly being adopted as prices continue to drop. Deploying solar plus storage *without* governmental subsidies is close at hand. Solar PV is at or below grid parity in many places around the world including here in the United States, Australia, and many European countries. And utilities have a new role when it comes to the generation, transmission, and distribution of energy in the twenty-first century. Their function (and an increasingly larger part of future profits) will come from managing sophisticated energy services like energy-efficient smart appliances, smart EV charging systems, and energy storage management. To migrate to this new environment, utilities and regulators need to be on the same page. New business models that redefine today's grid services will allow utilities to continue to maintain and operate their distribution businesses. New markets for energy services will provide new sources of utility revenue. The overall benefit of the smart grid of the twenty-first century is a more reliable, optimized, and secure grid. Customers are becoming more knowledgeable about their energy use, how to save energy, and sustainability. In many cases, they are generating and managing their electricity themselves. In the twenty-first century, energy customers will see much more of an "energy marketplace." Utilities have to rethink how to allocate costs, design new rates, and continue to provide customer value. Their decisions will impact future grid investments. They will also affect the customer-utility relationship. When it comes to sources of electricity, today's customers want greater choices, greener choices, and control over those choices.

A LOOK OUT TO 2050

The year 2050 is just around the corner. If I'm still here, I'll be 97. Regardless, the energy picture will look a lot different than it does today. Let's try and quantify some of those differences. Solar energy will be one of the two predominant forms of power generation, the other being wind. Every flat or south-facing building structure will have solar panels on the roof and south-facing walls. Manufacturers are already producing glass panels that capture the sun's energy, turn it to electricity, and allow building occupants to look through them. At the same time, these panels are thermal blocks. They keep the temperature on the outside from affecting inside temperatures.

The amount of electricity produced by covering building roofs with panels will be substantial. Walmart alone has about 5,400 stores as of this writing.[2] The average one is 42,000 square feet. That's a total of 226.8 million square feet. A rough estimate means Walmart can cover its rooftops with 3.1 GW worth of solar panels. These would produce a total power output of 4.4 TWh per year. The average nuclear power plant produces 12.2 TWh per year. So Walmart's stores would produce about one-third of the power of a single nuclear plant. This would be enough power to provide Walmart with 100 percent of its electricity needs.[3] In 2018, Walmart has solar panels on about 500 of its stores located in 22 states and Puerto Rico, so it has a little further to go. In comparison, IKEA has installed solar on 90 percent of its US locations. Other companies have gone even further. Amazon, Microsoft, Facebook, Apple, and Google have all either set or achieved a 100 percent renewable energy goal with regard to operations.[4]

Offshore wind, especially along the Eastern seaboard of the United States, will rapidly increase over the next several decades. It's starting in Massachusetts, where you can find the greatest offshore wind speeds in the entire country. No wonder Massachusetts is looking to procure as much as 800 megawatts (MW) of offshore wind. And that's just for starters. Three companies are competing for offshore wind contracts in Massachusetts.

One of the leading contenders is Vineyard Wind. It hopes to install an offshore wind farm roughly 14 miles south of Martha's Vineyard and approximately 30 miles from the shores of Cape Cod. It will cover an area of 160,000 acres. The turbine array will consist of state-of-the-art offshore turbines spaced roughly 0.8 miles apart. Every turbine will generate at least 8 MW of power. The turbines will be connected to an offshore substation that will collect power from the array. An undersea high-voltage cable will transmit the power to a grid connection point on the mainland.[5] The proposal is under review by more than 30 federal, state, local, and tribal organizations and will need more than 25 permits. It is scheduled to begin construction sometime next year.

When Vineyard Wind is operational, it will be the second offshore wind farm to go online in the United States. The first was a tiny, five-turbine system off of the Rhode Island coast, called the Block Island Wind project. Together, they are a drop in the bucket compared to the 25 offshore wind project proposals the US Department of Energy has received. If all are built, they will have a collective generating capacity of 24 gigawatts.[6] That's enough clean energy to power 16.8 million homes.[7] And once offshore wind really gets going, that number will increase.

But solar and wind are just the tip of the new energy iceberg. By 2050, there could be over 20 new sources of energy powering various segments of the global economy. These include hydrogen fuel cells, nuclear fusion, and small modular nuclear fission reactors. Fossil fuels will still be part of our energy mix 30 years from now. But its overall share will be rapidly decreasing at the expense of clean, renewable sources. Even though electricity demand could double by 2050, developments in energy efficiency will result in few additional fossil fuel-powered generating plants. The global scramble for oil and gas resources will have dwindled to almost nothing, greatly simplifying geopolitics. By 2050, technologies that improve sustainably generated electricity from wind, sun, heat, water, and geothermal sources will be what matters.

In addition to how we generate our energy, how we move around in our environment is also part of the energy disruption triangle. In many cities, the amount of air pollution from vehicles is intolerable. London and Beijing charge car owners additional fees to drive in the city center. China is leading the way in replacing all of its diesel-belching, public transportation buses with quiet, clean electric ones.

The Chinese government is keenly focused on increasing EV sales. Why? Most of the citizens in its large cities are choking on gasoline and diesel fumes from fossil fuel vehicles. But curbing pollution isn't the only reason China is focused on EVs. It wants to be the world's leading producer of EVs, as it is for other consumer items.

Both EVs and the battery storage sector are benefitting from a virtuous circle. As battery costs drop, they encourage EV purchases and battery storage deployment. That drives additional demand. Manufacturing increases and costs drop. Nowhere is this more apparent than in China. The company at the forefront of both sectors there is the BYD Company LTD. It's the world's largest manufacturer of EVs and electric buses.

Electric buses? At the end of 2015, China had 98 percent of the 173,000 electric buses operating in the world. Yes, in 2016 China's cities bought 115,700 of them, followed by another 89,546 in 2017.[8] Shenzhen's bus fleet is 100 percent electric, with 16,359 on the road. That's more buses than the *total* bus fleets of the top five North American cities.[9] Right now, 20 percent of China's buses are electric. It wouldn't surprise me if they were all electric five years from now.

Globally, BYD is quickly expanding. On December 10, 2017, BYD announced it was setting up a factory in Morocco on a 125-acre site. The factory will build all-electric passenger cars, trucks, and buses. It will employ 2,500 people. The project is Africa's first EV manufacturing facility. And vehicles made there will be sold in Morocco and exported to other countries.[10]

BYD is already China's largest manufacturer of passenger EVs and electric buses. This past September, the Chinese government said it wants to end the sale of ICE-powered vehicles. It hasn't set a date yet, but it's certain that China will not want to be perceived as being behind

European countries. Many of those have announced an ICE-ban by 2030. I expect China will set a date that is equal to or even more aggressive than that.

New environmental rules that are already in effect in China will also supercharge EV sales. But China isn't stopping with ramping up EV and electric bus sales. It's also betting big on energy storage, and so is BYD. Worldwide, BYD has installed 550 megawatt-hours of energy storage systems. It currently holds a 25 percent share of the US energy storage market. It has plans to introduce residential energy storage systems late this year or early in 2018. BYD is manufacturing electric buses and electric trucks at its Lancaster, California, plant. The plant can produce 1,500 buses per year. The factory has been expanded to meet increased demand and is now three times the size it was in 2015.[11] I expect BYD soon to be the overall world leader in EVs, electric buses, and energy storage products.

By 2050, you won't be able to buy a new vehicle with an internal combustion engine. They will be relegated to museums and car shows. Even by 2030, just 12 short years from now, nearly half of all vehicles sold will be EVs, by my estimates. And then, let's consider the huge misalignment of crude oil demand in the face of meeting a 2D carbon budget, or the estimated amount of carbon dioxide the world can emit without rising more than 2°C above preindustrial global temperature levels. By some estimates, approximately $2.3 trillion – about one-third – of potential oil company capital expenditures (capex) through 2025 won't be necessary to deploy in a 2D scenario. Some companies have a capex exposure of 10 percent or less. A few have an exposure of 60 percent or even more.[12] Oil companies will be relegated to selling their products to chemical companies. The chemical industry will be the only source of demand growth for fossil fuels. Some oil companies are already rethinking future demand growth strategies. They are shifting their focus toward natural gas. They clearly are seeing the writing on the wall. But solar plus storage is now a cheaper power generating solution than a natural gas peaker plant.

For the last 100 years, the only investors in the energy sector were large players: public utilities and governments. Today, many state governments, like the federal government, are strapped for cash. They have little or no money available to invest in energy infrastructure. But that's actually good news. When governments get involved, progress tends to slow down. So where are the billions that will be needed for the twenty-first-century grid upgrades going to come from? Fortunately, many pension funds along with private equity concerns are stepping up to the plate. During the past five years, private equity investment in the energy sector has topped $200 billion. Exciting new ideas and technology-driven business models are finding readily available cash from like-minded investors.

The disintegration of the twentieth-century energy business model is turning large utilities upside down. Today, their strategies must include cities and towns, progressive companies, and sustainably focused homeowners. These users are generating their own power from renewables, and in some cases, selling it back to the grid. This raises questions about rate changes that will be needed. Legacy assets that are no longer required must be properly dismantled and disposed of. It's only fair that the users highlighted above should share in those costs. No more will we see multibillion-dollar investments in massive fossil fuel or nuclear power plants that need to produce power for 50 years. It's just too risky of a proposition, and energy technology is changing too rapidly. Smaller investments mean less risk and little if any legacy disposal costs.

DEMAND DISRUPTION IS AT HAND

As I write this in 2018, we are seeing energy demand disruption. New technologies like solar, wind, and storage and sophisticated control software are disrupting the energy status quo. And it will happen even if renewable subsidies end as planned. The cost of solar, wind, EVs, energy storage, and energy efficiency are all continuing to fall. By the time you read this book, they will all be less expensive than they were when I started writing. But utilities are facing revenue reduction of between $18 and $48 billion by 2025.[13] What's the difference between the low estimate and the high estimate? The answer is practical limitations that will keep some customers from being able to disengage from their utility. Even though the economics of distributed energy technologies are improving as I write, many would-be customers have practical limitations that will keep them from being able to address part or all of their energy consumption via solar or wind plus storage. They may lack the amount or orientation of enough roof space to install solar panels. Or their electric load may be too great to be able to meet 24-hour energy needs via storage.

Another big problem, and perhaps the biggest, is government policy, or lack thereof, when it comes to renewable energy. I don't believe existing subsidies for solar and wind will be extended, and could even be curtailed from here. Even if solar or wind plus storage is economically viable, some backward-thinking utilities won't advertise that fact. All they see is a near-term reduction in generating revenues. They'll miss out on all the longer-term benefits and revenue streams. So how is the energy disruption triangle going to play out?

We are going to see a continued deployment of solar. Costs are nearly at or below parity everywhere in the United States. Many individual states still have subsidies encouraging the adoption of solar. Many states have renewable energy mandates, forcing utilities to install grid-scale solar or purchase energy from independent power producers who have solar installations. America's businesses are continuing to adopt solar at a rapid rate.

Along with solar, energy storage is quickly becoming a necessary addition to any renewable energy generation system. California already has a storage mandate to go along with its solar mandate. Other states are rapidly following California's lead. The prospect of replacing an expensive natural gas peaker plant with a field of solar panels and battery storage units at a fraction of the cost is a compelling investment thesis.

So what's going to happen from here? The adoption of renewable energy in the form of solar, EVs, and storage has too much momentum to stall, much less shift into reverse. It's the energy disruption triangle, and it's happening now. The fact that it's rapidly increasing in adoption shows that it can and will happen without any support from Washington. It's all because of scale.

Ten years ago, renewable energy and EVs were things a few nerds fooled around with. By the end of June 2018, Tesla was producing 5,000 Model 3s *per week*. And it *still* had reservations for 420,000 more. As Elon Musk wrote in a memo to employees, "I think we just became a real car company."[14]

Solar plus storage is becoming the go-to system configuration when it comes to future energy generation. Utilities and planners are thinking of that first, not as an afterthought. In July 2018, one of California's utilities, PG&E, announced its intentions to procure 567.5 MW of energy storage. Once installed, it will eliminate three natural gas–fired power plants. The four storage systems will provide 2,270 MWh of storage. All are expected to be online by 2020.[15] As the scale of EV and solar adoption continues to increase, manufacturing technology will continue to drive costs down, fostering even more adoption.

Just imagine what it must have been like when electricity first came through your neighborhood. First, everybody got a light bulb or two. Then, in Edinburgh, Scotland, in 1893, Alan MacMasters invented the electric toaster.[16] About the same time, Guglielmo Marconi invented radio communication, and every family bought the electric radio.[17] By 1922, dairy farmers were able to purchase Herbert McCornack's surge milking machine.[18] And so it went from there.

Fast-forward 120 years or so from the early electricity days. Today, we have so many appliances, tools, and now cars that use electricity; the list is too numerous to count. Electricity has become crucial to our personal and business lives. We all are concerned when the power goes out. All we can think of is when it will come back on. When it is on, we completely forget about it and, within an hour or two, take its presence completely for granted.

But there's one difference today. Most countries and scientists recognize the very real threat of global warming from the continuing use of fossil fuels. As an engineer, it all makes perfect sense to me. The solution to the problem also makes perfect sense. The biggest problem society faces today is one of ignorance. Believing that global warming will just go away won't make it happen. Governments at the federal, state, and local levels all need to adopt initiatives to bring sustainability to the forefront of our daily lives. It's the only way that we can be sure that our existence on the earth continues forever. If you are already living sustainably, good for you. Tell all your friends how easy it is, and how much money you're saving on your electric bill. Take them for a ride in your EV. As soon as they step on the accelerator, they're going to want their own. Show them your solar panels and your energy storage panel. Go test drive an EV and take your kids along.

If you're not living sustainably, start. Your children and grandchildren and great-grandchildren will thank you.

INVESTORS, TAKE NOTE

These days, the author spends a lot of time writing and speaking about energy. However, outside of this book, nearly everything he writes is about investing in energy and technology companies. Potential investors in disruptive energy sectors will want to check out David Fessler's research and recommendations at http://www.oxfordclub .com. If you'd like to see where David is speaking at next, please go to https://oxfordvoyager.com/events/.

NOTES

1. https://www.seia.org/research-resources/solar-market-insight-report-2018-q2
2. pv-magazine-usa.com/2018/04/23/walmart-to-host-solar-power-on-130-more-sites/
3. www.reddit.com/r/askscience/comments/zg7n9/how_much_electricity_would_be_created_per_day_if/
4. pv-magazine-usa.com/2018/04/23/walmart-to-host-solar-power-on-130-more-sites/
5. www.vineyardwind.com/the-project/
6. e360.yale.edu/features/after-an-uncertain-start-u-s-offshore-wind-is-powering-up
7. www.quora.com/How-many-homes-can-one-gigawatt-in-energy-capacity-provide-for
8. https://www.google.com/url?sa=t&rct=j&q=&esrc=s&source=web&cd=2&ved=2ahUKEwilnoHmuITeAhVLneAKHePnDswQFjABegQIBhAE&url=https%3A%2F%2Fevobsession.com%2Fchina-100-electric-bus-sales-drop-to-89546-in-2017%2F&usg=AOvVaw0ygYngfN5mwbAyK-VTnbNG
9. www.bloomberg.com/view/articles/2017-12-08/china-goes-all-in-on-the-transit-revolution
10. northafricapost.com/21176-another-chinese-giant-sets-electric-transportation-eco-system-morocco.html
11. cleantechnica.com/2017/10/07/byd-triples-the-size-of-lancaster-bus-factory/
12. www.carbontracker.org/wp-content/uploads/2017/06/2D-of-separation_PRI-CTI_report_correct_4.pdf
13. www.accenture.com/t20171213T064437Z__w__/us-en/_acnmedia/Accenture/Conversion-Assets/DotCom/Documents/Global/PDF/Dualpub_14/Accenture-Digitally-Enabled-Grid-Utilities-Survive-Energy-Demand-Disruption.pdf#zoom=50
14. www.wsj.com/articles/tesla-sets-new-model-3-target-of-6-000-a-week-1530544090
15. esnaexpo.com/press-release/54
16. www.mirror.co.uk/news/uk-news/made-in-the-uk-the-life-changing-everyday-innovations-1294240
17. https://public.wsu.edu/~bryan.mclaughlin/Radio/Who_Invented_Radio.html
18. surgemilker.com/history.html

Glossary

alternating current (AC):   electricity that reverses its direction at regular intervals

autonomous EV: an electric vehicle that does not require a human operator due to its uses of artificial intelligence, sensors, and GPS

busbar: a metal strip or bar used in electrical power distribution, either of high voltage equipment at switchyards or of low voltage equipment at battery banks

Carbon Disclosure Project: a UK-based organization that discloses the environmental impact of companies around the world

carbon filament: a form of incandescent lighting that is capable of operating at higher temperatures

chlorofluorocarbons (CFCs):   chemicals that are harmful to the ozone due to the release of chlorine atoms exposed to UV radiation, resulting, for instance, from the compounds of carbon, hydrogen, chlorine, and fluorine typically used in refrigerants and aerosol propellants.

compound annual growth rate (CAGR):   a measure of growth of an investment over a specific time period

compressed air energy storage (CAES):   a method of energy storage that compresses air at high pressures and stores it in large underground caverns, depleted wells, or aquifers

concentrated solar power (CSP):   the use of thousands of mirrors to focus the sun's rays on a tank of molten salt mounted on a solar tower

concentrating collectors: power systems that generates electricity using heat rather than light via mirrors and lenses that concentrate sunlight onto a thermal receiver

conversion efficiency: a measure of how well a solar cell converts the sun's energy into electricity by converting photons into electrons

direct current (DC): electricity that flows in only one direction

distribution infrastructure: the part of the electric grid that moves electricity from transmission substations to individual customers

dual-rate electric system: an electric system through which you'll pay more for electricity you use during peak hours (usually 8 a.m. to 8 p.m.) and substantially less for what you use during off-peak hours (8 p.m. to 8 a.m.)

electric grid: an interconnected network designed to deliver electricity from producers to consumers

electromagnetic: the interrelation of electrical and magnetic forces or effects

energy storage array: a system in which the capture of energy generated at one time is stored for use at a later time

Exide battery: high-quality brand of lead-acid battery

feed-in tariff: a government policy mechanism, the purpose of which is to attract and accelerate investment in renewable energy

Fessler's First Law of Technology: Technology marches on.

Fessler's Second Law of Technology: When it comes to technology, changes happen much faster than anyone expects they will.

Fessler's Third Law of Technology: New technology is almost always disruptive and transformative.

flat-plate collector: a heat exchanger that generates electricity by capturing solar energy and using it to heat water for bathing, washing, and heating

fluorescent: the production of light while it is being exposed to external radiation

fossil fuels: natural fuels (e.g., coal, gas) formed from the remains of living organisms

frequency fault: an abrupt change of frequency in a power grid, usually due to a generator failure

generation infrastructure: the part of the electric grid that produces power, including large, legacy fossil fuel and natural gas power plants as well as wind farms and solar power plants

gigafactory: initially used to describe Tesla's giant battery factory in Nevada but now used to describe any battery manufacturing plant anywhere

greenhouse gas (GHG):   a gas that warms the earth's surface by absorbing infrared radiation

grid parity: when an alternative form of energy can generate power at a levelized cost of electricity that is less than or equal to the price of power from existing baseload sources

gross domestic product (GDP):   the total value of goods and services provided over a period of time, usually one year

hertz: in the international system of units, it is the unit of frequency, equal to one cycle per second

Hornsdale Power Reserve: Tesla's big energy storage battery in South Australia

incandescent: the production of light as a result of a carbon or tungsten filament being heated

inertial response: a large synchronous generator contains a large heavy rotating mass that acts to overcome any instantaneous imbalance between supply and demand on an electric grid

internal combustion engine (ICE):   an engine that generates power through the use of gasoline, oil, or other fuel with air inside the engine

inverter: an electronic device that changes direct current to alternating current

investment tax credit: a dollar-for-dollar reduction in income taxes paid to the federal government based on the amount of money invested in solar property

Level 1 charger: a charger operating at the L1 level using 120 volt, alternating current (AC) power

Level 2 charger: a charger operating at the L2 level using 240 volt, AC power

liquid air: technique using electricity produced by wind farms in the middle of the night when demand is low to compress and cool nitrogen in the air down close to $-200°C$

lithium carbonate equivalent: the content of lithium within a lithium compound

microprocessor: a component that contains all the functions of a central processing unit of a computer

nameplate capacity: intended maximum output of a solar power station

nanotechnology: the understanding of the fundamental physics, chemistry, and technology of nanometer-scale objects

nominal frequency: the desired center frequency of an oscillator

nuclear power: power generated by nuclear reactors that can be converted to electric power

organic photovoltaic device: a combination of light-sensitive polymers mixed together to absorb light, setting their electricity generating abilities in motion

peaker plant: a power plant that generally only runs in times of high energy demand

photodiode: a semiconductor diode that changes its electrical resistance when exposed to light

photoelectric: involving the emission of electrons when light shines on a material

photon: a particle that carries energy and represents a quantum of light

photovoltaic (PV): the production of electricity by the combination of two substances exposed to light

p-n junction: one of the basic building blocks of semiconductor devices

pneumatic: containing or operated by pressurized air or gas

polycrystalline silicon: a high purity form of silicon used as a raw material

power grid: a network of power lines connecting multiple generating stations to loads

power plant: the location or apparatus in which power is generated for distribution

Power Purchase Agreement (PPA): a long-term (usually 20 years) contract between the entity generating electricity (the seller) and a second party looking to purchase electricity (the buyer)

Production Tax Credit: an inflation-adjusted per-kilowatt-hour tax credit for electricity generated by solar energy

Public Utility Regulatory Policies Act: created in the United States in response to the 1973 energy crisis with the purpose to reduce energy's demand on fossil fuels via conservation, use of domestic energy sources, and renewable energy

pumped hydroelectricity: a type of water-powered energy storage used by utilities for load balancing, in which water is pumped from a lower elevation reservoir to a higher one during periods of off-peak power when rates are lower

reflectance efficiency: the measure of a solar cell's surface effectiveness in reflecting the sun's radiant energy

regenerative braking: when the car's electric motor is turned into a generator that can then recover energy from the slowing down of the vehicle, and thus energy is transferred back into the battery pack

regional transmission organization (RTO):   a US-based system monitored by the Federal Energy Regulatory Commission in which the operator coordinates, monitors, and controls the movement and transmission of electricity over a multistate grid network

Renewable Energy Sources Act: an act passed in Germany as Erneuerbare-Energien-Gesetz (EEG) to guarantee solar energy customers a connection to the power grid and a remuneration for power produced for 20 years

renewable portfolio standards (RPS):   a regulation that requires an increase in the production of energy from renewable energy sources to fossil and nuclear electric generation

semiconductor: a solid material or substance that conducts energy between an insulator and most metals

smog: certain atmospheric pollutants combined with smoke and haze or fog

soft costs: expenses comprising the inverters that change the direct current (DC) power into alternating current (AC) power that is grid compatible, as well as the mounting hardware, grid connection fees, and labor

solar cell: a device used to produce electricity via solar radiation

soldering: the process of joining two or more items together by melting and putting a filler metal into the joint

steam locomotive: a type of railway train that uses a steam engine to produce power

Supercharger: Tesla's DC fast-charging station, proprietary for Tesla EV owners only

sustainable mobility: transportation methods that significantly reduce energy consumption

Swanson's law: stating that every time there is a doubling of panel production and shipment, there is a 20 percent drop in panel costs

synchronous generator: a power generator in which mechanical power output is converted from other power sources into electrical power for the grid

synchronous inertia: rotational inertia provided by heavy synchronous generators that protect a power grid against frequency perturbations

synthetic (or emulated) inertia: frequency stability on a power grid supplied by means other than large rotational thermal synchronous generators

thermal power plant: a power plant with a generator in which heat energy is converted to electric power

thermal synchronous generator: an electrical machine that converts mechanical power from a steam turbine into AC electrical power at a specific voltage and frequency, and which always runs at a constant speed called the synchronous speed

thin-film solar cell: a second generation solar cell made out of thin layers of photovoltaic material

transistor: a semiconductor device capable of regulating current or voltage flow and may act as a switch for electronic signals

transmission infrastructure: the part of the electric grid that moves electricity from generators over long distances to load centers

turbine (water, steam): a device used to convert potential or kinetic energy of water or steam into electrical energy

ultimate efficiency: an efficiency limit that normal photovoltaic systems are subject to

ultraviolet (UV):   having a shorter wavelength than the violet end of the visible spectrum but longer than that of X-rays

utility-scale solar: generally any installation greater than 1 MW in size that supplies power to the grid at the utility level, rather than at the distribution level

value of solar (VOS):   totals all of the benefits and costs of distributed solar and assigns a true cost

wideband radar system: a system incorporated in Tesla EVs that detects other cars, people, and other objects

Index